Internet Messaging

ISBN 0-13-978610-4

90000

Prentice Hall PTR
Internet Infrastructure Series
Paul Mockapetris, Series Advisor

Luotonen   *Web Proxy Servers*

Rose and Strom   *Internet Messaging:*
                                From the Desktop to the Enterprise

Internet Messaging

Marshall Rose

David Strom

Paul Mockapetris, *Series Advisor*

Prentice Hall PTR, Upper Saddle River, NJ 07458
http://www.phptr.com

Library of Congress Cataloging-in-Publication Data

Rose, Marshall T.
  Internet messaging: from the Desktop to the Enterprise/ Marshall T. Rose,
David Strom.
        p. cm. -- (Prentice Hall PTR internet infrastructure series)
  Includes index.
  ISBN 0-13-978610-4 (alk. paper)
  1. Electronic mail systems. 2. Internet (Computer network)
I. Strom, David. II. Title III. Series
TK 5105.73.R6623 1998
005.7'1369--dc21   98-19174
                                          CIP

Editorial/Production Supervision: *Kathleen M. Caren*
Acquisitions Editor: *Mary Franz*
Editorial Assistant: *Noreen Regina*
Series Advisor: *Paul Mockapetris*
Marketing Manager: *Miles Williams*
Manufacturing Buyer: *Alexis Heydt*
Cover Design:
Cover Design Direction: *Jerry Votta*
Series Design: *Meg Van Arsdale*
Page Layout: *Bear Mountain Type*

© 1998 Prentice Hall PTR
Prentice-Hall, Inc., A Simon & Schuster Company
Upper Saddle River, NJ 07458

Prentice Hall books are widley used by permission by corporations and government agencies for training,
marketing, and resale. The publisher offers discounts on this book when ordered in bulk quantities.
For more information, contact:

Corporate Sales Department,
Prentice Hall PTR
One Lake Street
Upper Saddle River, NJ 07458
Phone: 800-382-3419; FAX: 201-236-714
E-mail (Internet): corpsales@prenhall.com

Printed in the United States of America

10 9 8 7 6 5 4 3 2 1

ISBN 0-13-978610-4

Prentice-Hall International (UK) Limited, London
Prentice-Hall of Australia Pty. Limited, Sydney
Prentice-Hall Canada Inc., Toronto
Prentice-Hall Hispanoamericana, S.A., Mexico
Prentice-Hall of India Private Limited, New Delhi
Prentice-Hall of Japan, Inc., Tokyo
Simon & Schuster Asia Pte. Ltd., Singapore
Editora Prentice-Hall do Brasil, Ltda., Rio de Janeiro

Table of Contents

List of Figures

Chapter 3: Messaging on the Desktop: Sending

Chapter 4: Messaging on the Desktop: Identity and Privacy

Chapter 8: Closing

List of Product Tables

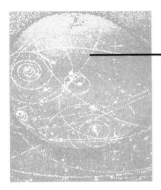

Foreword

by Penn Jillette

I picked up a ton of great tips to make my email more efficient by reading the manuscript for Marshall and David's book. But I'm just an individual guy, so email administrators should be as happy with this book as an email administrator could be empowered to be.

I sent the authors a message and learned another trick. If you receive some mail, send back an automatic answer saying that a certain code word must appear in the RE: line. Then when you receive another message with the code word, just don't answer. The thinking is: The correspondent is probably just some tech-dilettante, comedy-magic guy trying to waste your time with an e-howdy. He'll just think he typed the wrong address (and maybe he did). The technique works; I wrote the foreword anyway and less time was wasted.

After reading the whole book (at least you read a bound copy, I had to read it on paper printed on one side—so much for the paperless office—and held together by a freakishly large and therefore valuable rubber band), it's time to incorporate the tips and tricks (another tech term) into our e-lives. We must not forget that even with all the email problems we've just read about (most of which some of us don't even have and some of which most of us don't even have), email is still the greatest thing ever invented in the history of the world. "What about fire?" you say. And I answer, what good would it be without an email to "come and get it?" You give another try with "the wheel." Yeah, where would we want to go that we wouldn't have to confirm through a quick message? "Smallpox and Polio vaccine," you whisper, growing weaker and more desperate. Don't make me laugh, I have chapped lips. Email is the best.

I've been on email since a very rich and famous computer friend (it's even better to name-drop when you don't even need the name) said to me in 1985, "Shouldn't a guy like you have an ARPANET address?" (It wasn't ARPANET anymore by then, but being a future-thinking entrepreneur, he wanted to give me a better story for now, here in the future.) I was set up with *Penn@MediaLab.MIT.edu*. (Go ahead. Try to send something there. You're better off mailing to Marshall and David. It'll just bounce; my address has changed).

Before email, I was like Judy Jetson—a different age, sex and number of dimensions, but we were both on the phone all the time with our ponytails knotted high on our respective heads. The phone is nice, I guess. You can pick up emotions without sideways smiley winks, but the two people on the phone are rarely in the same mood: I feel like chatting and you want me dead. Email solves all that. I can read your messages when I'm in the mood to chat, and you can save my messages to help prove your case in court.

I feel that email, although often used for business, is more intimate than voice phone. When I see your words, they are in my font and color on my computer, and the computer feels like part of my brain. Telephone is talking; email is whispering thoughts directly into my mind. My email friendships are more solid than my few remaining phone friendships (phone phriendships?).

Penn and Teller (I guess I'm kind of talking about myself in the third person, but it's OK—I'm in show biz) run our whole business with email. All our staff and crew members are online, and the tours are often coordinated through email messages from one floor of a Hyatt to another by way of a system designed to go all the way around the world to sidestep a nuclear bomb. It may not be the most efficient way to run a business, but it'll get you the chance to write a foreword to an email book. Teller and I wrote three books through email. We read each other's chapters as attachments and did all the editing with messages (he cut out my best stuff).

I live on the road. And I keep track of all my business and keep in touch with all my friends using email. It seems to me that life on the road must have been very lonely and businesses must have been in a shambles before it. But I haven't checked *www.lifeB4Email.com*. I love email. I kiss it. And this book makes it even better. Now, if Marshall and David can just improve chocolate and sex, they'll really be talking.

OK, that's it—I have to email this in.

Preface

Welcome to *Internet Messaging*. This is a book about how you can use email on your desktop, in your enterprise and throughout the Internet.

Internet messaging provides a rich and widespread infrastructure for collaboration. It offers a variety of services—from personal messaging to distribution lists to exotic mail-based applications, and from simple textual memos to complex multimedia objects. It operates under a variety of circumstances and connection speeds, from computers using dedicated high-speed links or local area networks to roaming users of dialup lines. The Internet messaging infrastructure is widespread because it connects the commercial, government, research and education sectors in every continent on the globe. Despite the tremendous differences in end-user equipment, messaging formats and the like, it all manages to work together.

There's a lot of technology that goes into making the Internet messaging infrastructure a success. The objective of this book is to present it to you in a fashion that is understandable and accurate. Let's not confuse accuracy and detail; it's important that we provide you with information that is correct. But it's just as important that we don't allow technical nuances to obscure the larger picture. So, we've taken care that we emphasize the fundamentals. Similarly, because this is a practical book, we focus on those issues that may affect you in your daily life or your strategic planning. In essence: We talk about standards, but only as a means to an ends; and we don't talk about bits and bytes, unless they serve some larger relevance to you as a user.

Our strategy in organizing this book is simple. We started with 12 problems that appear to be rather consistent throughout the user community. We organized the 12 problems into six categories and developed a taxonomy to relate the categories. Each category was written as a chapter. We hope this provides an effective way for you to approach the information we're presenting. Since we've cross-referenced related issues in each chapter, the organization of this book allows you a fair amount of random access (read: "flipping") between chapters. So, after you've read the first chapter that introduces the taxonomy and categories, you can skip to different chapters based on your concerns of the moment.

Who we are

In the interests of full disclosure, you should know our background and experience.

David Strom has used more than 15 different email products for about a dozen different employers over 18 years of work. These products span a wide range, from the early IBM-host based DISOSS and PROFS systems and character-based MCIMail and AT&T Easylink, to LAN-based products such as cc:Mail and 3+OpenMail, to more recent Internet-based products. He runs his own consulting practice and has been using Eudora on both Macintosh and now Windows95 for the past several years as his principal email product, although he has been known to occasionally run Pine and Netscape Messenger.

Strom's background is in technical product research and testing—he has tested hundreds of computer products, including Internet software, network operating systems, PC systems and communication applications. He advises computer vendors on product design and strategy. In the past decade, he has written close to 1,000 articles for various computer trade magazines on a wide variety of networking and communications topics. Before becoming a consultant, he founded CMP Media's *Network Computing* magazine and hired its first staff of editors. He has also run new product research for Transamerica Occidental Life Insurance and worked as an analyst and in-house consultant in information-center and end-user computing departments.

Marshall Rose has participated in the design and implementation of half a dozen email products—and he is a heavy user of them. These products span a wide range, from the ground-breaking MH system (starting with the 1981 edition, which still has useful features not found in "modern" products), to the Safe-Tcl package used to write mail-enabled applications (such as exploders and spam filters), to First Virtual's Internet Payment Systems (the first Internet-based payment system, which, coincidentally, made heavy use of email). In parallel, he also uses email packages on both the Macintosh and Windows systems, although he currently favors Outlook Express on Windows95.

Rose's background is in Internet technologies. He's authored more than 60 Internet Requests for Comment (RFCs), implemented most of them, and productized or provisioned many of them. Although the majority of his work is in email, he's also worked in directory services and network management. He also runs his own consulting business, but spends most of his time at First Virtual, where he leads a group developing interactive, reactive and transactive advertising technologies that are just as at home in email as on the Web.

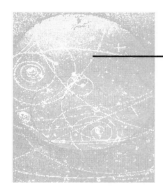

Acknowledgments

There have been several reviewers who spent considerable time correcting our draft manuscript, including Bill Frezza, Steve Birgfeld, Gary Gunnerson and Thomas Powell. Copy editing was expertly provided by Michael Perreca.

Marshall wrote this book in his spare time, as an employee of First Virtual Holdings Inc., the e-messaging company he cofounded back in 1994. Although a lot of First Virtual's technology is email-based, there's nothing specific to First Virtual in this book, with the exception of some of the future applications described in Chapter 8.

Marshall learned to sail back in late 1996, despite being extraordinarily predisposed to motion sickness. (In fact, his physician prescribes medication to combat this malady.) In late 1997, Marshall bought a small auxiliary sloop (read: "a sailing vessel with a single mast and a tiny, interior diesel engine") that he named *Azaka*. He wrote most of his portions of the book while recommissioning the boat (although a small boat, it now carries more electronics and safety gear than most airplanes). The reason this is relevant is that he did most of the actual writing on his boat using a laptop and cable Internet connection. Although the Internet service provider is branded as @Home, in this instance it would be more accurate to refer to it as @Boat. Amusingly enough, Marshall wasn't the first boat owner in San Diego to have a cable Internet connection, but he probably placed in the first 25 of his kind.

Finally, Marshall thanks David for collaborating with him on this book. After having written seven books about Internet technologies, Marshall had begun to get tired of writing, but David convinced him that there was more to say. In addition, David did more than his fair share of the work!

David wrote this book in his spare time, too—although it never seemed like there was anything but time to write. Unlike Marshall who wrote most of his chapters in one place, David wrote in several cities, using a combination of his own machines as well as borrowed computers—since he has given up on using a laptop for the past year. This is his first book, and he isn't sure he wants to consider a second anytime soon. Nonetheless, having Marshall as a writing partner has been a thrill and an inspiration.

April 1998
San Diego, California, and Port Washington, New York

Introduction: The Rising Chaos of Email

In the past decade, email has become the lifeblood of modern business communications. No longer the province of geeks and technocrats, email is now as necessary as the telephone for the average working man and woman. In some cases, email has become more important than the telephone, fax and pager for connecting far-flung empires across time zones and cultures.

If this surprises you, count the number of messages you've sent and received via email over the past week and compare that to the number of faxes or phone calls you've made. Or examine which deals would not have happened without email between the parties involved. Or consider how you could have written your last report without sending a draft copy to your colleagues via email. Or imagine how the last department meeting could have been scheduled without checking calendars via email. The list goes on and on.

A good slogan for the early 1990s could have been "email happens." Email was used by a relatively small minority of corporate workers and in a few select businesses. Today, email *matters*, and email matters big time for many of us. Without it, we couldn't conduct our business, stay in touch with our families and friends, and get on with our lives.

These days, email users can be found in any place of business and across the entire spectrum of workers. What once was a technical curiosity is now common cocktail-party conversation, and it is rare these days to exchange business cards without an imprinted email address, usually right below the telephone number.

The phenomenal growth and popularity of the Internet has been largely due to the growth and popularity of email usage over this past decade. Email is still the Internet's most popular application when measured both by the number of its users and the frequency of usage. While the Web has received a great deal of attention and press, email is the real untold Internet success story.

Everyone from your grandparents to your business associates has an email identity—and in many cases more than one. Almost all of these email addresses, regardless of the system and provider, are connected to each other via the public Internet. Studies put this number in the tens of millions of users: Depending on whom you believe, it could easily reach 100 million by the end of the millennium. The largest collection of email addresses, logged by America Online, exceeded 10 million users by the fall of 1997, and is still adding thousands of users daily.

The success of email is relatively recent and the result of several factors. First and foremost is the ability to send email to anyone in the world. In 1990, most email systems had little or poor connectivity to the Internet. Indeed, ordinary businesses were prohibited from obtaining Internet access, and service providers were few and mostly relegated to academic and government circles. The concept of purchasing a vanity domain name to match one's business name or trademarks was unheard of, and the Web still had yet to be invented. The vast majority of the world's countries had poor or no Internet connectivity.

The early 1990s saw little agreement on how major email systems should be connected to each other. Most of the corporate email users ran on disconnected systems that used their own software, such as mainframe-based IBM's PROFS and DISOSS, and LAN-based cc:Mail (before it was purchased by Lotus, and before Lotus was purchased by IBM) and Network Courier (before it was purchased by Microsoft and renamed Exchange). A few brave souls ran UNIX-based email systems, usually at universities or government research laboratories.

In addition to these proprietary systems, corporations also made use of one or more of various independent email service providers, such as MCIMail, AT&T's Easylink and CompuServe. When email system operators connected to each other or to the Internet, they did so on an experimental basis with little fanfare. For example, MCIMail operated an Internet gateway for its customers without much publicity or support for many years.

But over the past decade the Internet became popular and obvious as the glue that would bind these disparate systems. Internet service providers were established in droves, and countries loosened government monopolies on data communications, making corporate investment in Internet access easier, cheaper and more competitive. At the same time, the Web was taking off, making it acceptable and expected for corporations to have their own Internet Web presence and run Internet applications from every corporate desktop.

While the Internet was becoming more affordable and useful, corporations began to augment or replace their proprietary email systems with more open ones, or connected their systems to the Internet to communicate beyond their own borders. The "@" sign became a household word, and rattling off one's email identity in the form of *user@example.com* became commonplace. (One of the more curious circumstances is hearing two America Online users tell each other their address, in the form of *joe@aol.com*—even though everything after the "@" is unnecessary.)

As email became more functional, it also became a more accepted means of corporate communications. Today we send invoices via email rather than fax them or send originals via postal mail. We email answers to our customers' queries, and we don't think twice about sending email to friends and business associates around the world. We now get email composed entirely in another language besides English. And, as matter of fact, this entire book was created with a series of email messages!

In the early 1990s, email systems were mostly the province of the Information System (IS) professional and had little penetration in the warp and woof of corporate culture. Few CEOs would admit to using email, and those that did often had their administrative assistants or secretaries operate the computer to collect and send messages. (Many still do!) But email became essential as the corporate *Diaspora* increased: Branch offices in different time zones, telecommuters, international affiliates and different work hours from the usual 9-to-5 all rely on email to get work done and information communicated across the enterprise.

But this *Diaspora* isn't just limited to individual corporations. Nowadays, workgroups are composed of teams from many different corporations that need to develop a product, come to agree on how to treat a common customer or resolve a dispute. The tie that binds these workers is email first and foremost. Those workers that don't have a readily accessible email address are quickly left out of the loop and fall behind the curve. Those who don't know how to make use of email's more subtle features can waste hours or lose information.

A DAY IN YOUR EMAIL ADMINISTRATOR'S LIFE

We aren't going to spend a lot of time convincing you of the importance of email: If you are reading this book, you probably already agree with us. But let us illustrate some of the typical problems that you might experience during an average day as the email administrator for your corporation.

You wake up to the alarm at 6:30 a.m. and try to turn it off before your spouse wakes up too. Out of bed, you pad down to the den and turn on your computer. In a few moments, you bring up your dialing software and connect to the Internet, and then proceed to download your messages. Not bad—only 134 messages since you checked late last night. Most of them are just status reports and chitchat, along with a few of the usual annoying get-rich-quick schemes and porn site invitations that you wish you could stop coming into your corporate email network but in the meantime routinely delete. You remind yourself once again that you should investigate some blocking software sometime soon to see if that might eliminate these messages.

One message that you really need to read is 3 gigabytes long—luckily you learned how to set up your mail program to ignore long messages, otherwise you would be waiting until lunchtime before it could finish downloading.

Another message contains a rather curious attachment that you can't read. You suspect it is from your colleague down in the finance department, who loves to try out the latest and greatest email software and annoy you with these messages that prove that you are still behind the times and not running something that is up-to-date. He mentions something about a Java applet that you might not be able to view—that will have to wait. You really don't feel like trying to track this problem down, and you wish that your pal in finance would stop downloading the latest and greatest email products and stick to the standard email software that you keep trying to enforce on the overall corporation.

In the past he sent you email messages that were formatted with hypertext markup tags—the language of the Web. You couldn't read those either, but they usually turned out to be greeting cards or contain lots of odd fonts that really didn't make much difference to you. All you saw was plain text, which took away some of the impact but was good enough for you to read.

This morning you have a purpose in your email quest: You are looking for the latest version of a proposal from your London office colleagues. London is trying to install a new version of your corporate email software, and they are already well past their lunch hour and eagerly awaiting your pearls of wisdom. One of them sent you the proposal as a Microsoft Word attachment, which you need to make some quick changes to this morning so that the folks overseas can approve and send back to corporate headquarters to start the purchase process.

London is using Word because they want to format the proposal properly. If they just sent you the text inside the body of a message, you would be able to read the text but wouldn't be able to approve the format. You make a mental note to tell them to send you both in the future—a note that somehow never makes it into your consciousness for the rest of the day.

Unfortunately, London has upgraded to the latest version of Word, while your home machine back is still running the older version. Of course, the file formats are incompatible, and you'll have to wait until you get to the office and try to find someone in your department that has a more recent copy to read the document. Luckily, it fits on a floppy disk that you can take with you. You quickly save it to a floppy, but in your rush to get out of the house, you leave it at home.

Just as you finish with your replies, you look up at the clock—7:43. It is time to take a shower and wake the family for the day's activities. You down a quick breakfast and head into the office, where you spend the next three hours in meetings, away from your desk. Your company has nine different email systems, and you are trying to eliminate a few of them and simplify supporting all this software. You had originally wanted to bring everyone over to a single email product, but you have given up on that goal as next to impossible. Still, it would be nice if you could remove a few islands of staunch supporters and cut down on the number of products.

Finally, you get back to your office and have a chance to check your email again. Luckily, your office has a high-speed connection to the Internet, so that 3-gigabyte file doesn't ruin the rest of your day or tie up your machine. Unfortunately, it turns out that the file is an .EXE file, and you don't particularly want to run it. The last time you downloaded an executable program it contained a virus that messed up your machine for several days until your IT department could clean it up. Further, you have another 140 messages to plow through while you gobble down a quick sandwich and get that Word document off to London, which has been calling (three times!) while you were out all morning.

Too bad you forgot that disk back home with the proposal. You ask London to resend the file, meanwhile using the time to track down your local Word support person to find out how to convert a new Word document into an older one. You know that these support people will be hard to track down. Last you saw these people, they were spending most of their time trying to upgrade users of older versions of Word installed around the corporation. You thought you had problems with nine different email products? There are almost as many different word processing products scattered around the enterprise.

By the time you find someone to help you and are done getting your corrections into your document, you miss the workday in London.

As the day wears on, you realize that tomorrow you'll be on a plane to Omaha doing staff evaluations and you'll need to get a laptop ready to bring along so you can get some work done while you are out. Unfortunately, IT doesn't have anything decent to loan you and you forgot to ask one of your staff members to bring in a department laptop from home. Now you'll have to either do without one or run around the building attempting to borrow one for the next few days.

And your day continues.

EMAIL CHAOS

In our description above, email plays a central role in the workday. And along with that new focus comes a heavy responsibility. Many of us now use email to keep track of our "to do" lists, organize our calendar and meeting schedule, and notify us of pending problem areas. Email has become a heavy weight on our shoulders, as we deal with the frustration of incorporating it into our working lives.

Our scenario mentions several of the problems surrounding email's use, such as when the time comes to send a graphics file as an attachment or to send a document from our word processor. We often hear corporate workers complain of having "too much email," whether that means tens or hundreds of daily messages. A reasonable working definition for too much is more email than you can handle at a single sitting, whether that is hours or minutes. In our example, getting several hundred daily messages isn't uncommon in many high-tech companies, and is certainly more than anyone wants to deal with in a single session.

Some of us have become obsessive about checking our email at night and on weekends, extending the workday as we spend hours answering and reviewing messages to stay current with the flow. Indeed, during a typical weekend for one of us it wasn't a surprise that email queries sent on a Saturday afternoon were answered by all of our correspondents before Sunday evening! Many of you fear long business trips without being able to get to your email and the resulting message backlog that will greet you on your return.

In our scene, we were able to filter (by size) the extra-long message while at home with a slower modem connection. However, this isn't always the typical situation, and you need to have a solid understanding of the tools that are available to help organize and filter your email bonanza.

And finding your coworkers' email identity is often easier to accomplish over the phone than any other means. Making small mistakes in addressing often leads to consequences that can be anywhere from annoying to disastrous.

All of this makes for lots of pain and suffering when you want to take control over your email destiny.

In our scenario, we saw alternating periods of fortune and misfortune, depending on the behavior of various email systems, operators, users and software. And as much as we'd like to imagine otherwise, this is the way email generally works for us: Some days the email gods are smiling and we can get our work done, and some days we can't.

Some of these problems are substandard desktop software. But some of the blame lies squarely with the rise of the Internet. As the Internet has become the de facto means of intercorporate communications, other proprietary email systems have declined. And we have seen first-hand the situation that is common in many of today's corporations that have to maintain multiple email systems from different vendors, either by choice or by default.

In the early, primitive days of email you didn't have any choice when it came to running a particular email product: If the corporate enterprise was running PROFS, you ran PROFS. But the Internet has changed that equation, providing freedom of choice for email software. Now you can switch products at the drop of a hat and still be connected. Freedom of choice is nice, but you might end up trading one series of problems for another. And not all the functions present in proprietary systems easily translate into Internet-based products. For example, one of the benefits of using PROFS was the simple enterprisewide calendar system that was maintained for every user. No Internet-based product has been deployed that can match this functionality.

And some of the blame lies with computer manufacturers themselves, who have bulked up their machines with multiple copies of email products,[1] Internet access software, Web browsers and other things that you don't really need. It used to be that buying a new computer meant adding the software you needed to make it productive. These days, the first thing a new computer user does is delete this unnecessary software.

We've seen all of these problems first-hand. We have both used email for more than a decade in various working environments with various systems. And while both of us consider ourselves very experienced and email-savvy, we've have been stuck with our share of email problems. We've sent plenty of messages that didn't arrive for one reason or another. We've both tried to open many unreadable attachments or mangled messages. We've tried to fax from our email systems unsuccessfully and failed to receive faxes as email messages. We've seen this happen to our friends and colleagues, some of whom are very experienced computer users. In fact, the level of computer expertise isn't relevant when it comes to using email effectively. We all could use some help.

Out of these frustrations we have written this book.

We want to help make email more joy than jail in your working life.

We want to provide you with lots of practical information on how to make you productive using email and solve some common problems with simple fixes that are often hidden inside software you already own.

We want you, as the individual email user, to understand what options and features are available on other products than the one you are using at the moment. You might want to switch products, or lobby your corporate email administrator to consider alternatives.

We also want to give advice to the corporate email administrator who has to deal with making systemwide changes as technology matures or as needs evolve within his or her corporation. If you are such a person, you'll be able to compare products and features and see if it is worthwhile to switch products or upgrade to a newer version.

Finally, email is about communicating with others. We want you to understand the capabilities and constraints under which your correspondents operate so that you can communicate effectively. Unfortunately, the power of email is limited by the least common denominator between your systems, rather the combination of the two. So, sometimes it is more effective to raise your overall functionality by giving your correspondents better software!

100% PURE INTERNET

There aren't many simple answers to these issues, which is one of the reasons why this book is the length it is. But having said that, we'll suggest a goal, which we call "100% pure Internet." In brief, this means that, to the largest extent possible, you should select products that faithfully implement Internet standards and protocols as their native mode.

Having a 100% pure system also means you have the freedom to choose your products. If you were to start using one of these products for reading and sending messages, you could easily switch to one of the others with very little loss of functionality. That's the beauty of being 100% pure Internet.

If you can avoid using an application gateway, do so! If you can avoid converting between different messaging technologies, do so! If you are using an enterprise email system that is running on something other than Internet protocols and standards, try to convert to one that is!

Granted, no system or series of products is completely 100% pure Internet, although a few come close. And no email system is perfect, no matter what its purity level might be.

What about those systems that aren't 100% pure? For example, Lotus Notes, Novell GroupWise and Microsoft Exchange are all fine email systems but use their own protocols, message formats and transports. While they can work with Internet-based email through the use of gateways, they aren't 100% pure—not even close.

Notes, GroupWise and Exchange are very popular, mainly because they contain many features not found in the 100% pure products, such as integrated calendars, message recall and acknowledgment receipts.

Nevertheless, after all the email products we've used (more on that in a moment), we still think that the goal of a 100% pure Internet system is worthwhile. With such a system, you'll find yourself saving time and energy when it comes to technical support, and you'll find a better series of products overall.

The "How Can I" Matrix: Organize And Simplify Your Email Life			
	Receiving	**Sending**	**General**
Desktop	**Chapter 2:** ✔ **How can I** manage incoming email? ✔ **How can I** comprehend error messages and correct them?	**Chapter 3:** ✔ **How can I** use email to become my own push publisher? (manage mail lists) ✔ **How can I** integrate email with other desktop apps, such as calendars, schedules, address books, PIMs, Pilots, etc.	**Chapter 4:** ✔ **How can I** exchange messages securely? ✔ **How can I** manage more than one email identity?
Enterprise	**Chapter 5:** ✔ **How can I** access my email remotely (and presumably over slow speed connects)? ✔ **How can I** successfully use email as a means to enhance technical support and customer relations?	**Chapter 6:** ✔ **How can I** know your email address without having to call you on the phone first? ✔ **How can I** integrate email with other messaging services, such as fax, paging, etc.?	**Chapter 7:** ✔ **How can I** be sure that you can reliably and safely view my attachments and formatted messages? ✔ **How can I** determine the level of Internet-readiness for my enterprise email system?

HOW THIS BOOK IS ORGANIZED

We realize that you want answers to your everyday problems to try to become more productive and use email in new and exciting ways.

The only way we know how to help improve your email life is to first bring some order to it. So we have created a special "How Can I" matrix of six different cells, in two rows and three columns.

If you have a specific business problem, you should be able to find its solution in one particular cell of our matrix, and then go to the particular chapter that covers that situation. Don't feel obligated to read through our entire book if you need answers to one or two questions!

For example, if you can't receive attachments reliably, Chapter 7 on general enterprise email issues will cover this problem.

Use our "How Can I" matrix as both a reference guide to your own email universe as well as the organizing theme for this book. Each cell of the matrix contains two questions that strike at the heart of common email issues and will serve as the basis of a series of six subject chapters that will address each group of questions.

Our matrix recognizes that email is both personal and corporate: There are times you'll have questions about something involving your own desktop configuration or setup, and other times when your entire enterprise will want to standardize on a particular application or method. So, one axis for our matrix is desktop vs. enterprise issues. The other axis differentiates email issues into those involving receiving, sending or general email issues.

Chapter 2 looks at desktop-receiving issues, something that touches us all. How do we manage to pare down the sheer volume of email we receive and make it easier to sort through the time-sensitive ones from the trivial? How can we understand the various error messages that we receive and figure out which ones are genuine problems and which ones are just informing us of temporary situations?

Chapter 3 examines desktop-sending issues. It covers the two issues about using email to become one's own publisher to broadcast content. It also looks at ways that we can integrate email into other desktop applications to broaden our computing experience. We'll examine ways you can make use of the latest round of portable devices, such as the 3Com Palm-Pilot and Rolodex REX.

Chapter 4 rounds out the desktop issues with two general problems about exchanging secure messages and managing multiple email identities. By secure messages we mean the ability to encrypt, send and decrypt messages and documents to prevent others from snooping on your correspondence. And these days having more than one email identity is essential to getting one's work done—something well known to many America Online users.

Chapter 5 begins our enterprise-receiving discussion and examines how we can access our email remotely without spending lots of time waiting and redialing. We also talk about how corporations can make use of email to enhance customer support and relations by incorporating email into their Web site and support systems.

Chapter 6 covers enterprise-sending issues, such as how we can figure out someone else's email address without having to first call them on the phone. We also look at ways to integrate email into messaging applications such as fax, paging and voicemail.

Chapter 7 finishes out enterprise coverage with two general problems: being able to reliably view attachments and richly formatted messages. This covers the issues surrounding receiving viruses as email attachments as well. We'll cover how various groupware products such as Notes, GroupWise and Exchange work with Internet-based email. And we look at how corporations can determine the level of Internet-readiness with their email systems.

Finally, in Chapter 8, we have some closing words of advice.

The discussion in each chapter is divided into five sections: First, a brief introduction that lays the groundwork and presents an overview of some of the issues; then a more complete discussion of the two problems covered in that chapter, along with an explanation of particular software and hardware products that contribute to the problem. These explanations can't cover every email product, of course, but we assume that most of you will be running Windows95/98 or NT-based products.

We have chosen the most recent versions of the most popular email products to use in our examples and illustrations of both the potential problems and the intended solutions. Our list includes the following versions of software available in January 1998:

- Microsoft Outlook Express, the version that comes with Internet Explorer 4.01
- Netscape Messenger, version 4.04, which comes with the complete Communicator package
- Qualcomm's Eudora Pro, version 4.0
- Lotus' cc:Mail, version 8.1
- CompuServe's WinCIM, version 3.02
- America Online, version 3.0

These six products represent the most popular email software in use today [2]. They also show the wide range of how email is used. Three of the products—Outlook Express, Messenger and Eudora—are 100% pure Internet products, making use of Internet email standards, servers and protocols.

Two of the products, America Online and CompuServe, are software used for their own proprietary networks. While you can use both products to send and receive email over the Internet, they have lots of other features than doing email. For example, you can use either product to participate in group discussions and chat rooms. With either product you are tied to an email identity on their own network. If you want to change neighborhoods and move to a new network, you have to find some other software. Finally, cc:Mail is primarily a LAN-based email product. You need a cc:Mail server to connect to and exchange messages.

We cover Notes, GroupWise and Exchange software in Chapter 7, particularly focusing on how they relate to exchanging Internet messages.

In every chapter we cover the relevant standards that have been put into place for each situation. In many cases these standards don't solve the problem, and in some cases they are the cause of the errant behavior we describe. We propose some solutions, tricks and tips to get around the problems posed at the beginning of the chapter, and we end with some predictions as to where the future is headed.

WHO THIS BOOK IS FOR

Writing any book assumes a certain audience and skill level.

Our primary focus is with corporate and business email users, although much of what we have to say applies to personal use as well. This book is designed as a primer for the IS professional as well as savvy end user. We assume that you and your co-workers are trying to communicate with your customers and business partners, and you have a pressing need for such communication that goes beyond mere personal correspondence.

Many of our examples work equally well in large multinational corporations as well as smaller offices and departments. Where they diverge, we'll say so. We will try to provide advice that will work in the widest possible circumstances, but when it doesn't fit specific circumstances, we'll let you know.

We assume that corporations will have more than one email network, including multiple servers, software versions and operating systems. We do assume that most corporate networks are at least running Internet protocols on their email servers, if not on most of their desktops as well. This mixture of protocols, LAN-based email, standalone and laptop users, and various networked email systems is the hard reality of many corporate email environments these days, despite many best efforts at trying to simplify the situation.

We'll examine what corporate email administrators can do to improve their systems, whether they are large or small. Sometimes this will be a fairly simple step. Sometimes this will involve specific changes to particular servers or systems.

We assume you already have some sort of email software on your computer (hopefully it is one of the applications listed earlier). Maybe you use more than one email product: one at home and one at work. Or maybe your company is in the process of weaning you off one product and recommending using another. We try to incorporate specific information on a variety of products. Our interest is in making you more productive and giving practical advice, rather than convincing you to use one email product over another. We'll certainly give you our opinions about the relative differences in functions, features and ease of use of the specific products mentioned earlier: We won't shy away from our opinions, nor disguise them as facts when they aren't.

As we mentioned earlier, we use the most current version of six different products to illustrate both problems and solutions in our discussion. If you are using an earlier version, you can use this book to decide whether any particular set of features is worthwhile for you to upgrade to these newer versions, or perhaps switch to another product entirely.

We don't assume you know the details about various Internet protocols or how to reconfigure your operating system to support them, and we'll explain these details as we go along. And we'll provide plenty of links to other Web sites with more information, details about particular products or protocols, and further reading.

While we assume that you are using Windows95/98 or NT operating systems and software, we'll make mention of other products when appropriate relating to earlier 16-bit Windows 3.1 as well as Macintosh and UNIX desktop configurations.

WHAT THIS BOOK ISN'T ABOUT

We aren't going to give you tips about how to compose your messages properly—this so-called "netiquette" and online manners are best left to other books or just plain common sense.

We aren't writing a book for first-time email users, going through all the ways to use email effectively as business communications or how to justify an initial investment in email technologies. There are plenty of books already written about these topics. But we also don't assume that you are an email expert, as we mentioned above.

This isn't a book for how to set up and run an enterprise email network. While many of our tips and hints are geared toward enterprise users, if you need to learn how to set up a system from scratch, this book isn't going to provide a great deal of insight. But if you currently administer an enterprise email system, then many of the things we'll describe will help to improve the lives of your email users.

We aren't going to replace the instruction manuals and other software documentation that shows you how to use the many features of your email software.[3]

We aren't writing a book about the ins and outs of using America Online or Eudora or Outlook Express—we don't particularly care which email software you have running and whether you have a constant high-speed connection to the Internet or a slower modem with intermittent access. Plus, there are already plenty of books that explain these choices.

This book isn't about how to surf the Internet, run various Internet applications such as news readers and chat programs, or where to download the best shareware programs that do the same. While there certainly are many other Internet applications other than email, we are focused on just how to use email effectively.

And if you are looking for tips and tricks on picking the right Internet provider, this isn't the book for you either—there are plenty of that sort on the shelves as well.

WHAT IS ON OUR WEB SITE

This book covers technologies that are subject to changes: Software programs get new features and are upgraded almost weekly it seems. Trying to stay on top of these changes is difficult, and impossible to do so in print. We will make use of the Web site at *www.everythingemail.net* to track these changes to the various programs mentioned here. When we find something new and noteworthy, we'll post this information on the Web site.

The Web site also has links to other products mentioned in the book, offering specific solutions to various email problems. We'll try our best to keep these links accurate, although that might not always be possible.

Endnotes

1. This is especially true when it comes to multiple copies of email products and other Internet software. Perhaps no vendor has done more than Microsoft here—sometimes new computers come with multiple Microsoft email products pre-installed, such as Windows Messaging, Exchange email software for Microsoft Network, the full version of Outlook 97 and 98, and even Outlook Express, part of the version 4 Internet Explorer Web browser. Adding to the confusion is that the names are almost meaningless as a guide toward their functionality: Outlook Express has features not found in the "full" Outlook 97 product, for example.

2. There is a wide variety of other email products, including many that are either freely available or at low cost. A good place to start is at *www.imc.org/demoware.html*.

3. We suggest that instead of buying yet another book with these instructions, just review the help files and documentation with the software if you are stuck with a problem.

2

Messaging on the Desktop: Receiving

In this chapter, we consider two central issues of receiving email on the desktop: How to manage your incoming messages and how to interpret reports of unsuccessful attempts to deliver your messages. These two topics are a good place to begin for desktop issues. It is almost a certainty that before you send your first message from a new account that there will be messages waiting for you; and, despite two decades of research and development in email systems, manual intervention is often required when these systems encounter problems.

INTRODUCTION

To begin, it is important to understand something of the origins of email in order to understand the present state of affairs.

As quaint as it seems now, the original designers of the Internet's predecessor, the ARPAnet, didn't envision messaging as a significant application in the network. Rather, their focus was on tightly coupled applications communicating in real time. When email was developed, it was used primarily for "interpersonal communication." As such, the underlying mechanisms—the protocols and conventions—allowed for a fair amount of human interpretation. For example, Internet messages are structured as human-readable text, rather than using a concise binary notation. This orientation allows for great flexibility, but it is also a weakness: It is perhaps too forgiving of errors in implementation and operation.

To compound matters, although many people (including both authors) use email as their primary means of remote communications, few tools on the desktop are well equipped to deal with a continuous stream of email. The reason is insidious: In addition to receiving messages intended solely for the recipient, people also receive both discussion group (mailing list) traffic and newsgroup traffic on their desktop. As use of internetworking technology continues to grow in the Internet, intranet and extranet sectors, the volume of all three message sources continues to grow.

As described in Chapter 1, these two trends paint a horrific scenario awaiting many of you when you sit down to read your incoming messages. One goal throughout this chapter will be to illustrate the techniques used for managing this messaging morass.

Regrettably, this is an area where products have few standards to rely on in order to produce solutions. As paradoxical as it may seem, Internet messaging standards provide little guidance on how messages should be handled once received. It is up to the authors of desktop messaging software to provide proprietary mechanisms to aid their customers. Regrettably, if either history or the market is any judge, few products are ready for the challenge. The discussion of this, which follows next, is painful.

However, some solutions exist, and we shall consider them in detail. Filtering, based on both originator and recipient addresses is examined, as well as the use of whitelists and blacklists. Both are proven to be useful as first line management techniques. There are, of course, other tricks to be considered to minimize the amount of time you must devote to receiving incoming messages.

One of the great advantages of Internet messaging[1] is its inclusive nature: Proprietary and legacy messaging systems can be connected to an Internet messaging system through the use of specialized software, termed "application gateways." An application gateway for email is responsible for translating between the protocols and conventions of one messaging system to another. Sometimes the translation is algorithmic, for example converting from one data format to another. Sometimes the translation is heuristic, in which the rules applied work in some, but not all, circumstances. Sometimes either the algorithms or heuristics are "lossy", which simply means that if a message makes a round-trip through a messaging gateway, then the new messaging coming back won't be identical to the message that originally went through. Naturally, the limitations of such gateways may result in messages not being delivered.

In addition to the issues of technology mismatches, there are many operational reasons why some messages aren't delivered. For example, the recipient's mailbox might be full, the recipient's messaging relay (the computer system that accepts mail on his or her behalf) might be unavailable for an extended period of time (e.g., due to network outage or hardware failure), and so on. In all cases, the best possible outcome is for an "error report" to be returned to the originator. However, depending on the circumstances, a likely case may be for nothing to be returned to the originator. For example, an error report might not be able to be generated or sent back. In some cases, of course, the message may actually be delivered to the user's mailbox, but a catastrophe might occur (e.g., disk failure). For our purposes, this chapter considers what happens if an error report is delivered to the originator. In this case, the recipient of such a message might choose to take action.[2] In this area, Internet messaging standards provide some guidance to users. Most notably, there is a standardized format for error reports, which indicates the mailbox that didn't receive the message along with some reasons as to why the message wasn't delivered.

Although the reasons vary, in point of practice the only interesting information is whether the program that created the error report deduced that the error is transient or permanent. Transient errors include such matters as a locked or overflowing mailbox, an inability to access a local database, and so on. An indication of a transient error means that you can try sending the same message again to the recipient in question and perhaps it will be successfully delivered. In contrast, permanent errors indicate that something must change in the message before a successful outcome is possible, for example the recipient's address isn't recognized, perhaps because it is misspelled.

So, let us now consider these issues in greater detail, along with aspects of the systems that cause them.

PROBLEMS

As we mentioned in the Introduction, we all think we get too much email. Of course, everyone's threshold for what constitutes "too much" is different—we've seen some people go ballistic over a single message, while others are a lot more tolerant. Nevertheless, we all like to think that we have control over our inbox, if only so we can spend more time elsewhere in our computing lives.

For now, let's look at four sources of message clutter:

1. Mailing List Traffic

2. Unsolicited Commercial Email

3. Large Attachments

4. Error Reports

These aren't the sole sources of unwanted messages, but they do account for the majority of the problems you are likely to encounter.

Mailing List Traffic

Mailing lists are the single biggest culprit to mailbox pollution. There are many reasons you might subscribe to a list—you are interested in the topic at the time, you think you want to participate with a particular community, or your department begins a discussion over a project or a client. It doesn't matter. Eventually, your interest wanes, or the number of messages begins to get out of control. And by the time you want your inbox left alone, you either have forgotten how to get off the list or you simply cannot.

Mailing lists come in handy, because in a single operation you can send the same message to an entire group. It is a powerful way to try to coordinate activities of several people or when you need to correspond frequently with multiple people at once.

But there is a problem with lists. When your recipients get your message, they can't always easily reply. Sometimes they don't want to reply to the entire list, but just the original sender of the message. Not all recipients have the skills to understand how to reply properly, and not all email programs work the same way when it comes to replying.

Here is an example. Suppose we have a mailing list of five individual addresses. When each person responds, a reply is sent to all five addresses and five new email messages are sent—in addition to sending this reply as another message to the sender's mailbox. What started out as a single, perhaps simple, request can quickly turn into 40 or 100 separate messages in short order.

Lists have other issues, too. Sometimes the list program will take a simple error and propagate it to the entire list. What if our list isn't just five people but 500 or 50,000 people? And what if among these 500 or 50,000 addresses are a few invalid ones: People do change their email identity often and don't necessarily inform everyone of the change. Worse yet, what if among these addresses are programs that respond to your original email, saying for example that the person is out of the country and won't be back for several days? Now you have one program (your mailing list) communicating back and forth with another (the vacation program).

You could easily end up with lots of useless mail messages, and all of these error messages could get transmitted back to the entire list, something that easily gets annoying.

The issue is how the mailing list software resolves the actual list of addresses. As we'll get into more detail in Chapter 3, each mailing list program has different ways of doing this. There are times when the entire set of addresses is replaced with an alias name, which is placed in one of the message header fields. And sometimes this alias name can only be used by the list owner, and sometimes it can be used by anyone who has already subscribed to the list.

Some products work differently: They hide all the recipient names and use a special list address in both the From: and To: fields. This special list address is yet another alias, but this time the alias contains just a single individual's address, called the list moderator or list owner, rather than to the entire list. This avoids the entire list receiving everyone's comments and error messages. But it does place a burden on the list moderator to forward meaningful replies to the entire list.

Other products place the addresses of the entire list in the cc: or Bcc: fields of the message header, and the moderator's address in the From:

field. You can see how lists need lots of maintenance and careful use to keep focused and accurate delivery of messages.

Every mailing list has its own personality, and many assume multiple personalities as the contributors to the list gain and lose interest or get motivated to post messages. Some lists are active with many tens or even hundreds of daily messages, and others will have one message a week. The problem is that you don't necessarily remember all the lists you have subscribed to over time, and tracking down this information can be almost impossible after the fact.

Unsolicited Commercial Email

There is a second problem with mailbox pollution—one that the popular press has latched onto—called "spam,"[3] or bulk mailings of unsolicited commercial messages. Typically these contain offers that are too good to be true (e.g., "make money fast!") or contain links to pornographic Web sites.

Unsolicited email is a fact of life for Internet users, and even the infrequent user of email will still receive such messages. How do these miscreants get your email address? Easily. They get them from postings on various newsgroups, from your Web site that lists your email address, from other email that you've sent over time or from sites where you've given your email address (e.g., in order to purchase a product). The vexing thing is that the more you use the Internet for your business and personal life, the more you'll end up getting unsolicited email. Our advice is to get used to it and don't get too bothered about it. It isn't worth getting worked up.

Once upon a time, we used to subscribe to each printed magazine with a different name, usually a middle initial that was keyed to the name of the magazine. In this way, we could tell which publication sold our name to which mailing list when the solicitations invariably arrived months later. Unfortunately, most of us can't easily track where email solicitations originate.[4] But they do add to the overall message load.

Part of the unsolicited email issue also concerns scams as well. Many Internet users have fallen for the "collect your free prize" email. All that is required is a credit card number to pay for "shipping and handling." And even when this email seems to come from legitimate sources, it isn't. Of course, you should treat all of these kinds of messages quickly by deleting them.

Sometimes this takes rather subtle and nasty turns: When Yahoo introduced its free email system for the general public, anyone could sign up and receive a *mailbox@yahoo.com*. It looked like the whole world was working at Yahoo's offices because in the past, Yahoo employees had that particular domain name for their email addresses. What happened was very predictable: Con artists posed as Yahoo employees, who had since changed all of their email address to *someone@yahoo-inc.com*. The con was to request a credit card number for some contest or another by replying to *contest-winner@yahoo.com* or some other legitimate-sounding mailbox.

The moral of this and any other spam story: If it sounds too good to be true, it certainly is. And don't give your mailbox password to anyone for whatever reason. Make sure you understand what you are intending to purchase if you intend to give someone your credit card number over the Internet as well.

Large Attachments

In our "day in the email life" scenario in Chapter 1, we mentioned a third problem for desktop mail users: getting messages with unanticipated large attachments, especially when using a slower-speed modem connection to retrieve your mail. This isn't a function of any particular software, but just a result of unfortunate circumstances.

Anything larger than 50 kilobytes takes too long to receive over a phone line, especially when you are at the end of a long day of travel in some hotel room, or when you are in a hurry trying to catch up with your email. We've been there before and it isn't pleasant. Figure that your average Internet dialup connection these days is around 25 kilobits per second. Given the overhead and other delays, you are usually lucky to get more than 10 kilobits per second—or about a kilobyte a second—transferred to your desktop over such a connection. That means a minute for that 50-kilobyte file, and usually longer.

You can't control what or when your correspondents will send—although we do have a few helpful strategies for you to consider later on in this chapter.

Attachments carry a second issue with them, besides their unwieldy size and length of time to collect them: the potential for virus infection of your system. Since attachments can be executable programs, they could contain—either maliciously or inadvertently—a virus. Does this happen?

Yes, including getting infections from places that you would otherwise trust, such as email from a bona-fide Microsoft employee.

Attachments can also contain other programs as well that could do just as much potential damage to your machine, such as poorly written Active X and Java applications. These could be contained in a page of HTML source code, and you may not recognize what they are doing until the damage is done.

By the way, notice we are careful to state that the attachment can carry a virus. We've seen lots of bogus email warning of the potential for something else: a virus contained inside the message body of the email itself. This isn't possible and it is a hoax that comes around every so often. But the infected attachments are very real.

These viruses usually come from unsuspected places, such as inside Word documents as macro viruses. The macro viruses can cause all sorts of odd behavior in your machine, from changing the way Word operates to minor annoyances such as changing the date and time stamp of your files. If you think this can't happen to you, check your Word Tools | Macro | Macros menus and see what is listed there. If blank, you are clean. If you have macros listed (and you have never created one), chances are it is a virus. A good way to tell is to delete it, then save and open a file and see if the same macro returns to the list. We saw one user's machine that had been infected with a macro for almost a year and had changed all of his Word files into templates. It didn't destroy any information, but he was lucky. And he got it from downloading an email attachment, which was a Word file.

If you don't open the attachment, you won't get infected. But, then again, what's the point? We'll have other solutions in Chapter 7.

Error Reports

A fourth potential polluter of your inbox is the various error reports that come back to you when something is wrong with the mail you've sent. Here the problem, as we said earlier, is that these errors were really never intended for humans to interpret, and after reading many of them you might be inclined to agree as well. The trick is trying to match the particular error with the particular piece of mail that you sent—whether it was just a few minutes ago or last week. Unfortunately, the type of software program you have on your desktop almost always doesn't help here— mail servers generate the error reports.

Compounding the problem are two things: time delay and hidden headers. Because the Internet isn't a predictable place, chances are that there will be some delay when an error message arrives back in your mailbox. This delay could be a few minutes, a few hours or even a few days, depending on the links between your mail server and your recipient's. And sometimes the same error message gets periodically returned, even though you only sent a single message.

Hidden headers also make it harder to understand what is happening. Each email software program has a way to "simplify" the header information in any message that you receive. This could hide information useful for diagnosing the error, in the cause of reducing clutter on your display.

For example, let's use Netscape Messenger. There are three different options (All, Brief and Normal) that you can use to display the header, found in Options|Show Headers. The All option, as you may think, displays the entire header:

```
Return-Path: <mailman2@cyber.fantasyzone.com>
Received: from cyber.fantasyzone.com
([209.37.113.6]) by mail.sohonet.com (Post.Office
MTA v3.1 release PO203a ID# 0-32347U500L100S10000)
with ESMTP id AAA91 for <david@strom.com>; Fri, 19
Dec 1997 18:23:52 -0500
Received: from Redline
(1Cust244.tnt13.atl2.da.uu.net [153.36.90.244]) by
cyber.fantasyzone.com (8.8.3/8.7.3) with SMTP id
SAA07690 for <david@strom.com>; Fri, 19 Dec 1997
18:02:32 -0500
Message-Id:
<199712192302.SAA07690@cyber.fantasyzone.com>
From: CEN <mailman2@cyber.fantasyzone.com>
To: <david@strom.com>
Date: Fri, 19 Dec 1997 18:00:00
Reply-To: mailman2@cyber.fantasyzone.com
Errors-To: mailman2@cyber.fantasyzone.com
X-Mailer: NetMailer v1.03 [D.R-
D988CAA968EA8988FAD928F]
Subject: FREE!! - Quality Adult Feeds For Your
Site! - FREE!!
Mime-Version: 1.0
Content-Type: text/plain; charset="us-ascii"
X-Mozilla-Status: 0001
Content-Length: 1532
```

Another option is to just display the subject and destination, eliminating the routing information and other useful things to try to track down how this message got to you:

```
FREE!! - Quality Adult Feeds For Your Site! -
FREE!! (CEN , 12/19/97 18:00)

To: <david@strom.com>
```

Besides matching cause and effect, you'll also have trouble distinguishing between messages that are informational and mostly warnings with those that describe some more critical situation. And not all situations are permanent. Take the examples of an error generated from a full mailbox[5] or a router disconnected from the Internet or a downed server, which are mostly temporary conditions. And then compare to an unknown user or unknown domain name, which might be more fatal.

Sometimes a chain of other Internet-related events can cause a temporary email problem: For example, when we received a message saying that the domain aol.com could not be found. Granted, it is unlikely that the entire America Online system would disappear overnight, so this was probably caused by a routing failure to AOL's name servers, rather than the company going out of business. However, while it may be obvious to most of us that AOL isn't going to disappear overnight, many other lesser-known domains could easily be turned off, change their name or be disconnected. How can you tell whether or not to resend your message? Sometimes, you can't.[6] Of course, some of the mistakes are your own doing. If you aren't a careful typist, it is very easy to make a small mistake in someone's email address. We've done it countless times and will probably continue to do it many more times in the future. Some email products make it easier to fill in names that they already have in their address books—such as Outlook Express—and others such as CompuServe's WinCIM and MacCIM[7] software make it harder to guess the exact syntax of your correspondents.

Outlook Express actually makes things too easy. To reply to a received message, you just click on the person's address that is highlighted inside the message. However, if this person either has the wrong Reply-to: address, or is using a poorly implemented mail gateway, then Outlook Express won't let you change the address in the message you are composing. You have to manually delete the new message and create another one from scratch!

We'll talk more about how to decode these error messages later on in this chapter. But first let's look at some of the standards that are relevant to receiving email on the desktop.

STANDARDS

There are no standards that describe the actions that desktop software *must* take when receiving email. However, there are considerable explanations in standards documents that describe how messages are structured and how they might be interpreted.

In this section, we'll primarily focus on the headers. In Chapter 3, we look at structured messages, such as encoded and multipart messages. Next, we'll look at error reports. Finally, we'll look at an example of how powerful receiving software can be built using only a basic understanding of the standards and some minimal database capabilities.

Headers

At the highest level, an Internet message contains *headers* and a *body*. The headers are pairs of names and values, and the body, like the headers, is textually represented. If non-ASCII values needed to be represented (e.g., characters from a non-U.S. character set or binary structures), then an ASCII encoding is used. Discussion of encodings occurs in Chapter 3— for now, let's assume that all information is simple text.

There are four simple rules to understanding how a message is structured:

1. A message starts with one or more headers.
2. Each header is named by a keyword and followed by a value. Header keywords are case insensitive. The structure of the value depends on the header keyword.
3. The header value can span multiple lines, but never starts at the beginning of a line. Spaces and tabs are ignored, e.g., there is no significance between a single space and multiple adjacent spaces.
4. The body, which needn't be present, starts after the first blank line.

During transmission, lines are terminated with carriage return/line feed pairs, though local software may choose different end-of-line representations. Also, as we described in our last section, it is very important to understand that while a message may contain many, many headers, the software you use to read email may show you only a subset of them! You may need to enable special options in order to see many of these headers. For example, many of the headers useful for diagnostics are carefully hidden so as to reduce clutter.

Although Rule 3 above suggests that there might be a plethora of different formats for header values, in practice there are only three:

1. Unstructured text
2. Dates
3. Mailboxes

The first format is, naturally, uninteresting. Although the standards indicate a number of formats for different header values, the only useful searching is simple textual matching.

The date format used in messages is a bizarre mix of human-friendly and machine-unambiguous, for example:

    Thu, 08 Jan 1998 14:33:01 −0800

(The human-friendly part tells you the day of the week.) The only interesting aspect of this format is that the year includes a century, and hence is "year 2000 compliant."

Mailbox Format

The mailbox format is rather complex. Fortunately, the core structure is simple:

    local@domain

The "local" part is sometimes called "the mailbox" and the "domain" part is sometimes called "the host." The key thing to remember is that the semantics of the local part are meaningful only at the final destination host and probably don't have any relationship to the semantics used at your site.

There are numerous embellishments to this basic format, primarily made in the interests of being human-friendly. For example, a phrase can often precede the mailbox if it is placed between angle brackets:

    Marshall Rose <mrose@example.com>

Due to the syntax rules for header values, the phrase may need to be placed between quotation marks, like "Marshall T. Rose." There is also a format for grouping together related addresses. However, its use is rather obscure, and it is not widely implemented. Here are two examples:

An Example: Strom <dstrom@example.com>, Rose
    <mrose@example.com>;

Another Example: ;

The first shows a group containing two addresses that are specified. The second shows a group containing an unspecified number of addresses. What is this grouping format for? Well, some software lets you compose a message using this format, and when the message is sent out, the addresses inside the group don't appear in the headers of the outgoing message. This has its uses, we suppose.[8]

Composition Headers

At a minimum, a message needs to contain only two headers, an indication of the date that the message was composed (i.e., Date:) and an indication of who the message is composed for (i.e., To: or Bcc:). In practice, however, when a message is composed, there are several headers that are present. Let's look at the most common ones:

- To: and cc: indicate primary and secondary recipients. Both contain a list of addresses separated by commas. The difference between the two is intent: a message sent to a primary recipient is intended to elicit some action from the recipient; in contrast, a message sent to a secondary recipient is for informational purposes.

This provides a useful filtering hint: Messages listing your address in To: should command your attention, all other things being equal.

- Bcc: indicates "blind copy" recipients, which is a list of addresses separated by commas. Bcc: is strange because it can contain no addresses whatsoever!

  This is an example of where the theory of the standards and the practice of products diverge considerably. The intent of the standards is that the Bcc: is used as a communications mechanism between the user and the composition program, i.e., "send a copy of this message to each of these recipients in the Bcc: and send it in such a way that none of the other recipients knows that you have done so." Unfortunately, the common practice is for the composition program to simply send a message to the all recipients (primary, secondary and blind copy) which simply omits the Bcc:. The problem with such an approach is two-fold: first, a blind copy recipient can accidentally reply to the message, inadvertently disclosing their status; and, second, since the blind copy recipient's address appears nowhere in the message they receive, it is harder to filter it. The solution is to send each blind copy recipients a separate message that contains the original message. We discuss how this is done in Chapter 3.

- From: and Reply-To: which indicate the address authoring the message and the address to which any replies should be sent. Although you might think each would be limited to one address, both allow multiple addresses to be present, separated by commas.

  Some composition programs allow the user to specify the From: for the message. However, this is an implementation-specific feature: some programs allow the user to type this information in directly; others give the user an "Account Management" paradigm in which different email users are configured and then one is selected for use with the message.

  When replying to a message, it is the recipient's discretion as to who should be included in the reply. If a Reply-To: address is present, then, at a minimum, that address should be included in the reply. If no Reply-To: is present, then the From: address should be included in the reply. Beyond that, the reply may include addresses from the To: and cc:.

  From: and Reply-To: are the best examples of how the standards try to support a messaging protocol between people. Although the distinction between these two headers seems subtle, the authors of the standard had a very specific human-interaction paradigm in mind when they specified them. Given proper implementation in user software, careful use of these headers results in the effortless continuation of a correspondence to the appropriate individuals.

- Subject: indicates the topic of this message. Although it is unstructured text, programs that communicate via email often place special text there.

When replying to a message, the Subject: of the original message is generally copied to the Subject: of the reply, and prefixed with a short string, such as "Re:." This allows the originator's software to correlate the original message to any replies.

- Keywords: and References: contain words and phrases to help recipients categorize messages. In theory, this allows the originator to filter incoming messages. In practice, these two headers are rarely used.

- Comments: contains arbitrary text. There is no standardized usage for this header—it is likely an example of kitchen-sink standardization.

- Date: is generated by the user's composition program and contains the date that the message was submitted for delivery.

- Message-ID: is generated by the user's composition program. It is a unique identifier for the message. The structure of Message-ID: looks just like an email address with angle brackets, for example <local@domain>.

  When replying, an In-Reply-To: is created that contains the Message-ID: and Date: of the message being replied to. This allows the originator's software to correlate the original message to any replies.

- Sender: is generated by the user's composition program, if the From: used in the message is different from the sender's identity. Unlike the other headers, which take addresses, Sender: takes a single address and it contains a mailbox without any textual embellishments.

  This alludes to an important difference that we discuss in Chapter 3: the difference between the user responsible for sending the message and the user responsible for authoring it.

So, which headers are mandatory and which optional? In practice, a new message contains To: and Subject: supplied by the user, along with From:, Date: and Message-ID supplied by the user's composition program. Replies generally contain headers generated only by the user's composition program: these four headers along with In-Reply-To:.

Trace Headers

There are two headers, which are useful for debugging problems with the messaging infrastructure, Return-Path: and Received:.

Return-Path: is added by the infrastructure just as it delivers a message to you. In indicates the user responsible for sending the message. It generally corresponds to Sender:. However, there may be reasons why it differs, which we'll discuss later on in this chapter.

Received: usually occurs more than once—in fact, it usually occurs several times in each message. Every time a process takes responsibility for delivering a message, it puts a new Received: at the front of the message. This means that all of the Received: comprise a reverse-chronological history of the message's transit through the infrastructure. Want to know why a message took so long to get delivered to you? Check out the Received: times. Keep in mind, however, that the clocks used to derive the dates and times are probably not synchronized.

Unfortunately, the syntax of Received: is a bit tedious: It consists of multiple keyword and value pairs separated by spaces. The keywords are:

- from, which indicates the domain that relayed the message;
- by, which indicates the domain that accepted the message;
- via and with, which indicate how the message was transferred between the two domains;
- id, the queue identifier used by the receiving domain; and,
- for, which indicates the mailbox for which the message was intended.

Of these, the from value always appears, and the for value appears generally only when the message passes through a mailing list. Following the list of keywords and values is a semi-colon and the date that the message was received. Later on in this chapter we'll look at some examples.

Other Useful Headers

There are literally another 50 or so defined headers in various standards, along with even more headers that are informally used. Many of these headers are used when converting messages to and from the Internet email infrastructure. We won't mention these because, frankly, they're uninteresting—if something can't be represented using one of the standardized headers we've already discussed, it's probably not going to be of any value.

Having said that, here are some headers that are useful:

- MIME-Version: and anything starting with Content- are discussed in Chapter 3. Whenever these are encountered, it means that the body of the message is usually something other than unstructured text.

- Fax: and Phone: contain textual representations of the originator's facsimile and voice phone numbers.

- Importance:, Priority:, X-Priority: and Precedence: all try to impart some notion of the importance or urgency of the message. Only the first two of these are defined in standards documents. With the exception of X-Priority, the values are keywords (e.g., Importance: takes on one of high, normal or low, and Priority: takes on urgent, normal or non-urgent).

- X-Mailer: is unstructured text that identifies the program used to compose the message.

Other Non-useful Headers

Anytime you see a header that starts with Resent-, watch out! This is another example of where the theory of the standards and the practice of most implementations are far apart. The theory is that these headers are used to specify additional recipients when a message is to be redistributed. The notion of "redistribution" is different from "forwarding." When something is forwarded, the paradigm is one of attaching a cover letter to a message. When something is redistributed, the notion is that the message is simply rerouted to additional recipients. This rerouting would be equivalent to resealing a physical envelope and writing a new address on the outside. Many implementations, for one reason or another, don't seem to distinguish between these two activities, and hence have opted not to provide a redistribution capability.

Privately-defined Headers

Finally, anytime you see a header that starts with X-, this is called an extension or privately defined header. We saw an example just moments ago with X-Priority:. These privately defined headers make sense for proprietary applications between users of the Internet email infrastructure. For example, you might tell your friends to use a special header if they want the messages they send to you to be processed specially.

Error Reports

Although the Internet messaging infrastructure was originally developed in 1982, it was only some 14 years later that there was any standardization of error report formats! At present, implementation of the relevant standards is still spotty. Although much of the email software minimally supports the formats, user agent support is largely nonexistent.

For our purposes, we'll look at the two building blocks of error reports: reply codes and structured reports. It turns out that, regardless of whether the error report is structured or not, if you understand the "theory of reply codes" then you know how to interpret most of the useful information available to you.

Reply Codes

A reply code is a three-digit sequence indicating whether or not an operation succeeded or failed. There are two variants of reply codes: the "original" kind, which is simply a three-digit number; and the "enhanced" kind, which is three digits separated by periods. You'll find the original kind in any unstructured error report; you find both the original and enhanced kind in any structured report. We'll start with the original kind of reply code first.

A good example of reply codes is how America Online (AOL) treats errors. When you try to send email to a nonexistent mailbox, you get the following reply from the AOL postmaster:

```
Date: Thu, 22 Jan 1998 09:17:30 -0500 (EST)From:
Mail Delivery Subsystem <MAILER-DAEMON@aol.com>To:
<david@strom.com>Subject: Returned mail: User
unknownAuto-Submitted: auto-generated (failure)


Your mail is being returned due to one or more non-
delivery conditions listed below:

1: Your recipient no longer exists on AOL.
   (SMTP 550 ... User Unknown)
2: Your recipient's mailbox is full.
   (SMTP 550 ... Mailbox Full)
3: Your recipient has blocked mail from you.
   (SMTP 550 ... is not accepting mail from this
   sender.)
4: Your site has been blocked from sending mail to
   AOL.
```

```
(SMTP 550 ... Delivery not authorized)

-AOL Postmaster

>>> RCPT To:<edconti@aol.com>
<<< 550 Mailbox not found
550 <edconti@aol.com>... User unknown
```

The 550 error code can be interpreted as follows. The first digit of a reply code is a *completion* indicator: It tells whether a particular operation completed, and, if so, whether it succeeded or failed. There are five possibilities:

- Positive preliminary (1): indicates that the operation is ready to be performed but is waiting for confirmation. You should never see this in practice.

- Positive completion (2): indicates that the operation successfully completed.

- Positive intermediate (3): indicates the operation is ready to be performed, but additional information is needed.

- Transient negative (4): indicates that the operation was not performed due to a transient problem. The operation may be retried, in identical form, at a later time.

- Permanent negative (5): indicates that the operation was not performed due to a permanent problem. The operation, if retried in identical form, will fail.

Of these, only codes 4 and 5 are of interest.

The second digit of a reply code is a *category* indicator: It tells why the operation succeeded, failed or didn't complete. There are four possibilities:

- Syntax (0): indicates that the reply deals with syntax-related issues, such as unimplemented commands or syntax errors. If you see this, then it is likely that someone is trying out some new software.

- Informational (1): indicates that the reply contains requested information. You should never see this in practice.

- Connections (2): indicates that the reply deals with the underlying transport service.

- Mail-related (5): indicates that the reply deals with the email software.

Of these, only codes 2 and 5 are of interest.

Finally, the third digit of a reply code is used to distinguish between different situations.

For our purposes, the interesting reply codes start with 42, 45 or 55. Something starting with 42 indicates that the network was having repeated problems. Something starting with 45 indicates that a system in the messaging infrastructure, probably the recipient's system was having problems. In both cases, it is believed to be a transient problem, so you might want to try again later (perhaps after calling someone). The reply codes starting with 55 are a bit more varied:

- 550: indicates one of two things—either the local part is unknown at the final destination host or the final destination host can't be found. In our example above, the mailbox no longer existed.

- 551: indicates a routing problem of some sort—the message was delivered to a host that knows of the recipient but also knows that the recipient isn't local.

- 552: indicates that there was insufficient storage available for the message.

- 553: indicates that the recipient's mailbox is "unavailable" (perhaps it is locked for some reason).

- 554: is a catchall—the message just couldn't be delivered.

These problems are all viewed as permanent, so you'll need to change something in your message before you send a new one.

The only real difference between the original and enhanced kind of reply codes is that the enhanced reply codes contain more detail. For example, while 550 doesn't distinguish between whether the local part or the domain part is unknown, 5.1.1 is used to indicate an unknown local part, and 5.1.2 is used to indicate an unknown domain part. We won't list the enhanced codes here for a simple reason: Any time that you encounter them, there also will be a textual explanation next to them.

Structured Reports

Although discussion of structured messages occurs in Chapter 3, a brief discussion of structured error reports is necessary. If an error report isn't structured, its body is plain text. There is usually some boilerplate words indicating that the message couldn't be delivered, the three-digit reply code (the original kind), a textual explanation and perhaps the original message is included at the end. Although this is probably easy enough for most people to read, it isn't useful to automated processes, such as mailing list software, which may want to do address list management. Hence, a structured format was developed.

A structured error report consists of two or three parts. The first part is a textual explanation as to the problem and includes the three-digit reply code. The second part looks like a small message—it has a collection of headers. These headers include precise information as to what the problem was and where it occurred. This information is carefully generated so as to be machine readable. The third part, if present, is the original message. Although the software available for today's users is still primitive when handling structured error reports, it is conceivable that future software will let the user edit the original message, based on what the problem was, and then resend it.

Since the "smarts" of a structured error report is in the second part, let's look at a brief example:

```
Reporting-MTA: dns; smtp.example.com
Arrival-Date: Sun, 11 Jan 1998 13:20:50 -0800 (PST)

Final-Recipient: rfc822; <bogus@example.com>
Action: failed
Status: 5.1.1
Remote-MTA: dns; pop.example.com
Diagnostic-Code: smtp; 550
<bogus@pop.example.com>… User unknown
Last-Attempt: Sun, 11 Jan 1998 13:20:51 -0800 (PST)
```

The first two lines identify the server that detected the problem along with the time that it took responsibility for delivering the message. The Final-Recipient: indicates for whom the message was destined. The next three lines indicate that the message couldn't be delivered ("failed"), that the reason is that the local part of the mailbox is invalid (5.1.1) and that the server "pop.example.com" refused to accept the message for delivery. The last two lines contain the reply code given by that server (550) and the time when the error was encountered.

An Example of a Custom System

As we have seen, there are relatively few rules defined by the standards as to how mail should be handled once received. Perhaps the only rules are those that discuss how replies are formed (e.g., looking for a Reply-To: before looking for a From:). Even so, there are a number of policies that can be implemented based on the headers we've seen thus far. Let's consider an example of a customized system that Rose has been using for many years. You should know that you're not going to find any commercial package that offers precisely these capabilities. Our purpose is to illustrate the power that is available simply through the thoughtful process of headers—perhaps some day everyone will be have systems that automatically do this!

First, we show in Figure 2.1 the algorithm pictorially:

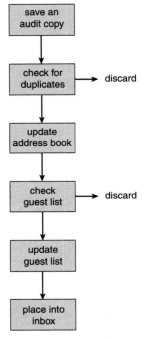

Figure 2.1   An algorithm for a custom system

And now, for the next few pages, here is the detailed description.

First, determine the originator of the message. Do this by looking through the Resent-From:, From:, Sender: and Return-Path: headers (in that order) and taking the first value you find. Extract the local and domain parts of the mailbox contained therein. Also look at the Subject: and strip out any extraneous white space encountered. Save a copy of the message to a local auditing file.

Next, determine the identity of the message. Do this by looking through the Resent-Message-ID: and Message-ID: headers (in that order) and taking the first value you find. Look in a database of message identities. If the identity is already there, discard the message and stop processing. Otherwise, add the identity to the database and continue processing.

Next, see if there is an entry for the originator in a database of incoming correspondents. Create or update the entry as appropriate, capturing the mailbox, any text associated with the mailbox and the X-Mailer: of the message. Capturing the text allows us to build a simple database of correspondents (to answer questions like "what is so-and-so's address"). Capturing the X-Mailer: value allows us to determine the capabilities of the address when sending future email.

In order to explain the next step, we need to define some terms. A "whitelist" is a list of mailboxes that are unconditionally allowed to send email to the user. Although many policies could be used to maintain a whitelist, only the simplest policy is actually implemented: Every time the user of this software sends a message, every addressee is added to the whitelist. The user can override this policy on a per-message basis. A "graylist" is a list of mailboxes that are temporarily allowed to send email to the user. Although many policies could be used to determine the length of stay on the graylist, a fixed two-week lifetime is used. We'll discuss how mailboxes are added to the graylist in a moment.

To continue, examine the local part of the originator to see if it looks like it is from an administrative account or automated process (e.g., "postmaster" or "listserv"). If so, pass it through. If not, look at the domain part of the originator to see if it is on a list of "friendly" hosts. If so, pass it through. If not, look at the originator mailbox to see if it is on a "whitelist" of correspondents. If so, pass it through. If not, look at the originator mailbox to see if it is on a "graylist" of correspondents. If so, pass it through. If not, see if the Subject: contains a password. If so, pass it through. If not, send back an automated reply to the originator, the message is discarded and no further processing is done.

The automated reply explains that the originator isn't on a "guest list" and that the user won't see their message. The reply tries to be friendly, because there is inevitably an adverse psychological reaction when someone receives such a message.[9] However, there are relatively few people who see such a reply, since this message usually is triggered by unsolicited commercial email. In the off chance that the originator has a legitimate reason to communicate with the user, the reply contains a "password" that can be used in the Subject: of a message to avoid the whitelist check. Finally, the automated reply is a structured message (we discuss these in Chapter 3), so that it includes a copy of the original message. This makes it fairly easy for someone to send it back to the user after he or she puts the password in the Subject:.

In addition, even if an automated reply should be sent, two checks are made to see if the message should simply be discarded. First, a quick attempt is made to check the validity of the originator mailbox. (We discuss how to do that in Chapter 6.) If the mailbox doesn't exist, then no reply is sent, which avoids any subsequent error report. Second, a check is made to see if an automated reply has been sent back to the originator within the past two weeks. If so, only odd numbered messages are replied to. This has the effect of breaking any mail loops that might occur if an automated process (such as a trouble-ticketing system) is replying to a message.

Let us say that the message passes the various tests (e.g., it is on the whitelist). Processing continues. The headers of the message are examined for all other recipient addresses in the To: and cc:. If any are found, they are placed on the graylist. This allows whitelisted correspondents to temporarily grant access to the user's mailbox. Otherwise, if one of these other recipients replies before the user gets a chance to, he or she would see an automated reply rejecting the message. Instead, the user has an opportunity to reply and whitelist the recipient automatically.

Next, a copy of the message is made available for the user to see. However, processing continues. If the message is structured and contains references to external body parts, then those parts are precached. This tends to allow faster access when the user actually reads the message. For example, if the message includes a reference to an image on a file server, that image will be fetched and placed into the user's image cache—typically before the user ever reads the message.

Finally, this user employs two workstations (one workstation runs UNIX and the other Windows). This particular process runs on UNIX. So, if the message contains attachments that can be read only on Windows, the message is automatically re-distributed to the email account associated with the Windows workstation.

Although seemingly complex, it should be noted that all of the sophistication is built on top of some very basic structures within the message. Very few headers are actually parsed. Much more extensive use is made of a database in order to maintain a whitelist, a graylist, and so on.

SOLUTIONS

Now that you understand some of the standards involved in creating message headers, let's move on to some practical ways you can manage your inbox. We'll examine the following areas:

1. Sorting and Viewing Messages
2. Keeping Track of Your Correspondence
3. Filtering Messages
4. How to Reply
5. Hidden Headers
6. Opting Out of Spam
7. What to Do With Errors

As we mentioned in Chapter 1, we will use six software programs in this chapter and in subsequent chapters to illustrate our solutions:

- Microsoft Outlook Express, the version that comes with Internet Explorer 4.01
- Netscape Messenger, version 4.04
- Qualcomm Eudora Pro, version 4.0
- Lotus' cc:Mail, version 8.1
- CompuServe's WinCIM, version 3.02
- America Online, version 3.0

We don't confine our discussion to these products exclusively, and, where appropriate, will mention other products, Internet sites and services that can help out.

Sorting and Viewing Messages

One of the most powerful mailbox management tools is already part of your existing email software, just underused or often ignored. The tool is the ability to sort messages by sender, by date or by size. You don't need to buy any new software, and often you don't even need to read the manual to figure out how it works. You just need to know a few simple tricks.

Sorting makes a great deal of sense, especially when you receive many messages at once, say, after a long trip or vacation. If you forgot to unsubscribe to a particular mailing list when you were away, you can sort your inbox and quickly gather up all these messages and delete them, or move them to another folder where they can be dealt with later when you have the time to read through them. You can look for messages from your boss, or a correspondent with whom you were expecting some information, without having to scroll through the entire list.

Not all email products allow you to sort on every possible thing, but most have fairly similar behavior. But before we start sorting, we should explain some tricks on how you can help view your messages. Let's take a look at how each product works.

Eudora has up to nine columns that can be displayed. You have complete control over which columns are shown and in what order. First, go to Tools | Options | Display and you'll see the window in Figure 2.2 where you can check or uncheck various parameters.

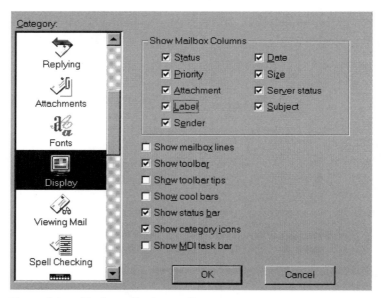

Figure 2.2   Eudora display options

The nine columns are:

- message status (if you reply to a message or forward it, an R or F will appear in this column, otherwise it will be blank),

- priority,

- whether or not an attachment is present,

- an arbitrary label,

- the sender (From:),

- the date sent,

- the message size,

- the server status (whether or not the message was completely delivered or if parts still remain on the server), and

- the message subject.

If we take a look at our inbox, we'll see the following display at the top of the window, shown in Figure 2.3:

Figure 2.3   Eudora mailbox title bar

Now, if you don't like the order or width that the columns are in, you can easily change it. You can widen or shorten the display in each column by using your mouse in the column label bar. This is useful when you want to look at a particular lengthy email address or want to examine more of the information in the subject heading, for example. Move your mouse to the line dividing two columns and you'll see your cursor change shape from an arrow to something with two arrows. You can then adjust the size of the column.

You can also adjust the size of the column so that the column no longer appears on your screen: If you don't particularly care to see which of your messages has attachments, for example, then you can remove the column entirely. (Or you can uncheck the box in the display options window.)

Finally, you can rearrange the order of the columns shown on the screen by clicking on the column title bar and dragging it to the left or the right. Say you want to have the sender be the first column shown and it comes up as the third. You just move it to the left.

Outlook Express, Messenger, cc:Mail and WinCIM have similar features when it comes to rearranging the columns. But, unlike Eudora, you can't easily remove or add columns, unless you reduce its size down to nothing. Let's look at each of their mailbox title bars.

The title bar in Outlook Express looks like what is shown in Figure 2.4. The first column indicates priority, the second with the paper clip indicates attachments.

Figure 2.4   Outlook Express mailbox title bar

The title bar for cc:Mail looks like what is shown in Figure 2.5, with a similar interpretation with Outlook Express.

Figure 2.5   cc:Mail mailbox title bar

Figure 2.6 shows CompuServe's WinCIM title bar:

Figure 2.6   WinCIM mailbox title bar

And Figure 2.7 shows Netscape's Messenger title bar:

Figure 2.7   Messenger mailbox title bar

After you get done rearranging things, you'll be glad to know that all of the products will remember the state of your mailbox view when you exit the program. This means that you don't have to spend a great deal of time adjusting things and moving columns around when you bring up your email software.

Notice we haven't said much about AOL so far. You can't do much with the America Online software, unfortunately. You are pretty much stuck with how it displays your messages.

Now, let's get things sorted out. Each of the programs operates somewhat differently when it comes to sorting.

AOL doesn't have the ability to sort messages. Messages are displayed in chronological order, beginning with the oldest messages and continuing to the newest ones. We think this runs the exact opposite of how most of us work, where we tend to react to the most recently received message first and let older ones hang around unnoticed.

However, you can rearrange your messages one by one. That is fine if you don't have very many of them in your inbox, but it can quickly get tedious. To move messages around, you first single-click on the message displayed in Mail | Read Incoming FlashMail window, and while holding down the mouse move the message up or down in the list. As you are moving the message around, you'll see your mouse icon change from a straight arrow to one that has a small rectangle attached to it. This indicates that you are moving the message around.

The other products have more flexibility. Outlook Express' inbox has five columns, shown in Figure 2.8. With each column, you can sort messages either in ascending or descending order. In the columns with worded labels, you merely click on the column label bar and you'll see a small arrow pointing up or down. Click on the bar again and the bar changes direction, indicating the sort order chosen and which column you are sorting first. It is that simple. If you want to use your right mouse button, you'll see a small menu (as shown in Figure 2.8) indicating your choice of ascending or descending order, and you can choose the appropriate order.

!	0	From △		Received
		(Web Server)	✓ Sort Ascending	12/18/97 1:59 ...
	0	David Strom	Sort Descending	12/31/97 11:08...
		Earthlink Support	Welcome to EarthLink Network!	12/19/97 6:09 ...
		ELN Webmaster	How to use your FREE webspace!	12/29/97 9:24 ...
		Microsoft Outlook ...	Security Features in Outlook Express	12/31/97 10:37...
		Microsoft Outlook ...	Welcome to Microsoft Outlook Express	12/31/97 10:37...
		Test Reply	New Users	8/22/95 10:31 ...
		webhelp@minds...	Setup for www.strom.w1.com	12/22/97 10:00...

Figure 2.8   Outlook Express sorting of messages

Eudora has a somewhat different approach to sorting. First you need to go to Edit | Sort menu, and you'll see a series of menus as shown in Figure 2.9.

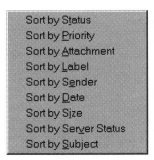

Sort by Status
Sort by Priority
Sort by Attachment
Sort by Label
Sort by Sender
Sort by Date
Sort by Size
Sort by Server Status
Sort by Subject

Figure 2.9   Eudora message sorting choices

You select which column you wish to sort from these menus. You can also just click your mouse on the particular column title bar, as with the other products. However, this just produces an ascending order. To reverse the sort order, you need to first hold down the Shift key before clicking on the heading title or menu option.

Messenger combines the methods in Outlook Express and Eudora. Using the mouse on the column headings, you can change the sort order as we explained in Outlook Express. And it has its own series of menus to control the sort order if you were to go into View|Sort commands. Finally, WinCIM uses arrows that point right or left, rather than up or down, to indicate the sort order, as shown in Figure 2.10.

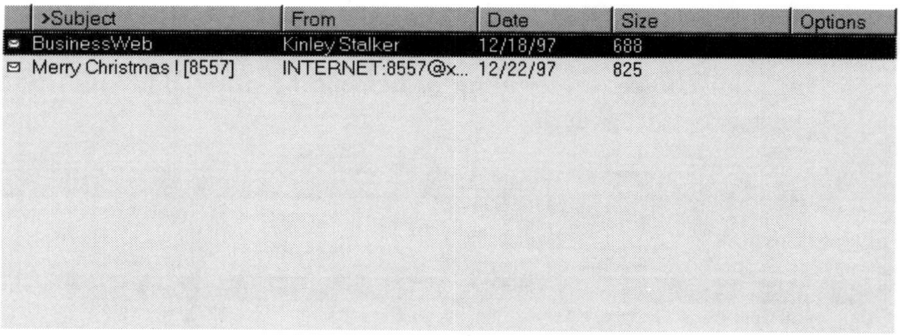

>Subject	From	Date	Size	Options
BusinessWeb	Kinley Stalker	12/18/97	688	
Merry Christmas ! [8557]	INTERNET:8557@x...	12/22/97	825	

Figure 2.10   WinCIM mailbox sorting choices

Keeping Track of Your Correspondence

Sorting your email is fine, but it doesn't really help organize all of your correspondence. We next need to introduce the concept of folders. The notion is really a simple one: You want to be able to keep track of your correspondence in a way that makes it easy to find a particular piece of mail that you received or sent. Folders are critical to managing your email life.

We can always tell the email veterans from those new to email by the way the veteran organizes his or her folders. It isn't enough to just have lots of folders. You need to organize them into groups according to project, client or type of business. For example, we have one folder that contains all of our published articles for a particular publication. The folder is separated into different folders, one for each article or series of articles. There is a separate folder with comments from readers, and another one with comments from editors and assignments.

All of our featured products support some use of folders in a variety of ways, which we will get into shortly. But we can't emphasize enough that you need to be organized yourself: No computerized system will do it for you if you aren't clear on what the division of topics will be: Let's see…does the invoice for the Example Company go into the invoices folder, the Example Company correspondence or both? Get this down before you create your first folder.

You also need to be concerned about how large your folders can get: Some of the products have trouble dealing with folders with thousands of messages in them. And having large folders makes it harder to back them up and make portable copies.

But before we describe how to do this, we should first mention that each email program has a number of tricks to automatically organize your daily life. You can set up your software to automatically save a copy of every piece of outgoing email in one folder, and save every piece of incoming email in another. In practice, we have found the copies of outgoing correspondence essential to keeping track of our business.

To set this up in Eudora, go to Tools | Options | Sending Mail Options and check the box next to Keep Copies. This will save a copy of every message you send to a special folder called Out. You can't change the name and you can't split up the Out folder into subfolders. It will just continue to grow. Eudora, by the way, distinguishes between mailboxes, which contain collections of messages and folders, which contain groups of mailboxes—just to confuse things. We'll keep this simple and call everything folders in this book.

If you don't want to keep copies of all your outgoing email, you can selectively make copies and place them in the Out folder. You can turn on a special button in the message toolbar. In Figure 2.11 the button looks like two small documents, to the left of the RR button. Press it in, and a copy is created. Press it out, and (unless you have already set up your options as above) a copy won't be created.

Figure 2.11 Eudora mailbox option buttons

You can also save a copy of your outgoing message to another folder if you feel so inclined. As you are composing your message, right-click anywhere in the message body. You will get a pop-up menu of choices, one of which will be Fcc, which leads you to a menu of all of your folders.

In Messenger, the path to accomplish this task is Edit | Preferences | Mail | Messages, where you'll see a check box to specify automatically keeping copies of your outgoing mail and a list box to choose the folder that these go in.

With cc:Mail, all of your messages are automatically copied to the Sent folder. You can delete these after a specified period of days, or keep them forever by going to File | Tools | User Preferences | Special Folders and choosing the Never delete button as shown in Figure 2.12.

Figure 2.12   cc:Mail option for deleting messages

To examine AOL messages you have already sent, you need to be connected to the AOL network. Then go to Members | Mail Preferences. Here you can check boxes to make a copy of all outgoing and incoming mail in your local folders of these names. In Figure 2.13 you can also retain copies of correspondence that you have sent for a specified period of days.

    ☑ **Confirm mail after it has been sent**

    ☑ **Close mail after it has been sent**

    ☐ **Retain all mail I send in my Personal Filing Cabinet**

    ☐ **Retain all mail I read in my Personal Filing Cabinet**

    ☑ **Use AOL style quoting in mail**

       Keep my "old mail" online 3 ⧩ **days after I read it**

                OK **Cancel**

Figure 2.13   AOL preferences

In WinCIM, the path is Access | Preferences | Mail, where you will see a box to check for where you want to keep copies of your outgoing messages. Like Messenger, you can specify a particular folder name for this repository. See Figure 2.14.

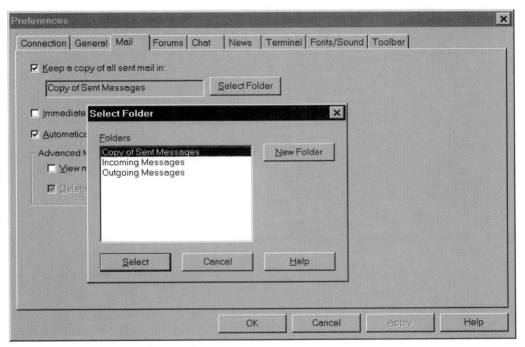

Figure 2.14   WinCIM folder preferences

Finally, in Outlook Express you go to Tools | Options | Send and check the box next to save a copy of messages in the Sent Items folder. Like Eudora, you can't change the name of this folder.

So, how do you create folders anyway? In Eudora, the command is simple: Mailbox | New. You'll get a dialogue box to name your new folder, and there is a check box underneath that will create a folder (instead of a mailbox). That's it. Now the folder will show up on your menu of mailboxes, as well as in the special folder windowpane to the left of your messages.

There is one caveat here: If you create a mailbox, you can't change your mind later and turn it into a folder or collection of mailboxes. You'll have to create a new folder and then copy the messages from your old mailbox to the new folder.

Creating folders in the other programs is just as simple. In Netscape Messenger, the command is File | New Folder. You'll see the dialogue box as shown in Figure 2.15, which gives you the choice of whether to make it a folder by itself or a subfolder within one of your existing folders.

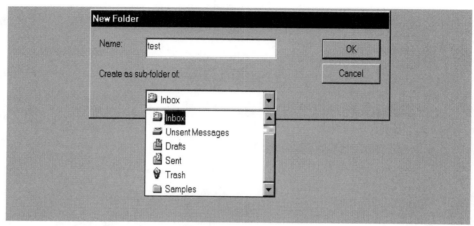

Figure 2.15   Messenger folder preferences

In Outlook Express, the path is File | Folder | New. This brings up a dialogue box where you can choose to add a new folder to your list, or create a new subfolder inside of one of your existing folders. In cc:Mail, the easiest way to create a new folder is to move your mouse to the left-hand windowpane showing the list of folders and right-click. Then you'll see an option to create a new folder.

AOL has folders, and they are visible in its Personal Filing Cabinet, which can be found from the File menu. This contains mail that you have already downloaded via Flash sessions, as well as files you have downloaded, your favorite places or bookmarks to specific AOL and Internet resources, and any Internet newsgroups that you subscribe to. AOL downloads incoming mail into a folder of that name. You can then move copies of these messages into other folders that you create. First, click on the Add Folder button at the bottom of the Filing Cabinet screen as shown in Figure 2.16. Next, type the name of the folder in the small window that appears. You can expand and contract the folder view, just as you would do so in Windows Explorer, and drag and drop files from one folder to the next.

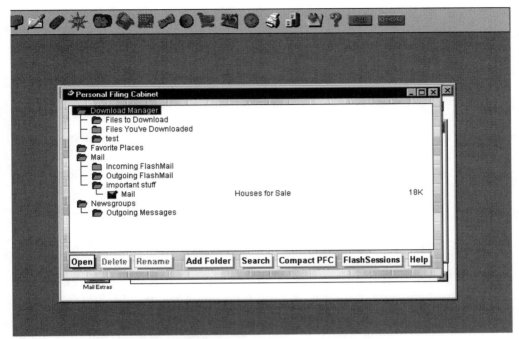

Figure 2.16   AOL filing cabinet options

CompuServe WinCIM puts all of its folders into a special place called the Filing Cabinet, which is easily reached from the File menu. It is a little confusing, especially since the incoming mail can be found in the Mail portion of the program, but you can create new folders inside the Filing Cabinet with the appropriate button at the top of the screen.

Once you have a few folders, you can start moving messages into them and organizing your email life. There are two ways to do this: manually, using the various commands in each product, or automatically, via a series of filters. We'll get into more details about this latter operation in Chapter 5.

Filtering Messages

Folders are a nice, simple mechanism for keeping order in your email working life. But it doesn't do anything to stem the flow of email that comes into your mailbox, and you first have to download your email before you can sort it into folders.

A much more proactive solution is to use filtering technology. Filtering works in real time, as the messages are being received, and operates on each message according to a series of rules. Typically, the filtering routine examines the message header for particular text string matches: You want to delete all email from hotmail.com, for example, because you are tired of receiving spam messages from these accounts. So you would set up a filter to examine the From: field in all incoming headers and delete the message.

We'll have more to say about filters when we get to Chapter 5 and talk about enterprise solutions. But for now we want to review how filters are implemented in each of our featured products. Some of the products come with a variety of means to filter incoming, and in some cases outgoing, messages too.

Perhaps the strongest filtering product is Eudora, and recent versions have continued to improve its ability to process mail. One of the nice features about Eudora is that you can filter incoming and outgoing messages. You go to Tools | Filters and fill out the dialogue box by choosing a series of rather extensive menus, as shown in Figure 2.17. You can inspect any portion of the email message: For example, you can look for messages from a certain recipient (even if that recipient is in a cc: field and not just the From: field) or text strings inside the message body. You can specify up to two different criteria and two different fields to examine.

You can also specify up to five different actions once your selection criteria are met: You can print the message, forward it to another user, copy it to a folder, and so forth. When it comes to filtering, Eudora knows what it is doing: the filters are easy to set up and obvious to use.

Eudora also can limit the size of messages received. You go to Tools | Options | Checking Mail and specify the maximum size of the message you wish to download. Once you check the box next to this parameter, Eudora will only download the first bit of the message body, with a message such as:

```
WARNING: The remainder of this message has not been
transferred.

The estimated size of this message is 146362 bytes.

Click on the server retrieve icon above and check
mail again to get the whole thing. If the server
retrieve icon is not showing, then this message is
no longer on the server.
```

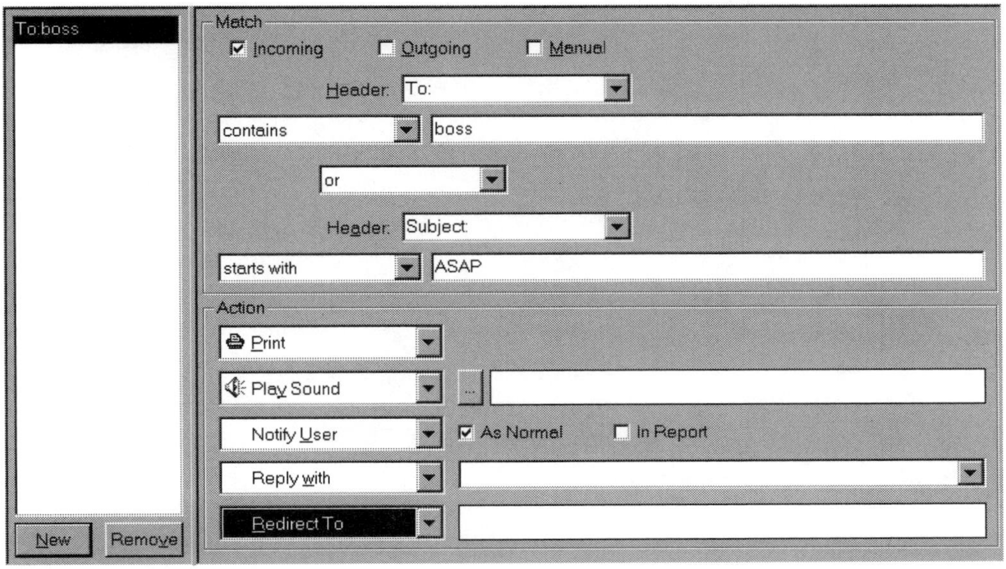

Figure 2.17   Eudora filter options

If you want to download the entire message, you have a rather strange process to go through. First, find the icon mentioned—it is located just to the right of the BLAHBLAHBLAH icon at the top of the screen, and has an arrow. You need to click on this icon, then close the message, and then recheck your messages to download the large message in its entirety. However, Eudora places a second message in your inbox, which means you now have to delete the truncated message, otherwise you might get confused over which was which. If you want to delete the message without downloading it again, there is a second icon next to the server retrieve icon which you need to click. Again, you also need to recheck your mail, and the large message will be deleted from your server.

cc:Mail has two places that you'll need to configure to set up filtering. And to make matters more confusing, it calls them rules. But cc:Mail has an impressive collection of activities as well. They are less obvious to set up than Eudora's, but you create as flexible a situation with as many different actions as you'd like once your message meets your criteria. You can also schedule the rules to be run at specific times, say, after you download your messages or at certain times of the day. Go to Create | Rule. (See Figure 2.18.)

Figure 2.18   cc:Mail rules options

A separate set of commands is used to set up the filter on message size. Go to Actions | Connect | Set Filters. There you will find a place to receive messages only if they are less than a certain size. You check the box next to this statement and fill in the size, such as 40 kilobytes, as shown in Figure 2.19. You can also receive messages from particular recipients or containing particular subjects, and just download the message headers. This is something that cc:Mail has had for a long time, and only now are the Internet Message Access Protocol (IMAP)-based products getting around to supporting this feature. We'll have more to say on IMAP in Chapter 5.

Figure 2.19   cc:Mail filter options

Outlook Express filters are contained in its Inbox Assistant. You go to Tools | Inbox Assistant | Add to create a new filter. You can select messages by various header fields by simply filling out the form on screen as shown in Figure 2.20, and check various actions, such as prevent large messages from being downloaded.

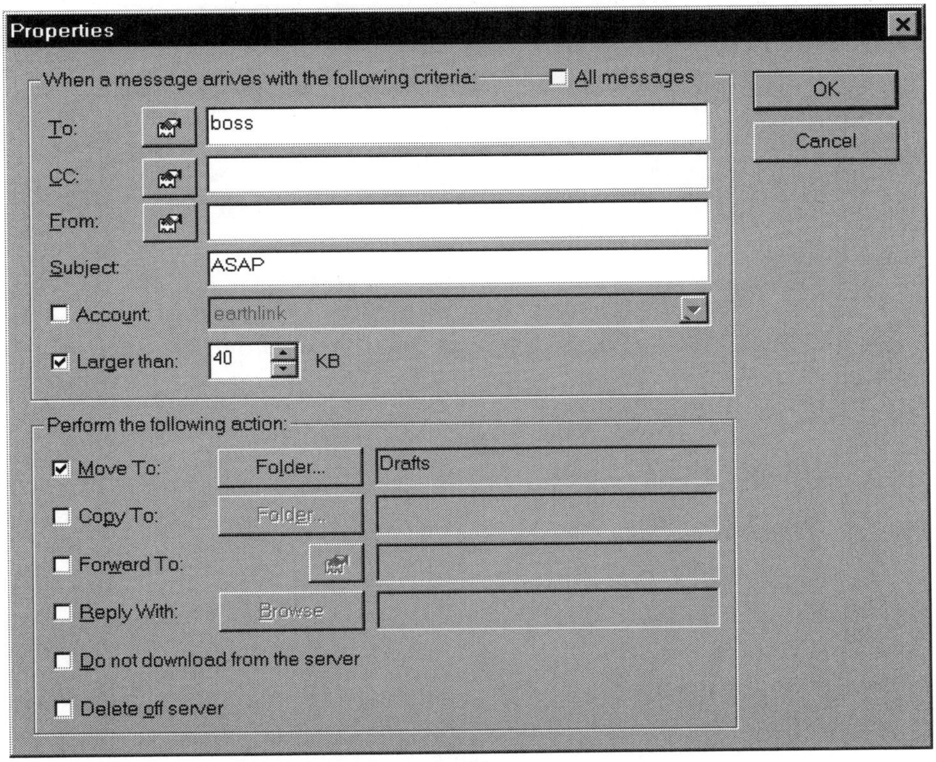

Figure 2.20   Outlook Express filter options

Netscape Messenger's filters can be found in Edit | Mail Filters | New, and has a similar layout to Eudora's. You can specify many different selection criteria (Eudora has up to two), but only one action per filter, and a limited number of actions at that (see Figure 2.21). The way you do this is by clicking on the more button on this screen, which creates a new row that you can specify the header and selection criteria. You have a separate place in the Edit | Preferences | Mail options to specify whether you want to download and leave a copy of your messages on your server.

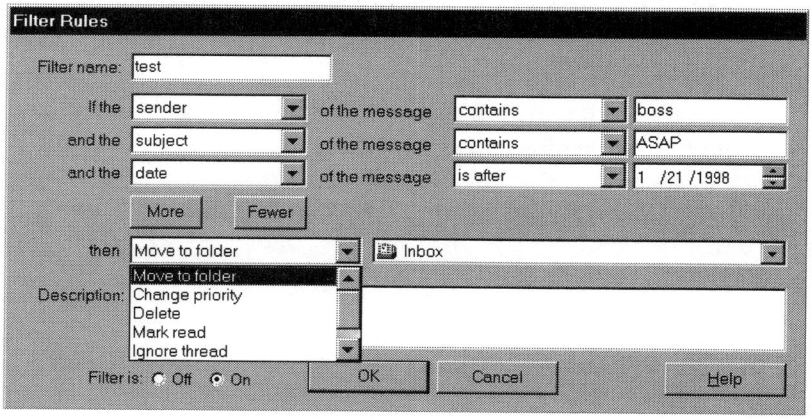

Figure 2.21   Messenger filter options

AOL and CompuServe have no filtering feature other than the ability to file specific messages in specific folders when they are received.

How to Reply

As we mentioned earlier in this chapter, every email program has the ability to either reply to just the sender (the address shown in the From: field) or reply to everyone mentioned in the To:, cc: and From: fields. Please master this difference and pay attention when you are replying, and you'll save yourself a great deal of abuse and unwanted messages down the road.

It sounds so simple, and certainly we all conceptually understand the difference between replying to a single author or to a larger list. But we've made the mistake countless times in the past and hope that we are more careful now. Some of this is just plain email etiquette: You don't need to reply to everyone all the time, unless there is a specific reason to include everyone in the loop. Let's look how the software programs actually work.

In Netscape's email software, for example, there are two buttons labeled accordingly: click on the Reply button (or Control-R) and you'll just reply to the sender. Press Control-Shift-R and your message will go to everyone also mentioned in the To: field. You can also use the menus, go to Message | Reply and you'll see the two options there.

The same is true of Microsoft's Outlook Express, except the buttons there are labeled Reply to Author and Reply to All (with the same keystrokes as Netscape's software if you don't want to click the buttons).

Depending on what version of Eudora's software you are using, there is a special switch in the configuration menu shown in Figure 2.22 (at Tools | Options | Replying) to automatically change all replies to reply to all. If you don't turn on this switch, you will just reply to the originator of the message. You can also turn on other options, such as making copies of the message to the original folder or mailbox where it originated, and whether you want to include yourself on any replies.

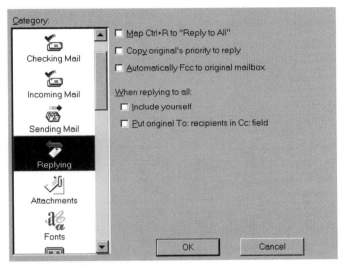

Figure 2.22   **Eudora reply options**

When you compose a reply with the AOL software, you have two choices: to reply to the original author or to reply to everyone. The buttons are labeled as such and are located to the left of the message window.

CompuServe's WinCIM has a series of buttons across the top of the screen when you open any particular received message. The buttons are clearly labeled, as shown in Figure 2.23.

Figure 2.23   **WinCIM reply buttons**

cc:Mail just has a reply function, which is found at Create | Reply. And like Outlook Express, you can also automatically add outgoing correspondents to your address book.

But what happens when you want to reply to mixture of internal (to your corporation) and external addresses? Or Internet and non-Internet addresses? We'll have more to say about how to handle Internet gateways in Chapter 7, but for now we offer a few words of wisdom.

One way is to first recognize the format of the address, and make sure that it has both a local mailbox and a domain name, separated by an @ sign. Local mailboxes don't need to have any domain name (if the message is being sent within the domain and using the same host), but it doesn't hurt to type it in anyway.[10]

Email gateways add their own series of characters to the message header. These characters may be superfluous when sending your message, or they may be essential. Before you hit the send button to speed your message on its way, make sure that the address in the header is actually what you expect it to be and has not been mangled by the gateway. Sometimes you actually might receive a message that has been forwarded from the gateway administrator—and you do not necessarily want to bother this person with your replies!

Speaking of checking your header to check that your message is going to the right recipient, you should note that some email products do not recognize redirected messages and tend to reply to the originator of the chain of correspondence. You might not want to send your comments to this person, but to the person who sent you the redirected email. Again, we have made this mistake more times than we would like to admit.

And to help speed your replies, several products have the ability to automatically populate your address books with your correspondents' addresses. We'll get into further details about this in Chapter 3.

Hidden Headers

As we mentioned earlier in the chapter, each software program can hide the information present in the message header. Sometimes this is done as a matter of convenience to the user, but often it obscures the nature of any email problem as we described.

Why would you want to examine the headers? There are lots of reasons. You may have trouble with sending a reply back to your correspondents: If you examine the header, you might find out that someone mistyped the Reply To: address and you can find the originating From: address with the correct email address. Or you may be trying to track down the origins of a spammer, or someone who has come through a gateway that mangled the header.

Let's show you how to alter the display when you really need to examine the header and determine what is happening.

In Netscape Messenger, the command is View | Headers, and, as we stated earlier, there are three options. The command takes effect for all the messages in all of your mailboxes, and if you decide to view all of the header information, Messenger formats the header in a somewhat annoying center-based justification.

Eudora can change the display of its headers on individual messages, and then only on ones in your inbox. The button is a rather quaint one labeled BLAHBLAHBLAH. When you press the button at the top of the screen, you see the entire header. Press it again and a brief header is shown. If you like to see the entire headers by default, you won't be able to do that in Eudora (unlike Messenger): Every time you leave the message display, it will revert back to the brief format. Figure 2.24 shows the full header displayed.

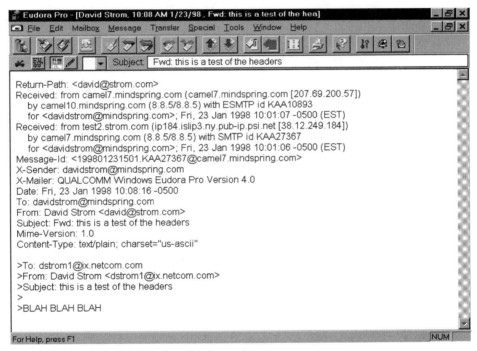

Figure 2.24 **Eudora full header display option**

Outlook Express doesn't display much in the way of headers by default. If you need more, you'll have to go looking for the complete header information in an odd place. First, you need to bring up the screen with your message in it, by double-clicking on the entry in your inbox. Next, go to File | Properties and choose the tab labeled Details. You'll see a screen similar to the one shown in Figure 2.25. Pressing the message source button at the bottom of this box will bring up a copy of the complete message, headers included.

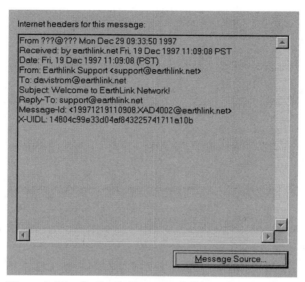

Figure 2.25   Outlook Express full header display option

CompuServe, cc:Mail and AOL offer no control over how headers are viewed, and you receive the full details anyway. AOL at least puts the entire header from any Internet message at the bottom of the message, which is a nice compromise.

Opting Out of Spam

Now that you have some understanding of the ways your own email software can help you manage your messages, it is time to look at other solutions. And one of the biggest frustrations is dealing with spam.

Spam is unfortunately a fact of modern Internet life. And, given the number of email users, it isn't hard to see the opportunity and risk/rewards are way out of whack when it comes to trying to control spam. What makes spam hard to fight is that a spammer doesn't have a physical office: He or she could literally be doing business the next minute under a completely new identity. You have no way of knowing, and if you try to block mail from *somethingbad.com*, the spammer could open a new domain at *somethingbad2.com* and you'll still get his or her messages.

But there are some tricks. One of them is to never have an AOL account, which seems to draw spammers like flies around honey. If you do, we recommend that you avoid being online in any of the chat rooms. For some reason, that brings attention to your address.

AOL isn't the only attraction for spammers. Another place is the Web, and we recommend that you never place your email address on any Web page. This is because there are several programs now that will search through your Web site and collect email addresses.[11]

Another tactic is to set up a filter to delete any messages that come from typical spam addresses, such as *hotmail.com*. But this could also delete messages from legitimate correspondents on these domains, too.

There are several Web sites that will put you on lists to avoid spam. We have tried these lists, but not every spammer will check first to see if you have opted out of mass mailings. You can find a list of these sites at Yahoo, under Junk Email Registration Services. Some of these sites carry rather interesting domain names, such as *nothankyou.com* and *junk-mail.com*. We're not sure that listing your email address there will do anything, but if you have some spare time, it might be worth trying.[12]

Certainly, spam is aggravating. None of us likes to have our mailboxes polluted with these messages, and frustration can certainly mount. However, you need to keep cool and not go nuts trying to fight spam. We think Scott Hazen Mueller has several good suggestions on what *not* to do when fighting.

```
Don't threaten violence or vandalism; don't
mailbomb the site; don't mailbomb the alleged
spammer, who may be an innocent third party such as
myself [due to spoofing one's email address]; don't
ping-storm or SYN-flood the site; don't hack into
the site; don't try in any way to bring the site
down illegally. And, above all else, don't use spam
to fight spam. This also applies in Usenet - don't
follow up to spam postings, lest your posting also
become spam. (from spam.abuse.net/spam/dontdo.html)
```

One of our correspondents uses the following tactic whenever he receives spam. He forwards a copy of every message, including the complete header information, to two email addresses. First, he sends one to the postmaster of his own ISP, as a defensive measure to block any other incoming email from the spammer. Second, he sends a copy to *abuse@example.com*, where example.com is the originating domain name of the spammer. In most cases he gets a note back a few days later that says the abuser's account has been terminated. He has no idea whether this is really true or just a placebo, but at least it gives him some satisfaction.

All in all, there aren't any perfect solutions, unless you are willing to set up your own custom system as we have described earlier in this chapter.

What to Do With Errors

Our final series of solutions has to do with taking care of error messages that you might receive. We all get them, and some of us more than others. The trick is in understanding how to match a particular set of decisions to the type of message you receive. You don't want to keep sending email that doesn't go anywhere, or doesn't go where it is intended.

We cover in this section errors dealing mostly with misaddressed mail or with those dealing with badly formed message headers. In Chapter 7 we'll cover problems relating to attachments and how to resolve these errors.

As we mentioned earlier in this chapter, figuring out what error message was generated by which piece of email you sent isn't always easy. There could be days in between when you tried to send your message and when you received the error report, or you could get multiple error reports for a single piece of email. We really don't have any good advice here, other than to try to sort your outgoing messages by recipient and try to match that recipient's domain name with the one from your error report. Sometimes you could spend more time tracking down the error than in composing the original message!

Let's look at some sample error messages we have received and try to decode them. First is a report that is probably one of the more helpful ones we've seen:

```
Subject: Returned mail: Service unavailable
From: Mail Delivery Subsystem <MAILER-
DAEMON@pgh.nauticom.net>

The original message was received at Wed, 7 Jan
1998 17:53:14 -0500 (EST)from [208.215.131.25]
Your email message could not be delivered. Common
causes are listed below:

User Unknown:             The username you entered is
                          not valid on the system
                          you addressed the email to.
```

```
                              (ie USER@somehost.com -
                              USER does not exist.)

Host Unknown:                 The hostname you entered is
                              not valid or there is a
                              problem with the user's
                              service provider.
                              (ie user@SOMEHOST.COM -
                              SOMEHOST.COM does not
                              exist.)

Disk Quota Exceeded:          The user you entered has
                              used up his/her available
                              disk space for their
                              account on their Internet
                              Service Provider.

Below you will find the error that caused your
message not to be delivered:
   ----- The following addresses had permanent
fatal errors -----
<ryhome@viper.nauticom.net>
   ----- Transcript of session follows -----
fclose: Disc quota exceeded
binmail: cannot append to /usr/spool/mail/ryhome
Mail saved in dead.letter
554 <ryhome@viper.nauticom.net>... Service
unavailable

Reporting-MTA: dns; pgh.nauticom.net
Received-From-MTA: DNS; [208.215.131.25]
Arrival-Date: Wed, 7 Jan 1998 17:53:14 -0500 (EST)
Final-Recipient: RFC822; ryhome@pgh.nauticom.net
Action: failed
Status: 5.5.0
```

Here we see the actual three-digit error codes explained in detail, along with the actual error. However, the message is somewhat confusing and we almost have too much information. Do we think that the real reason is that the disk quota was exceeded, meaning that someone's mailbox ran out of room and we should try to resend our message later? That is one interpretation. We also see, further down in the message a 554 error—which, as we described earlier, could mean just about anything. Here it is labeled as a service unavailable error, which could mean a full disk quota or several other things. Finally, there is the 5.5.0 error in the last line of the report.

Our diagnosis: a full disk quota. We should resend this message in a few hours and see if it gets through.

How about this message:

```
From: Mail Delivery Subsystem <MAILER-
DAEMON@ix.netcom.com>
Subject: Returned mail: Mailbox full, Please try
later.
Auto-Submitted: auto-generated (failure)

The original message was received at Thu, 22 Jan
1998 06:14:53 -0800 (PST)
from caldera.com [207.179.18.1]

    ----- The following addresses had permanent
fatal errors -----
<sparksb@ix.netcom.com>

    ----- Transcript of session follows -----
554 <sparksb@ix.netcom.com>... Mailbox full, Please
try later.
```

This seems clearer. Once again, our diagnosis is a full disk quota. But this time we don't have to have a medical degree to find it. The error message even tells us to try again later. Here is another example of a full mailbox, this time from CompuServe:

```
From: CompuServe Postmaster
<postmaster@compuserve.com>
Subject: Undeliverable Message:  ? EMDNRM - Mail
Delivery Failure. No room in mailbox. 72631,73--
Web Informant #96, 18 December 1997 (Truth in
advertising?)
Sender: auto.reply@compuserve.com
```

Again, a very clear statement of the problem, and contained in the Subject line as well, so we don't have to go searching through the message text itself. Take a look at this message:

```
From: Mail
Administrator<Postmaster@magnum.sohonet.com>
Subject: Mail System Error - Returned Mail

This Message was undeliverable due to the
```

```
following reason:
Each of the following recipients was rejected by a
remote mail server.
The reasons given by the server are included to
help you determine why
each recipient was rejected.
```

```
     Recipient: <Mstrange@fonorola.net>
     Reason:    User unknown
```

This is a relatively easy call. The user name no longer exists at the particular domain name. We need to find out what happened to this user and change his address. Diagnosis: Someone has changed his address and is no longer home.

```
From: Mail
Administrator<Postmaster@magnum.sohonet.com>
Subject: Mail System Error - Returned Mail
```

```
This Message was undeliverable due to the
following reason:
```

```
Your message was not delivered because the Domain
Name System
(DNS) for the destination computer is not
configured correctly.
The following is a list of reasons why this error
message could
have been generated. If you do not understand the
explanations
listed here, please contact your system
administrator for help.
```

```
     - The host does not have any mail exchanger
       (MX) or address (A) records in the DNS.
     - The host has valid MX records, but none of
       the mail exchangers listed have valid A
       records.
     - There was a transient error with the DNS
       that caused one of the above to appear to
       be true.
```

```
You may want to try sending your message again to
see if the
problem was only temporary.
     DNS for host sv.tbgi.com is mis-configured
```

```
The following recipients did not receive this
message:
     <SRBENJ@sv.tbgi.com>
```

This looks like a problem, but it is relatively minor. The most likely cause of the error is the third reason in the list, a "transient error" with the particular domain name server that supports this host. Diagnosis: a random Internet error. We should try to resend the message tomorrow.

```
From: Mail
Administrator<Postmaster@magnum.sohonet.com>
Subject: Mail System Error - Returned Mail

This Message was undeliverable due to the
following reason:

Your message was not delivered because the DNS
records for the destination computer could not be
found. Carefully check that the address was
spelled correctly, and try sending it again if
there were any mistakes.

It is also possible that a network problem caused
this situation, so if you are sure the address is
correct you might want to try to send it again. If
the problem continues, contact your friendly
system administrator.

     Host cliffo.vip.best.com not found
```

This could be more serious problem than the previous message. It could be something similar, a "transient" error that will be corrected in a few hours. Or it could be that this host is no longer available and will never return. Recommended action: Try to resend the message tomorrow and see if the same error is reported.

```
From: Mailer-Daemon@homegate.net (Mail Delivery
Subsystem)
Subject: Returned mail: Cannot send message for 5
days

The original message was received at Fri, 12 Dec
1997 21:31:19 GMT from localhost [127.0.0.1]

     ----- The following addresses had delivery
problems -----
```

```
<prs@homegate.net>   (unrecoverable error)

    ----- Transcript of session follows -----
<prs@homegate.net>... Deferred: Connection refused
by hk.homegate.net
Message could not be delivered for 5 days
Message will be deleted from queue
```

This is a very hard report to track down the exact cause. This stems from a message that was sent five days earlier. In the meantime, our host attempted to deliver it and finally couldn't. It could be a persistent routing problem between our host and the recipient's host that is keeping mail away, although after five days you have to wonder what is going on out there at HomeGate. Recommended action: Try again after a few more days.

```
From: postmaster@proxim.com
X-Mailer: ccMail Link to SMTP R8.00.01
Subject: cc:Mail Link to SMTP Undeliverable Message
Message is undeliverable.
Reason: User "dant@proxim.com" is not found in the
cc:Mail Directory.
```

This is our first example of how an Internet gateway responds to problems, in this case the Internet gateway for cc:Mail. The reason is pretty clear: This is another case of a user who has changed his address or who is no longer with the company. Recommended action: Find out where this person has moved to and change his address in our records.

Let's look at another gateway error report:

```
From: postmaster@smtp-ima.symantec.com
Subject: unable to deliver mail

This message was returned to you for the following
reasons:
    Unknown recipient: hsherman@symantec.com
The original message follows.
Received: from Mailer.symantec.com (198.6.49.5) by
smtp-ima.symantec.com with SMTP
  (IMA Internet Exchange 2.11 Enterprise) id
000132DC; Thu, 18 Dec 97 08:13:33 -0800
[original message follows]
```

Again, it seems as if the user has moved on and email address has changed. What is nice about this message is that following the error report is our original message, so we can track down what we sent. The same is true of the following message, this time from Microsoft Exchange's Internet gateway.

```
From: System Administrator
<postmaster@CASTELLE.com>
Subject: Undeliverable
X-Mailer: Internet Mail Service (5.0.1457.3)
X-MS-Embedded-Report:

Your message

  To:       paul.singh@castelle.com
  Subject: Info Press pricing
  Sent:    Wed, 21 Jan 1998 07:15:12 -0800

did not reach the following recipient(s):

paul.singh@castelle.com on Wed, 21 Jan 1998
07:51:07 -0800
    Unable to deliver the message due to a
communications failure
    MSEXCH:IMS:CASTELLE:SANTA_CLARA:NT02 0
(000C05A6) Unknown Recipient
```

The Internet gateway reports back its own error code—this one a C05A6. This is definitely "a user no longer at this address" situation, and Exchange usually labels itself there in the last line (MSEXCH).

We've covered quite a few different areas surrounding the issues over receiving messages. Let's look at what future developments will be.

FUTURES

A recurring theme throughout this chapter (and indeed, the whole book) is that there is a large gap between the functionality provided by Internet messaging standards and the solutions desired by the marketplace. It is the goal of successful products to use the standards as a basis for achieving those solutions.

The Problem of Unsolicited Email

For our purposes, the standards provide a stable and extensible basis for message headers. The challenge to product implementers is using those standards to manage incoming mail effectively. We have seen mixed results in this field. While filtering is a useful technique for dealing with mail that you expect, it is less than optimal for dealing with mail that you don't expect. In particular, an intelligent adversary [13] can usually devise messages that don't get caught by the filters you have. Although one can view this as an evolutionary process of cat-and-mouse, it begs the question as to why we should have to deal with this situation at all.

Companies that offer a "mailbox concentrator" service, such as Critical Path (*www.criticalpath.net*), offer one possible response. The idea here is that a service provider hosts hundreds of thousands of mailboxes, and when unsolicited commercial email is detected, the service provider deletes that message from all of its mailboxes. The "detection" part can either be manual (a user forwards the message to the provider) or automatic (based on the Received: headers, the number of times the message is seen, and so on). This is an interesting, but suboptimal, solution to the problem: It requires either manual intervention or relies on heuristics that can easily return false positives.

Regrettably there aren't any commercial products that provide the functionality seen in the one-off implementation we discussed earlier in the chapter. The key in developing such a product is in having an intuitive user interface to allow each mailbox user to customize the behavior of the incoming mail processor. Since mailbox concentrator services typically offer a Web-based interface to their users, this may be a natural combination of features. So, our first prediction is that this juxtaposition will occur: Mailbox service will increasingly become outsourced and those services will figure out new ways to reduce the clutter of unsolicited messages.

The Problem of Handling Errors Gracefully

Unfortunately, only recently have the standards begun to be useful with respect to error reports. Not surprisingly, no products exist that allow users to automatically recover from the errors reported. Further, few products are able to even render the new style of error report in a fashion that is easy for users to read.

In this sense, the situation for users is worse than before: You still have to deal with the old style of error reports (textual and without any rules as to how they are organized), and you also have to deal with the new style that doesn't render easily. In all cases, the process is manual. The only beneficiaries of the new style are mailing list maintainers, since recent upgrades to some different packages are able to interpret the new format automatically and unsubscribe addressees associated with permanent failures.

So, this leads us to a second prediction: User software will start handling these error reports automatically. There are several possibilities here. In some cases, the software could simply report the error, along with a suggested action, directly to the user. In other cases, for temporary failures, the message could be automatically resent.

Endnotes

1. One hope is that there are some advantages, otherwise why would so many willingly subject themselves to so much pain? It is not uncommon in some corporate settings for the phrase "You have mail" to invoke a facial apoplexy in at least one person present.

2. Presumably this action involves examining the message to determine the reason for the failure and possible corrective action, if any. In addition to the technical options discussed here, we won't dwell on some other, more satisfying options. These include: calling up the CIO's boss and demanding that the CIO be terminated for cause (having selected a corporate email system that isn't 100% pure Internet); calling up the CIO and demanding that the network operations director be terminated for cause (having under-provisioned the local storage on the intranet, or the number of redundant links to the Internet); or both. The point, of course, is that technology only takes us so far, and very often the problems we face aren't of a technical nature.

3. The term spam originated from a famous Monty Python routine, and the proper noun is a trademark of the Hormel Corp. A better term perhaps would be SPUME, which Brad Templeton coined for "system polluting unsolicited mass email." He defines SPUME as "performing a bulk mailing to a list of people to whom you are a stranger, and who did not request to be on the list."

4. Actually, Rose's desktop email system allows him to configure an *infinite* number of mailboxes automatically. Hence, each and every time he supplies his email address to someone other than a friend or colleague, one of these special, easily traceable addresses is sent.

5. Some CompuServe accounts are particularly prone to this, especially unused ones.

6. Sometimes you just have to use the telephone and call up your correspondent to find out what is going on!

7. CompuServe has a particularly arcane system of addressing messages to recipients that are on Internet-based mail systems or elsewhere besides CompuServe. While America Online makes use of the *user@example.com* system of domain names for all recipients beyond its own borders, with CompuServe you must first insert the label INTERNET: before any address intended to the Internet. The WinCIM and MacCIM client software does prompt you for what kind of system your recipient is on, but it still can get quite confusing. We'll discuss this topic in greater detail in Chapter 7.

8. But its value is probably not worth the confusion it introduces. For example, Outlook Express uses semi-colons rather than commas to separate addresses when displaying them to the user. Why its implementers made such a choice is a matter of some speculation—none of it of a complimentary nature.

9. Long ago, there was no need to lock the doors of one's house. Not so long ago, no one used answering machines or caller ID to screen incoming phone calls. Times change.

10. Not using the domain name can result in trouble when a message is forwarded outside your domain. Those recipients will have a harder time replying to these abbreviated addresses.

11. This is not an easy problem to solve, but here is one solution. Substitute a JavaScript program that displays your email address for the actual text that appears on your page. Our thanks to NetBITS—this originally appeared in issue #15 (*www.netbits.com*).

```
<script language=javascript>

<!--

// SpamProof Mail Script 1.0 by Joseph McLean
<flux@thecentre.com> - freeware

// Linktext is the text you want folks to see and click
upon.

// email1 & email2 are the text on either side of your
email address's @ sign.


var linktext = "Email Me!";

var email1 = "jsmith";

var email2 = "example.com";


document.write("<a href=" + "mail" + "to:" + email1 +
"@" + email2 + ">" + linktext + "</a>")

//-->

</script>
```

This chunk of code can be pasted into your Web page's HTML at any point that you would want to include a mailto: link. Some old browsers don't support JavaScript, but they won't hit an error—the mail link will simply be invisible (as it is to the spiders).

12. For more helpful hints about how to deal with spam mail, see Paul Hoffman and Dave Crocker's paper called "Unsolicited Bulk Email: Mechanisms for Control" at *www.imc.org/ube-sol.html*. For lots of additional links, information on legislation, and other details about the spam, see the article in *SunWorld* entitled, "Controlling unsolicited bulk email," at *www.sun.com/sunworldonline/swol-08-1997/ swol-08-junkemail.htm*. This suggestion for removing your email address from your Web pages is just to avoid any personal spam: You still want to have some email address on your Web pages for your customers to contact you—an issue that we will cover in more detail in Chapter 5.

13. An amusing euphemism for referring to a spammer. Regardless, the term "intelligent adversary" is a half-truth in any event.

Messaging on the Desktop: Sending

In this chapter, we consider two central issues of sending email on the desktop: how to use email as a publication mechanism and how to integrate messaging with other desktop applications.

These two topics provide a good exposition of the power of email. First, they move from simple one-on-one exchanges to one-to-many exchanges; and, second, they move from textual exchanges to desktop automation.

INTRODUCTION

To begin, let us consider a minor but important observation from Chapter 2: It is almost as easy to send a message to many recipients as it is to one recipient.

Einar A. Stefferud founded the original mailing list in the Internet, MsgGroup, in 1979. What Stefferud and many other of the Internet's earliest pioneers recognized was that unlike the world of physical messaging, the originator is able to automate the sending process. This original mailing list, now termed a discussion group, was formed out of necessity: The researchers wishing to make extensive use of email needed a forum in which to exchange ideas as to how the technology should be developed. Although MsgGroup was used to discuss all aspects of Internet messaging, at times it could be viewed as a discussion group to talk about the technology that made discussion groups possible.

For our purposes, the trick of it is primarily ease of use at the sending desktop. The actual Internet messaging infrastructure—the systems that relay messages between desktops—is blissfully unconcerned as to whether a given message is to be delivered to one recipient or to many. Because of its ubiquity, email is by far the preferred "push" technology for the Internet.[1] However, publishing using messaging as the distribution mechanism is not without problems.

One lesson we shall learn is that list management is difficult. Two issues demonstrate this problem quite handily. The first issue is drawn from Chapter 2: Interpreting error reports is hard to do. The second issue deals with the problem of address maintenance, in the absence of delivery errors. Surprisingly few people can accurately enter their email address. There are perhaps several reasons for this, for example, difficult to spell or remember mailboxes, confusion between hyphens ("-") and underscores ("_") and so on. Furthermore, email addresses change frequently; empirical evidence suggests that they change more frequently than any other addressing artifact, including physical delivery addresses, postal addresses, telephone numbers, and so on.

Address management for mailing lists is largely centralized. As a consequence, "subscription"—the ability to manage a database of addresses—is the hard part; in contrast, "publishing"—sending the actual messages—is largely a nonissue.

Of course, once you can publish via email, why publish only text as your content? Why not publish other things via messaging? In Chapter 7, we look at using hypertext markup language (HTML) and other formats for email publication. However, for now, we'll consider things from a slightly different perspective—publishing to other applications.

From an architectural perspective, originators and recipients are simply "users." A user might be a person or perhaps a program, such as a calendar or scheduling program. Historically, the term "mail-enabled applications" was used to refer to programs that received and processed mail.

As might be expected, because email is a "best-effort" delivery service, the originating program must be aware of both error reports and silent drops. In the former case, it must be able to interpret the indicated cause of failure and act accordingly. In the latter case, it must contain some kind of algorithm to achieve reliability through retransmission. In practice, however, it is difficult to achieve optimal results without a long traffic history with which to make predictions. A momentary network failure might result in a message being queued for retry several hours later.

Furthermore, the lack of rigorous adherence to standards makes it difficult to write these programs. As a simple example, consider a scheduling program that mails several possibilities as to when a meeting might take place. In the usual case, a corresponding scheduling program would receive the message, consult its appointments database, perhaps consult the people involved and then send a reply indicating whether a meeting is scheduled or not. Now, suppose that a different process receives this message, for example an automated process that simply replies "I am out of the office until next week." There is no information present in either the original message, or in the reply, to indicate to the Internet messaging infrastructure that there is a misconfiguration. Hopefully, on the theory that the originating scheduling program does extensive error checking, the ill-conceived reply will be detected.[2]

So, let us now consider these issues in greater detail along with aspects of the systems that cause them.

PROBLEMS

You start out with what you think is a simple enough task: You wish to publish a weekly electronic newsletter for your department. You have recognized the need for your newsletter ever since several of your colleagues asked you the same series of questions about project status. For the moment, you compose a separate email message whenever you get a request from one of your coworkers. It's tedious, even using the cut and paste features of your word processor so that you don't have to retype the message. But you'd like something more elegant.

How do you do it without spending a great deal of time and money for new software? You don't want to build any new systems, let alone maintain them for this task.

Think for a moment what a print publisher goes through in the process of getting out a new edition of a magazine or a newspaper. He or she first has to know the intended audience of the publication, either by doing surveys or by interviewing subscribers directly, so that the content matches the readers' interests. Then he or she has to have writers prepare the content, editors correct it and other people produce it in a form that is pleasing to the eye, taking into consideration choice of graphics, colors and format. Then a printer has to produce the pages, collate them and mail them to the readers. That is a lot of work.

An electronic publisher goes through a similar process, whether on the small scale of our departmental newsletter, or on a bigger scale with an audience of thousands of readers. The only difference is the end product is bits, not paper. But still someone must take the time to understand the needs of the intended audience, prepare the content and make it pleasant to read. And the content has to be delivered to the readers as well.

The challenge of being your own publisher isn't the only issue faced when sending email from your desktop. You also have to keep track of various email address lists and try to figure out ways to send email directly from your desktop applications. We'll cover these issues in this section.

Push Technology

If we had asked the question of being your own newsletter publisher in early 1997, the popular answer would have been to make use of a "push technology" product. Defined as automated delivery and/or notification of information via the Internet, many companies came out that winter with push products. What a difference a year makes: Many of these companies are either out of business or rapidly trying to redefine their purpose. Push technology has gone from hypeful to hopeless in less time than high fashion changes.

The idea behind push is as simple as our posed problem: sending content, whether it is a page of HTML or a series of advertising images in the form of animated screen savers, automatically to a given audience of users' desktops. The particular stream of content is called a channel, and many of the push products have both a means of creating your own channel (such as the Example Corporation's Human Resource Newsletter) and becoming a subscriber to other people's channels. Channels could be private, within the corporate intranet, or public, such as the ESPN sports scores and Dow Industrials average. These channels vary tremendously. They could contain pointers to particular Web pages out on the Internet, or contain the actual information, such as graphics and text, that would be saved to your own hard disk.[3]

Yet the implementation is all but easy. Push products really didn't have the publishing tools at all. You often didn't know who your audience was, couldn't tell what software they used to view your content and preparing content often took loads of time and was a "hit or miss" proposition. Most of the products couldn't even tell you whether your readers actually received your content, let alone if they spent any time reading it.

Push suffered from several issues. First and foremost, you want to get your information delivered to your email inbox, whatever and wherever that may be. While many push technologies install special software on your desktop or augment your browser with plug-ins or other software, most of us use our inboxes as ways to order our day's priorities. Given our already bloated hard disks full of other software, the incremental piece of push software was too much for many of us to handle. It seems like a small point, but it isn't. And we saw lots of users tired of getting so many cutesy screen-saver animations and other digital effluvia. They quickly turned the push channel off, uninstalled the software, and went back to using their email for some real work.

Most of the push products didn't really take advantage of email at all—they used the browser either as the control panel to tune in to a particular channel or as a container to deposit the information itself. This was a problem, because everyone uses different browser versions, different platforms and different configurations. Installing browser plug-ins is not always simple, and not every push vendor supported a wide enough range of operating system platforms either.

There are plenty of other problems with push implementations: How many push screens does it take to send a page of HTML to a particular desktop? How do push clients maintain and consolidate standard Web server log information in a way that can be useful to the Web server analyzers? Can a push publisher make any valid claims equating the value of desktops receiving their messages to the number of ad impressions delivered via Web banners?

Contrast this browser situation with email now. Email is pretty much a bread and butter application—this is why you are reading this book. Everyone's email does work differently, but getting messages sent doesn't require you to install extra software on your machine. You just send the message. Most email programs don't have plug-ins or extensions[4] that require you to become a part-time software installer and troubleshooter.

Second, push ate bandwidth like nothing else, and became a pox upon the network. Products like PointCast behaved so badly that any mention of them could cause a long string of curse words from many IS managers' lips. It wasn't unusual to see 15% or more of a corporation's overall T-1 circuit consumed with the network traffic resulting from PointCast software.

Push was hungry for bandwidth largely because of some sloppy programming on the part of its creators, who worked with fat Internet pipes and in small companies. Once this network *faux pas* was realized, the push creators moved quickly to cut their bandwidth consumption. However, by then the damage had been done, and corporate IS managers wanted little to do with some of these products.

Push also had no real standards to build upon—every vendor had its own scheme for notification and delivery of pushed content. This was especially true for Microsoft and Netscape, which developed their own incompatible software, protocols and systems. Some of the push prowess depended on the Web and HTML. Some worked at lower-level TCP/IP protocols. The wide variety of push differences continue to bedevil the push players, and even the applications developed for one company's early software versions aren't compatible with later ones.[5]

To make matters worse, few could agree on what push really means. What about products that didn't really send any content at all but polled a particular server at specific intervals: Shouldn't that be called scheduled pull? What about products that just organize Web sites that you have already visited: Shouldn't that be called something else?

We had an opportunity to use many of these products and personally meet with the CEOs from many push companies. We asked them the same question: How do you want to receive information from us, via your own software or via email? The universal answer was email. Not eating one's own dog food is the best reason we can find for avoiding the whole push arena entirely.

So what alternatives remain in a world without push? Email. And any notion of sending groups of email messages brings us to the problems with using mailing lists. Mailing lists are relatively simple to set up, as we'll show later in our section on solutions. But maintaining them and keeping their addresses current is another story entirely.

The real advantage that email brings to the push party is universal notification. We've seen an explosion of such services and uses of email by a wide variety of commercial and noncommercial vendors. For example, our favorite online bookstore Amazon.com can send you email when a new book matching certain criteria or from certain authors is published. GreetSt.com, an online greeting card company, can send you email to remind you not to miss sending that certain someone a birthday card.

We get daily email telling us the closing prices of our investment portfolio, and other email with news digests related to particular technologies. Most of the airlines have mailings set up to remind you of travel bargains, including American Airlines, which has different mailings for domestic and international fares. There is a site called RemindMe (*www.photo.net/philg/services.html*) that reminds people when to move their cars to avoid getting parking tickets. The site can also send reminders for other events at varying intervals before any particular date.

All of this has implications for managing mailing lists, which is our next topic.

Mailing Lists[6]

A mailing list is nothing more than a group of email addresses. Email sent to the mailing list name gets "exploded" or copied to every member on the list. There are several kinds of mailing lists that are in use today. One type is the kind that any of you use as part and parcel of your desktop email software. Typically, these lists are found in an address book of some sorts. The address book contains information on your correspondents, such as their actual name and email address, and perhaps other information including postal addresses and phone numbers. Most email software has similar techniques for creating lists: You go into their address books, create a new list name and proceed to add members to the list. When you want to send mail to a group, you first create the group, and then click on the group name in your address book or type it in explicitly in the mail program. That's not too difficult, now is it?

The trouble comes when a member's address changes and you don't necessary know when that happens. We've found that about 1% to 2% of our own mailing list changes every week. That doesn't sound like much, but it takes time to track down new addresses and make the changes. Given the other pressing needs of our workday, who wants to have to do list maintenance as well?

The typical situation is the error message you receive that contains a "bounce" message. As we discussed in Chapter 2, you don't always know why something is wrong with the message you sent. And you need to be able to match the error message and the recipient name with the suspect list that contains the incorrect information. Then you need to open up your address book of the email program that sent the message, find that list name, and either delete the now defunct recipient or figure out why his or her address is no longer valid. Did you make a typo? Did this person change jobs or job locations? Did this person decide to switch Internet providers and email identities? It sounds messy, and it is. And there really isn't any other way to automatically fix the problem either.

Tracking down changes in email addresses is time consuming, and we go into more details about these problems in Chapter 6.

But this is just the tip of the mailing list iceberg. There are plenty of other mailing lists besides the ones that you maintain inside your own email program. There are mailing list programs that operate on special email servers: These run without any human intervention. You send email to a special address, called the listserv address (named after a popular piece of software that is used for this purpose), which subscribes you to (or removes you from) the mailing list. Of course, this includes the exact instructions for these commands and where they are placed in your email message, depending on the listserv software being used.[7] If your email isn't formatted correctly, then the listserv can't process your instructions, and it sends back an email with a sometimes cryptic error report.

As we said, computers maintain listservs. This makes it easy for you to forget about them when you change your email address. Then the trouble begins when the listserv attempts to deliver mail to your old address. Eventually a carbon-based life form must manually intervene and remove your old and no longer functioning email address from the listserv. And, as we mentioned earlier, listservs have to be smart enough to ignore messages that are generated on your behalf by a machine, responding to the listserv broadcast mailing by saying that you are away from your office. Some aren't, and all sorts of havoc can occur whereby your out-of-office message gets sent to several hundred of your closest friends.

A third type of mailing list includes those that are maintained by mail system administrators for the convenience of the entire enterprise of email users. Typically, these are called "system aliases." Such lists—for example, "marketing" for the entire marketing department to send broadcasts—may also not reflect the current members of the department. These types of global lists are usually maintained and used by two different people within an organization. This lengthens or in some cases breaks the feedback cycle from sending a message to the list to receiving an error message to determining and making the correction. A simple solution would be to make sure that all lists can be maintained by the individuals that use them, but in practice (as we shall see later on in this chapter) that isn't always possible or even desirable.

There is a reason for the wide diversity of different mailing lists: They do different things because people have differing requirements. But that doesn't make things any easier, especially if you are contemplating using them for the first time.

This may all sound too technical for you. You are probably thinking, "Why do I care about these mailing lists? Just leave me alone and let me get on with answering my messages." Well, here is a short anecdote to illustrate that lists are becoming more pervasive and popular.

We all get those annual holiday newsletters from our family members and supposed friends. Some of them are annoying, to be sure, but many of us like to hear about what these people are doing. With the rise of email, some families have begun their own mailing lists, sending out messages, photos and periodic greetings to a group at once. The list is automatic—any family member that knows the list alias can send a message to the group. And the mailing list keeps everyone in touch without having to duplicate the message to everyone or remember individual email addresses. We know several families doing this, and the interesting thing is that the email addresses span different systems and networks.

Let's look at mailing lists from the standpoint of our print publisher perspective. With a mailing list, you generally know your audience, especially if you maintain the list addresses yourself. Even if a computer automatically signs up subscribers, generally there are ways for you as the list owner to periodically examine the list of addresses and make some assessment of who is on your list. Second, you have some control over how people view your content, because you understand the nature of email and how people read their mail. (Or you will after you finish reading this chapter.) And, finally, you have control over the delivery of your content.

With all these lists, it becomes hard for you to keep track of where you store your lists and to remember which list contains which members. Is Joe in marketing still on the corporate marketing list after he transferred to Chicago and has a new email address? Did Tom get taken off the distribution list because he was fired last week, or can he still receive his email? Where did I put the email that I got when I subscribed to that listserv many months ago, and why did I subscribe in the first place? You could easily make list maintenance a full-time job, and indeed in many corporations list maintenance is a big part of an email system administrator's workday.

Address Management

Compounding these problems is another series that relates to keeping track of your correspondent's addresses. When you start to think about this, you probably have email addresses tucked away in many different corners of your hard disk. The logical first place to start is in the address book or corporate directory of whatever email software you are using. But you might have more than one email program. Then which address book is the more current one? You also may have stored email information in whatever software you use to maintain your own Rolodex, contact manager, customer database or accounting system. You may even have email addresses stored in spreadsheets and Word documents. Remembering which address is the most current one for your correspondents is not always easy.

On top of this, there are times that you'd like to import addresses from other electronic sources, or export your email address book to other programs. We'll cover these issues later, but many products either don't allow this or don't have very sophisticated tools to cope with any kind of address book manipulation.

In the ideal world, you would like to be able to search through your address lists with a variety of methods. For example, as you type an address, the software automatically brings you to that portion of the list that matches what you type. In the early days of email, cc:Mail was one of the first products to offer such a feature and now more products have it.

Or perhaps you would like to use a search tool to find all matches with wildcards of particular addresses, as you would use the search tool in Windows Explorer or inside your word processor. For example, you would look for *@example.com to find all the addresses you know that are part of the example.com domain and work for the Example Corporation. Yes, it would be nice. Most products don't offer anywhere near the sophistication and utility of your average word processor or even a simple database for these kind of searches.

And we haven't even mentioned all the nonelectronic sources of email addresses, including your physical files that contain business cards, letterhead and scribbled notes with email addresses too. What a mess! In order for mailing lists to work, you need to centralize where all these addresses are kept, and work at keeping them up to date. We'll talk more about that later in the chapter.

Creating the list is only really half of the problem. The other half is understanding the process by which email gets sent to each member on the list. Some email products send a sequence of separate messages, one message to each recipient on the list. Some send a single message, with the entire list of recipients specified in the email To: field (or wherever you insert the list name in your email software). Some email products use a special alias address for the originator of a list message, while others put your own email address there. And we are all too familiar with spam that contains an invalid originating address.

Now, you may not really care about this for your own newsletter to the marketing department. It really doesn't matter whether the message comes from you or from an alias address, and you don't really care whether everyone's email address in the marketing department is listed in the header. But for wider and more professional efforts, you might.

Understanding this process is important because you may not want to have all your recipients see everyone else's email address. Scrolling through a long list of several thousand names isn't a very nice way to start off reading any message, and it is easier for a recipient to just delete it unread than try to find the actual beginning of message after the roll call of all the names. And you may not wish to let everyone know who is getting a particular message. We still receive various email from different public relations executives. What they have in common is that all of the person's key press contacts were enumerated on the message header, with both the actual name and the email address. Anyone could have copied these addresses down and used them to start a good mailing list to these contacts. Again, this gets back to our notion of the publishing process, and drawing parallels with the print world. What if a magazine was to fill its first several pages with a detailed list of its subscribers? You probably would be initially fascinated, but after the second or third time you'd skip ahead to the main content of the magazine, or maybe even cancel your subscription.

Desktop Scheduling and Email

We started out this section talking about ways to push-publish your content, and using an email mailing list as one method. But we aren't out of the woods yet. We'd also like to integrate email with our other desktop applications and be able to send messages directly from these applications. Here is an example:

Say we are trying to schedule a meeting among five different participants, three of whom are in other cities and would have to fly in for the meeting. We could call up (or send separate email) to each person, asking for dates of availability over the next week or so. That is cumbersome, time consuming and usually involves many calls or messages before we can come to a consensus on the open time slot. This sounds like a job for a computer program, and there are many now that perform this task to schedule meetings and keep track of calendars.

You'd like any program to work across your enterprise so that everyone's calendar is visible. But you'd also like to have different levels of access to your calendar. Some of your coworkers should be able to make and change your appointments without your explicit permission: They could be your administrative assistant or department secretary. For others, you would prefer that they only view your schedule and see when you are free, but not necessarily with whom you are meeting and when.

In the ideal world, you'd like this feature as part of your email software for several reasons. First, you'd like to receive notification of requests for your time through email, since you order your priorities according to other email messages that you receive. Second, you want to make use of the directories, address books and contact information that you maintain via email. There is no sense in having to recreate or retype any of this information if you have already created it for your email program. And, finally, you don't want to have to learn how to use yet another piece of software if you can leverage functions of existing programs such as email that you spend more of your time using.

Perhaps the best product for group scheduling was the IBM mainframe-based PROFS of yore. It did everything to integrate scheduling into the messaging environment. It had different levels of access so that your staff couldn't tell you were taking the day off to play golf, but your secretary could see this. The only problem is that it cost a bundle and only ran on IBM's big iron and proprietary mainframe networks.

Second best is Novell's GroupWise, which runs on a variety of platforms. Whether you want to create a meeting date or create a message, you use similar tools and menu commands. As participants confirm their attendance, you receive email with this information. You use the same directory for the meeting users that you have for your email users.

Unfortunately, the products that we have chosen for this book don't really help in this regard. The full version of Outlook 98 works in conjunction with Microsoft Exchange to do scheduling—but this piece is missing from the Outlook Express software. cc:Mail works in conjunction with Lotus' Organizer group scheduling program, but you still need to use the Organizer software to set up any schedules. And Netscape has its own Calendar Server that works in conjunction with a Web browser to view meetings. Again, another interface. Both cc:Mail and Netscape products, however, make use of the existing directory entries that you have for email—a small step forward.

Desktop Applications and Email

So much for scheduling. But there are other applications that we'd like to email enable. For example, how about sending our spreadsheets (or documents) directly to an email recipient, but doing so from inside the spreadsheet (or word processor) program itself? Microsoft and Lotus, among other desktop application vendors, have put this ability inside their Office suite of products.

Let's say we want to send a Word document to someone via Exchange. There are two ways to do this. If we are in Word, the command is File | Send To | Mail Recipient. In our case, this brings up an email message form in Microsoft Exchange with the name of our file as an attachment. A second way is to save the file in Word and close it. Then browse our files with Windows Explorer and right-click on the file name. You'll see a Send To option on the small menu that pops up beside the file name. Choose Exchange, and it will bring up the message form as before.

You still have to fill out the right address in the message form, and you still have to remember to send the message. But those are relatively small tasks, compared to trying to locate a file that you were just working on someplace on your hard disk.

If you have installed more than one email program on your computer, this might not always work the way we have described. You may have additional email programs listed on the Send To menu, depending on how you installed these programs.

The issue here is that you often don't realize how your desktop is configured until you try to make use of this integration feature and want to send a file from one of your applications. If your actions launch the right email software, that's all well and good. But if some other email program appears, then you are at a loss over what to do and how to fix it. Do you make some changes to your email configuration? Or is there something inside the operating system, such as a control panel dialogue box, that needs fixing?

Part of the blame for this confusion lies with some of the desktop integration "standards" such as VIM and MAPI, which we'll get into later in this chapter.

Spoofing Your Email

There is a final problem for sending desktop email, and it is an ugly one indeed. To begin, anyone can send email to your Simple Mail Transfer Protocol (SMTP) server, regardless of who the message is addressed to (i.e., the messages don't have to be going to a local address on your server). They don't need your email account password, they don't even need a valid email account name. They just have to know about your server and be able to access it over the Internet. They can even "author" messages with a From: containing your email address.

It is an unfortunate sign of our times that this behavior has become more frequent and used to nefarious means. Some spammers have caused legitimate email accounts to be canceled (or sites blacklisted), all because they hijacked these accounts in this fashion. And unsuspecting email users are sometimes blamed for other's actions.

This is not a new problem. Indeed, when one of us was a graduate student, one of our fellow students played a prank. He hijacked our student email account and sent an off-color message to another student, making it appear as if we had sent the message. The issue is that now almost anyone can do it, given the minimal effort to change the designated SMTP server information in any email software program.

ISPs have reacted to this situation by blocking users who try to send a message to the ISP's servers if the message's recipients are outside the ISP's network. This sounds like a good solution, until you consider the situation of the traveling user, who may use another provider to access the Internet and needs to make use of his or her account on the home ISP. This is just another thing to check when you sign up with a particular provider. If you do a great deal of traveling, make sure that your ISP has enough local access numbers in the cities you travel. We offer more hints about accessing your email account remotely in Chapter 5.

STANDARDS

There are no desktop-specific standards for sending email. There are, however, standards that describe how messages are relayed within the Internet messaging infrastructure. In the early days of Internet email, the origination of messages from the desktop to the Internet messaging infrastructure was considered a local matter. There were a number of platform-specific technologies for doing that. Today, however, the same protocol is used both for submitting messages to the Internet messaging infrastructure and for when the infrastructure relays those messages.[8] That standard is called the SMTP.

Before we consider SMTP in greater detail, it is useful for us to complete a topic that is introduced in Chapter 2. Chapter 2 describes structured message headers. The topic of messages with structured bodies was postponed. We now begin by considering that topic.

Structured Messages

The history of Internet email starts with only two sets of structures: the structure of an envelope for relaying messages throughout the infrastructure (we'll discuss this later on in this chapter); and the structure of headers used within a message (as we discussed in Chapter 2). Messages were assumed to be unstructured plain text. There are two underlying assumptions for such a system. First, that the message bodies contain characters used only for printing or formatting (commonly referred to as "printable ASCII"); and, second, that humans, rather than programs, are the ones processing the message when it is received.

Clearly, both of these are poor assumptions. This led to numerous systems being developed for "multimedia email" throughout the pre-modern Internet. After considerable experimentation, the community standardized one particular approach, called Multipurpose Internet Message Extensions (MIME).

Although there are some six or so documents that comprise the MIME standard, there are really only two key topics: labeling a message body so that a program can uniquely identify the type of content contained in the message; and encoding a message body so that if it contains nonprintable or binary characters, these can be safely transmitted via email.

Let's reiterate that for clarity: MIME structures and encodes data. The structuring part is done using a Content-Type:, and the encoding part is done using a Content-Transfer-Encoding:. We now look at each.

Content Types

The Content-type: header is used to identify the content value contained within a message. A content type is identified by:

- a type, which gives general guidance as to the resources required in order to process the content;

- a subtype, which refines the content; and,

- zero or more parameters, which allow for the customization of the content.

By convention, when people talk about a content type they say both the type and subtype. The two are separated by a solidus ("/"), for example text/plain or application/MSWord. There are seven predefined types and a several subtypes associated with each content type. The definition of the original content types is such that there probably won't be any-more than the original seven.

The multipart type is the most complex. It is used to convey a content value that contains subordinate parts. Basically, a multipart content, regardless of its subtype, contains zero or more body parts, each separated by a delimiter. Each of the body parts is structured in a similar fashion to an electronic mail message. Unlike a message, however, no header fields need be present. Hence, any of the body parts could start with a blank line. However, there are usually headers present and they should all be named with a prefix of Content-. If no Content- type: header is present, then the value text/plain is used as a default, which means that the body part contains unstructured ASCII text.

There are eight subtypes of multipart in common use. We'll describe five here. The others, multipart/encrypted, multipart/signed and multipart/related, are discussed in Chapters 4 and 7.

1. multipart/mixed, which indicates that the subordinate body parts should be processed in sequence.

2. multipart/parallel, which indicates that the subordinate body parts should be processed in parallel. However, if more than one body part requires exclusive access to a common resource (e.g., if two or more body parts requires access to the user's keyboard when rendering them), or if the software processing the message is incapable of simulating parallel processing, then sequential processing is acceptable.

3. multipart/digest, which indicates that each subordinate body part is an electronic message, having type message/rfc822 (discussed in just a moment). When messages are forwarded, this is the content type to use. Unfortunately, much "modern" desktop software simply includes the message as text—without actually structuring it as an included message. As a result, humans can figure out what's going on, but programs can't.

4. multipart/alternative, which indicates that while there are multiple subordinate body parts present, they all have identical semantic content. As such, only one should be processed. The body parts are ordered in terms of expressive power, with the least expressive content being the first, and the most expressive content being the last. The reason for this is to make things simpler for pre-MIME software. That desktop software will display the entire message to the user; hopefully, the first body part will be legible to a human.

5. multipart/report, which indicates that the message is an error report. This is the structured error report described in Chapter 2.

The easy way to think of the multipart type is that it is interpreted directly by the desktop software and the user should be completely unaware of its existence. The same is largely true of the next type, message, which has three commonly used subtypes and one unpopular subtype:

1. message/rfc822, which indicates that the content value is an electronic mail message. When forwarding messages, the multipart/digest content type is used and each subordinate body part is of type message/rfc822.

2. message/partial, which indicates that the content value is part of a fragmented message. When a message is too large to send, typically due to administrative controls, it can be divided into several fragments. Each fragment has a common id and a unique number. The final fragment must (and the other fragments usually do) have an indication as to the total number of fragments. Upon receiving all fragments, the original message can be reconstructed. The only particularly tricky part about the process is that the Content- headers and the Message-ID: of the original message is placed at the front of the value put in

the first fragment. This prevents any confusion between the headers identifying each fragment and the headers in the original message.

3. message/delivery-status, which is contained inside a structured error report. As described in Chapter 2, it's the second part of an error report that contains machine-readable information about the problems in delivering the message.

4. message/external-body, which indicates that the content value is a pointer to the content, rather than the actual value. This subtype is falling out of use. The reason is that it is proving easier to send a message containing HTML, which embeds a link to the external content rather than constructing a separate external body part.

As a note for protocol historians, this last subtype was developed at approximately the same time as the Web technologies. For various reasons, it didn't use the same syntax as the Web. This was, in retrospect, a mistake, given that an HTML fragment has equivalent functionality to an external body part.

The remaining content types are meaningful to the user. The standardized ones in common use are:

1. text/plain, which indicates that the content value is plain text. A parameter indicates which character set should be used when rendering the text. In general, the simplest character set that faithfully represents the value should be chosen. For example, the characters contained in the US-ASCII set are a subset of those contained in the ISO-8859-1 repertoire. If a message makes use of only those characters in the former character set, then that should be the character set indicated by the email program. However, as we'll see later in this chapter, not all products have been implemented in this fashion.

2. text/html, which indicates that the content value is from the HTML used by the Web. The same characters set issues apply as for text/plain.

3. text/richtext, which indicates that the content value is input to a simple text formatter. This is another casualty of the early development of MIME not foreseeing the popularity of HTML.

4. image/gif, which indicates that the content value is image data encoded using the Graphics Interchange Format (GIF).

5. image/jpeg, which indicates that the content value is image data encoded using the Joint Picture Experts Group (JPEG) format.

6. audio/*, which indicates that the content value is audio data encoded using the indicated subtype (and parameters). Originally, there was the audio/basic content, which was phone-quality, single-channel audio, but this lacks the sizzle required by the people marketing today's Internet.

7. video/*, which indicates that the content value is video encoded using the indicated subtype (and parameters).

As might be imagined, there are many subtypes of text, image, audio and video used for specialized applications throughout the Internet. However, we haven't yet described the seventh content type, which is where most of the customized behavior is found—the application type. Although the original intent of the application type was to convey a content value for mail-enabled applications, in practice anytime something needs to be sent that is more complex than one of these four types (text, image, audio or video), then the application type is used.

For example, if you need to send a spreadsheet, a word processing document or a slide presentation, then the company that wrote the authoring program has already registered the application subtype that conveys the appropriate kind of file.[9] Among other things, the MIME standard documents the procedure wherein a vendor may register content types with a registration authority. In addition, there is one other common subtype:

- application/octet-stream, which indicates that the content is arbitrary binary data. Parameters indicate a textual explanation of the contents. This subtype is generally used when the appropriate company has registered a specific application subtype.

In effect, the application/octet-stream type provides a simple file transfer facility over email.

Let's now look at two examples. First, let's combine these concepts and look at the structured error report from Chapter 2:·

- A structured error report consists of two or three subordinate body parts. So, we know that it's going to be a multipart content type. The particular content type is multipart/report.

- The first part is a textual explanation as to the problem and includes the three-digit reply code. The particular content type is text/plain.

- The second part looks like a small message—it has a collection of headers. These headers include precise information as to what the problem was and where it occurred. This information is carefully generated to be machine readable. The particular content type is message/delivery-status.

- The third part, if present, is the original message. The particular content type is message/rfc822.

Second, it should now be easy to see the "right" way to generate a Bcc: message:

1. Strip the Bcc: header out of the message, but remember the addresses contained therein.

2. Send that message to the recipient addresses in the To: and cc: fields.

3. For each address in the Bcc: header, construct a new message of type multipart/digest. It should have one subordinate body part, message/rfc822, which contains the message that was sent in the previous step.

4. The headers of each new message sent should be identical to the original message sent except that the Content-*: headers should be removed and replaced with a Content-Type: of multipart/digest and the To: and cc: headers should be replaced with a To: header containing the address of the Bcc: recipient.

Content Encodings

The Content-Transfer-Encoding: header, if present, indicates how the content value has been encoded. There are four general rules that govern encodings:

- The multipart and message content types are never encoded. This requirement makes it much easier for mail reading software to parse structured messages.

- There is no *a priori* binding between a content type and the mechanism used to encode its value. Although some content values may lend themselves toward a particular encoding, these are independent issues. For example, one could encode plain text using the same mechanism used to encode binary information. There is no particular efficiency gained by such an approach, but it does have the amusing side effect of preventing people with pre-MIME desktop software from reading your messages!

- One should view the encoding and decode of a content value as completely separate from processing the value. Hence, when processing an incoming message, the value is decoded to its native form prior to being processed as a particular content type.

- Although MIME allows for extensibility of transfer encodings, the definition of new mechanisms is strongly discouraged. MIME provides three standard encoding mechanisms: one useful when the value is printable and format characters, one useful when the value is mostly such characters and the third for content values that are primarily binary in nature.

The three encoding mechanisms are:

1. 7bit, which indicates that the content value conforms to the ASCII repertoire.

2. quoted-printable, which indicates that the content value is mostly (or entirely) from the ASCII character set. It is useful when a small percentage of the characters have the high-order bit set, or when it is possible that mail software somewhere down the line might transform some of the characters present. An example of the latter case might be if some non-Internet email system is involved.

3. base64, which indicates that the content value is arbitrary binary values. For every 24 bits of input, it generates a four-character sequence taken from a special subset of the ASCII characters. This character set was carefully chosen to have identical representation in all currently standardized character sets. Arguably, it is the safest transfer encoding for this reason.

One might reasonably ask at this point why arbitrary binary values couldn't be sent directly using the Internet messaging infrastructure. The answer is historical: Internet email grew up in an ASCII world. Message envelopes (to be discussed later in this chapter) and headers are all ASCII.[10] Although it may be more bandwidth-efficient to support native binary transfers, there are other efficiencies to consider, such as software compatibility. For example, the Internet messaging infrastructure is blissfully unconcerned with regard to the content values it carries, other than they are part of an ASCII stream.

Content Embellishments

There are a couple of other headers that MIME allows that increase functionality. These are:

- Content-Description: contains arbitrary text describing the content value.

- Content-Disposition: actually serves two purposes. First, it indicates whether a subordinate body part should be considered as an "inline content" or as an "attachment." In the former case, it should be processed with the rest of the message in sequence; in the latter case, it should be processed only when the user asks. For example, you might send a presentation to someone with some cover text. This could be sent as a multipart/mixed content type containing a text/plain and then some application-specific content value. The Content-Disposition: for the second value would mark it as an attachment.

- Secondly, Content-Disposition: conveys file system semantics for the content value, for example, the corresponding file's name, creation time, and so on.

- Content-ID: contains a unique identifier for the content value, just as Message-ID: contains a unique identifier for a message.

- Content-MD5: contains an integrity checksum for the content value. It is meant to detect inadvertent changes to the content value. An interloper can still make changes to the content value and then recompute the Content-MD5: value.

- MIME-Version:, which always takes the value 1.0—its mandatory presence and fixed value made for amusing discussion a decade ago.

Finally, there is one additional aspect of MIME that we've only touched on: character sets. We continue our discussion of them in Chapter 7.

Message Submission and Transfer

SMTP is the Internet's most venerable application-layer protocol. It lacks both the negotiation clumsiness of the Telnet protocol and the multi-channel fumbling of the file transfer protocol. Its simplicity and elegance often lead to robust operation in multivendor environments. Its design also heavily inspired another Internet email protocol, Post Office Protocol (POP), which is discussed in Chapter 5.

In order to understand SMTP, there are really only three basic concepts: the "where" of message envelopes, which describe the destination mailboxes; the "how" of address expansion, which describe the process whereby mailboxes are determined; and the "why" of protocol interactions, which describe the rules wherein responsibility for a message is transferred as it transits the Internet messaging infrastructure.

Message Envelopes

Because SMTP is a relaying protocol, it carries both the envelope and content of a message. The SMTP envelope is very simple. It contains:

- The email address of the use that caused the creation of this envelope termed the *originator* address. This corresponds to the Sender: field in the headers, if present.
- One or more *recipient* email addresses.

It must be *strongly emphasized* that there need be no relationship between the addresses in the SMTP envelope and any recipient addresses present in the headers of the message. In fact, it is entirely possible for the headers to contain no recipient addresses at all.[11]

Of historical interest, we note that SMTP also caries a "delivery mode" in the envelope, indicating how the message should be delivered, either to a mailbox or the recipient's "terminal," or both. In the modern Internet, only mailbox delivery is supported.

Address Expansion and Explosion

Thus far, we've been operating under the implicit assumption that there is a one-to-one relationship between an address in a message and the mailbox that receives the message. In the general case, this is perhaps true. However, when an SMTP server accepts responsibility for one of its local addresses, that address might actually be an *alias* that resolves to one or more other email addresses, termed the alias value. Any number of these email addresses might be a local recipient, or could be reachable through a remote site.

It is up to each local email server administrator as to how an SMTP server is configured to have aliases. However, when a local alias is encountered as a recipient address in an envelope, it replaces the alias address in the envelope with the email address given by the alias value. Note that the server must not modify the content during this process. This is termed *alias expansion*.

Some aliases are special in that they are actually mailing lists. A mailing list is a collection of one or more email addresses with an associated administrator. When an alias corresponding to a mailing list is encountered as a recipient address in the envelope, then *list explosion* occurs. A new envelope is created with an identical content. The new envelope's originator is set to the address of the mailing list's administrator. (This redirects any subsequent error reports to the entity responsible for the mailing list, rather than the originator of the message.) The recipient addresses in the envelope are set to the addresses given by the alias value (the list's subscribers). The alias is then removed from the original envelope. The new envelope is then re-examined by the SMTP server, as if it had just been submitted.

Finally, desktop software may also provide an aliasing facility. However, these aliases must be expanded prior to submitting the message to the infrastructure. Because this is a local desktop function, such aliases are removed from the relevant headers and replaced with their values. To summarize:

What	Who	How
System alias	SMTP server	Replace recipient addresses in envelope
Mailing list	SMTP server	New envelope with administrator as originator
Personal alias	Desktop software	Expand headers prior to submission

Protocol Interactions

There are four parts to an SMTP session:

1. Exchange relay identities.

2. Send the message envelope.

3. Send the message content or reset the envelope.

4. Release the session.

The actual commands used in SMTP aren't particularly interesting. What is interesting is how SMTP indicates whether a command succeeded or not. It uses the three-digit reply codes described in Chapter 2.

There are two other commands in vintage SMTP that are termed probe commands. The first allows you to verify the validity of a local mailbox at the server. The second allows you to expand the contents of a local alias at the server. In practice, neither of these commands is particularly useful. For "security" reasons most sites have disabled them. In theory, this is an acceptable policy. Unfortunately, in practice, the verify command sometimes gives out false positives or false negatives, depending on the implementation. As a consequence, an improved method of verifying a mailbox is to send an envelope and see if the recipient address generates an error. Either way, the envelope is then reset to avoid sending a message. Of course, not even this is reliable, since some servers are configured to accept all addresses and then later make a determination as to whether they are actually valid; if not, an error report is returned.

SMTP has an extension mechanism allowing a standardized way for evolving the protocol. Here is a list of some of the extensions that have been standardized:

- You can indicate whether you want to receive delivery reports when a message is received at the final SMTP server.

- You can indicate how big the message is you're going to send. If the message is too big for the server, either due to a physical limit (not enough disk space), or an administrative limit (user over quota), then you'll be told not to bother sending the message.

- If you'd rather see enhanced error codes (as described in Chapter 2), rather than the three-digit reply codes, you can request that.

There are also some rather esoteric ones dealing with increased efficiency (command pipelining) or perceived efficiency (8-bit transfers), but these are of interest only to messaging implementers.

More on Spoofing

Earlier in this chapter the concept of spoofing email accounts was discussed. The core technical issue in this topic is that SMTP servers talk to just about anyone. Furthermore, there is no strong authentication procedure for an SMTP session. As a consequence, it is trivial for someone to configure his or her desktop system to communicate with an arbitrary SMTP server on behalf of an arbitrary mailbox.

The consequence of this is simple: It is very easy to spoof email. Of course, a messaging administrator can look at the Received: headers to follow the path that the message took in the infrastructure and then reverse-engineer where the culprit interjected the message. Unfortunately, some sites might mistakenly view your site as the offending party and administratively blacklist it. In order to combat this, most SMTP servers are now configured with a list of recipient domains that they'll accept messages for. If someone tries to submit a message for a mailbox outside of those domains, it will be rejected. Although this doesn't solve the spoofing problem, it helps to prevent your site being mistaken for the culprit.

VIM AND MAPI

Our discussion has concentrated on various Internet-based standards that involve sending email. However, this isn't the complete story, much as we'd like to concentrate on 100% pure Internet email. There are two other standards that are worthy of mention, and they have nothing to do with the Internet whatsoever. They are the Vendor Independent Messaging (VIM) standard and the Mail Applications Protocol Interface (MAPI). Despite their names, they both try to accomplish the same task: to define a mechanism for how desktop applications can invoke an email program and send a message from within the application.

This sounds simple, but there is a lot of difficulty with actually implementing this interface. First off, figuring out what basic operating system services are available to most applications isn't easy, especially if you want to architect the same services on Windows 3.1, 32-bit Windows, UNIX and Macintoshes. Second, the notion of "sending a file" isn't implemented the same across applications. Despite these difficulties, Microsoft and Lotus came up with their own interfaces.

Both standards began their lives with different purposes. VIM began with Lotus' cc:Mail as a single interface that would work across all the various operating system platforms and for all of the various cc:Mail products. Microsoft of course wasn't satisfied with the way VIM was put together and created its own MAPI for Microsoft Mail, the precursor to Exchange and Outlook. MAPI became part of the Windows operating system applications interface and is now supported by most Windows-based email products, including cc:Mail, ironically. VIM is still being used by Lotus, although it seems to be in decline.

Both products install a series of dynamic linked libraries. This presents the challenge of keeping these files up-to-date, and ensuring that some application doesn't overwrite the latest version with some older version is always an interesting parlor game when it comes time to install some email software. When an application, say, a word processor, wants to send a file via email, it calls this library and sends the information to the email program.

When you install an email program on your desktop, it registers itself as a MAPI or VIM service provider. For the MAPI programs, once they are registered, the application will appear on the Send To: menu when you right-click your mouse on a file shown either on your desktop or Windows Explorer. VIM programs require special programming to work within applications.

There is a great deal more complexity behind these two programming interfaces, but for now we'll move on to examining some of the products and how they implement Internet standards and provide solutions for sending email.

SOLUTIONS

We have some simple solutions that can help prevent or at least postpone some of the problems mentioned earlier with sending email. They cover three different areas: where you keep your email addresses, how you maintain your mailing lists and how you set up and keep track of list servers.

The solutions covered in this chapter relate to maintaining addresses on your own desktop. Some of our discussion in Chapter 6 relating to enterprise directories and searching various public email directory servers is also appropriate in terms of populating your own directory.

Also, given our earlier discussion on standards, we want to emphasize that not every address book entry will be for a carbon life form: There are plenty of times when you wish to send email to a program or to a group of people. So, bear this in mind as you are reading some of our suggested implementations for creating and importing new addresses.

Before you can fix the address list problem, you need to first take stock of where these email addresses are maintained and decide which single place will become your email address repository. You have two choices here: You can use the address book built into one type of your email software, or you can maintain a separate address book in another piece of software, such as a database or contact manager.

Don't pick your email software as your central address book yet. Do some research and understand how address lists are created, how they need to be maintained and how you can get information into and out of the intended address book if you change your mind.

Creating Address Book Entries

The address books in both Netscape Messenger and Outlook Express function as a primitive contact manager. You can track all sorts of information about each member, including home and business postal address and phones, as well as random notes. Outlook Express' address book contains information on each person's digital certificates to authenticate messages from this particular person, while both Outlook Express and Messenger's address books also contain information that you need to connect to them and use the conferencing functions.

This may be more overkill than is necessary to run your email life, since in either case you don't need to have anything more for each contact than a name and an email address. With both products, adding individual names as well as mailing lists to your address book is very similar. In Outlook Express, you go to Tools | Address book and then click on the button to add a new mailing list. You then add individual members to it. You probably only want to fill out the first window as shown below, but if you want to add more information, there are several other screens that can contain business address and locations for doing desktop conferencing using Microsoft's NetMeeting product.

Outlook Express also has the ability to differentiate between those recipients that can only receive plain text messages and those that can receive HTML or formatted messages. You merely check the box at the bottom ("Send email using plain text only") shown in Figure 3.1. (We'll have more to say on this HTML email matter in Chapter 7.)

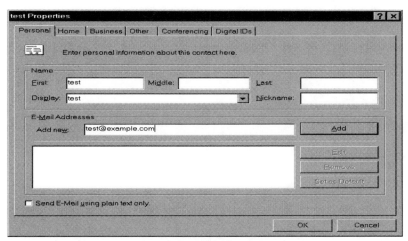

Figure 3.1   Outlook Express address book form

Outlook Express has two other nice features. First, you can automatically add your correspondents' addresses to your address book. Go to Tools I Options I General and check the box labeled as such. Second, Outlook Express is able to check the recipient's name that you type in the message header against the list of its names in either your Outlook Express address book or a public directory server. This isn't as useful as it sounds, but to perform the check, go to Tools I Check Names. Outlook Express will examine what you have typed with what is in your address book and also what is listed on a public directory server.[12] It sounds good in theory, but these public directories aren't quite as populated or as universal as they could be. And you'll need to be connected to the Internet at the time you compose your email—something that always isn't the case. Finally, if your address book entry isn't correct to begin with, this feature isn't going to help.

Earlier versions of Netscape Messenger, called Netscape Mail, had less capable address books than the one implemented in version 4. They also used a somewhat clunky drag-and-drop system to add names to your address book. In Messenger, you follow a similar routine to what we have just described for Outlook: You go to Communicator | Address book and then click on the button to create a new mailing list. You then can type in new addresses directly in this window, as shown in Figure 3.2.

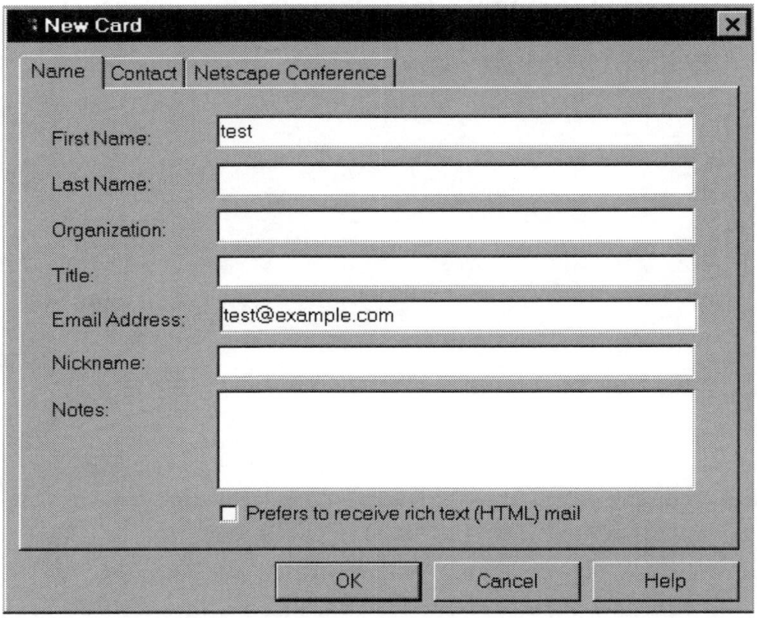

Figure 3.2   **Messenger address book form**

With both Eudora and America Online, you go to your address book and add your list name and recipients, separated by commas. For the AOL software, you don't have to specify anything more than their AOL screen names, or if you want to have a list that mixes AOL and Internet addresses, list their entire Internet address. In both Eudora and America Online software, the address book dialogue box is somewhat confusing, since the same window is used to specify either nicknames or aliases for single recipients or for the list. In AOL's case, you are asked for the "group name" when the group could just as easily contain a single address. With Eudora, it is the reverse: You are asked for a recipient's name that could also contain multiple addresses. The AOL screen is shown in Figure 3.3.

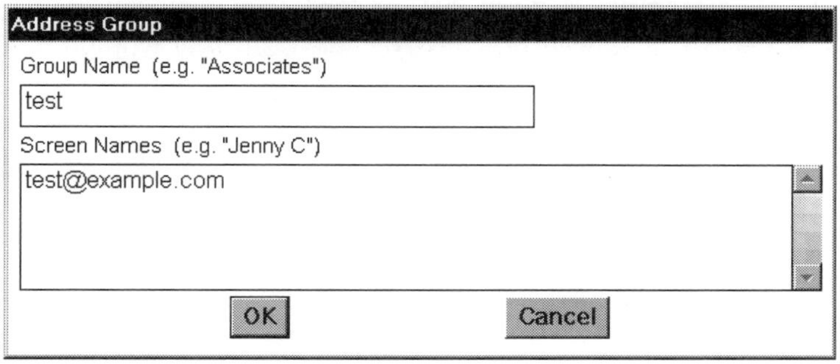

Address Group

Group Name (e.g. "Associates")

test

Screen Names (e.g. "Jenny C")

test@example.com

OK   Cancel

Figure 3.3   AOL address book form

With CompuServe's WinCIM, you go to Mail | Address Book | Add Entry. You choose to add either a mailing list or an individual address. For a new list, type the name and then press the button at the bottom of the window labeled Address Book to review existing addresses you wish to add. For adding new addresses, WinCIM also has a handy way to help you figure out how to set up mail to non-CompuServe users. First, you select from a pull-down list (see Figure 3.4) the system that your recipient is on (including Internet, Lotus Notes or one of several dozen different systems to which CompuServe connects). And any mailing list can contain a mixture of users on different systems, which is a useful feature. With the pure Internet products such as Messenger and Outlook Express, you have to rely on understanding the necessary syntax yourself if you want to send mail from the Internet to these other systems.

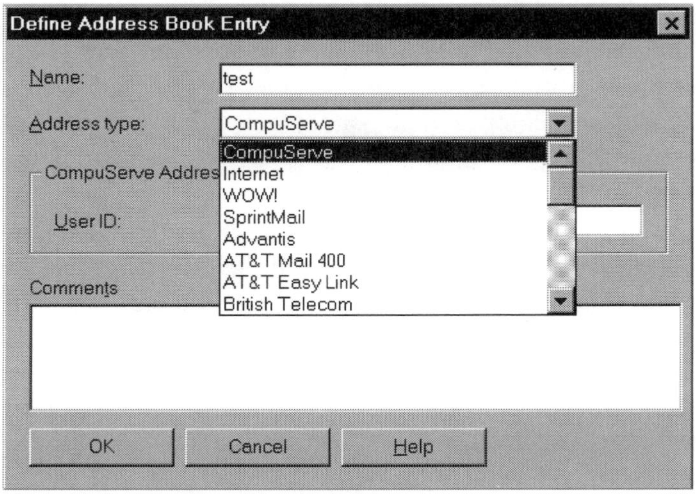

Define Address Book Entry   ×

Name: test

Address type: CompuServe   ▼
                 CompuServe   ▲
CompuServe Addres Internet
                 WOW!
User ID: SprintMail
                 Advantis
                 AT&T Mail 400
Comments   AT&T Easy Link
                 British Telecom   ▼

OK   Cancel   Help

Figure 3.4   WinCIM address book form

For example, to send mail to someone on the Internet from Compu-Serve with an address of *test@example.com*, you would select the Internet choice on the pull-down menu and type in *test@example.com* in the name field. If you now go to compose a new message to this person, you'll see that WinCIM has assembled INTERNET:test@example.com in the To: field of the message header.

With cc:Mail, there are two separate options under the Create menus, one for a private mailing list and one for a new address entry. For the former, you bring up a window where you have to name the list and proceed to add members from your cc:Mail address book. However, cc:Mail administrators are the only ones that can create and change shared or public address lists for multiple users.

For all of these products, making changes to your mailing lists is very easy. You double-click on the list name shown in the address book. This brings up the properties window of the list. Here you can add, remove and edit the names on that particular list.

What about searching for the right name through a large address book? Most of the products have implemented short cuts to make it easier to find the right name, although none is as fully featured as a true database program. With Outlook Express, in the Options | Send, you have a checkbox that can turn on the ability to automatically complete addresses when you are composing a new message. cc:Mail and Messenger do something similar by default.

In theory this sounds great, but once your address book contains several hundred or several thousand entries, it is cumbersome to try to track down a specific address, especially if you aren't sure of the exact spelling of the beginning of someone's name. Ideally, you'd like to search on a domain name, for example, or on some other parameter that isn't part of the email address itself. For that, you'll need a real database or contact manager, which we'll get to in a moment.

So far we have just concerned ourselves with manually adding entries into the address book. With some of the products, there are other mecha-nisms for automatically populating your address book. With Eudora, you highlight the message in your inbox and click on Special | Make Address Book Entry. The address shown in the From: section will be quickly added to your address book. Messenger has a similar feature, under Mes-sage | Add to Address Book. You can choose to add just the sender's email address or everyone in the header.

In WinCIM, you have a special button that appears when you are reading any message labeled Add Address. Clicking on this will bring up another window (shown above), where you can add any of the names in the message header, or even make changes to their alias, before you add them to your address book.

Outlook Express has a slightly different feature whereby you also can automatically add email addresses from all of the people to whom you send mail. You turn this feature on by going to Options | General and checking on the box to automatically add addresses of people to whom you reply.

These tips are helpful, but they don't really allow us to import multiple addresses in a single step. In Outlook Express, you choose File | Import | Address Book and see the screen as in Figure 3.5. There are several different address book formats to choose from, including several Microsoft and Netscape formats, as well as Eudora's and a comma-separated text file. You'll need to be able to locate your existing address book file before attempting to do this.

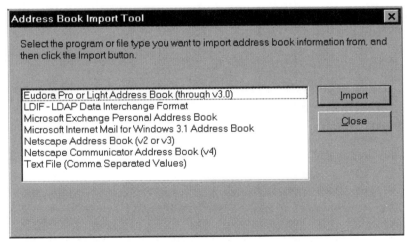

Figure 3.5   Outlook Express address book conversion options

The other products don't have this flexibility with importing information. Messenger, for example, imports address books from previous Netscape Mail software. A separate utility program imports addresses (and all of your messages in folders) from Eudora products. cc:Mail only adds entries automatically when it connects to a cc:Mail post office and synchronizes its entries with the ones in the post office. AOL and Win-

CIM don't have any import ability whatsoever. Eudora's address import feature is very primitive and we recommend not using it unless you are desperate to populate your address book.[13]

One alternative to using our featured products' own capabilities is to buy some additional software for populating your address books. Perhaps the most notable vendor is Puma Technology (*www.pumatech.com*), makers of IntelliSync products that work with any number of address book formats, contact managers, email products and handheld devices. Chances are good that if you need to move information from one place to another, you'll end up using their software.

How about going the opposite direction? You want to take the information in your current address book and export it to use in a new mail package, for instance. Again, Outlook Express is the most feature rich. File | Export brings up two choices. If you highlight a single entry before choosing the export command, you can save any single address to a special file in vCard format. This format is still catching on but can be useful when exchanging information with other systems. You can also choose to export the entire address book to one of two file formats: the Microsoft Exchange address book or a comma-separated file that could be read by many database programs.

There is another solution for maintaining address books: Ignore the features found in whatever email software you are using and run a separate piece of software that you use for maintaining all your contact information. A product such as ACT! (*www.symantec.com*), GoldMine (*www.goldminesw.com*) or even a Windows database such as Lotus Approach (*www.lotus.com/approach*) or Microsoft Access (*www.microsoft.com*) are all good tools for keeping track of contacts. When the time comes to send a message to someone, you look up his or her address in the contact program and then highlight it with your mouse. You can copy and paste it using Windows commands (either by clicking on the commands in the appropriate menus or using the Control-C to copy and Control-V to paste) into the header field of your email program.

One of us has been using Approach to do this task for several years. While it can be cumbersome to add many email addresses to a single message in this fashion, it has the advantage of being able to use a fully-featured database to select the right name, search various fields and export names and email addresses in the precise way we want.

There are other advantages as well. Using Approach, which runs on a .DBF file format, means we can export our address list to just about any other piece of software that can read a database file or comma-separated file. We aren't locked into using it forever as our needs change or as we move from one software product to another. It is also easy to go into this database and update any specific email address, based on the error report we have gotten from our last email with any particular correspondent. We can do all sorts of searches on our address list, including using wildcards and searching on any field that we have in the database—something that none of the email address books do very well. But we have to be diligent about updating the database when we learn of changes, and that takes some time.

Maintaining Your Lists

Let's move on to our second issue: how you intend to maintain your mailing lists. As we mentioned earlier in the chapter, the problem of keeping mailing lists up-to-date is reduced when the list creator and list user is one and the same person. Every time someone uses a list, there is a potential to learn about changes to the addresses on the list. Indeed, lists that aren't used often quickly go stale, given how many changes take place in one's email identity.

But sometimes this isn't possible. The cc:Mail administrator, or someone who has administrator status, as we mentioned earlier, must maintain the public lists for cc:Mail. In a large organization, this gets cumbersome, and these public lists—unless the administrator is on all of the lists—can easily get out of date.

If you use a database or a contact manager to maintain your addresses, you can make use of these programs' features to keep your lists up-to-date. For example, we have a few lists that we maintain in Lotus Approach. When the time comes to send mail to this list, we export the addresses we desire based on some preset selection criteria (all clients, or all people in a certain zip code or all people at a given corporation). Then the list is current as of the moment we last checked those particular email addresses.

If you want more flexibility in terms of address list creation and management, you'll have to purchase some additional list processing software. We've mentioned earlier the UNIX products, including listserv and majordomo, and covered some of the limitations of the various push publishing products. But there are other products that are available for

Windows and Macintosh desktops that you can run either in conjunction with your existing Internet email server or that include their own as part of the software.

A list of mailing list software vendors is shown below.

Mailing List Server Products

Vendor, URL	Product	Platform, Price
Fog City Software, *www.fogcity.com*	LetterRip v2.0	Macintosh, $295
Ipswitch, *www.ipswitch.com*	IMail	NT, $495
Internet Shopper, *www.ntmail.co.uk*	NTList	NT, 95, $200-500
L-Soft, *www.lsoft.com*	LISTSERV	NT, 95, UNIX, $600 and up
Mustang Software, *www.mustang.com*	Web Essentials ListCaster	NT, 95, $299
Pacific Software Publishing, *www.pspinc.com*	NewsMAIL v1.0	NT, $499
Revnet, *www.groupmaster.com*	GroupMaster v1.0	Web-based, pricing varies by size of list
Shelby Group, *www.shelby.com*	Lyris List Server	NT, 95, $495 and up
Soft Ventures, *www.softventures.com*	SVList	NT, 95, $30
StarNine Technologies, *www.starnine.com*	ListSTAR	Macintosh, $395

These products vary in terms of capabilities and ease of use. For example, SVList only runs with a single mailing list: If you need more than one, you have to run it multiple times from different directories. Newsmail works in conjunction with a Microsoft Internet Information Web server, which means that users with a Web browser can create and manage lists and send out messages to groups. That is an elegant way to approach the problem of maintaining a list, but you may not wish to run a Web server to do so. And Groupmaster is also Web based, but uses its own Web server to manage its messages.

Keeping Track of Your Subscriptions

We have one final suggestion, concerning how you keep track of the list-servs to which you subscribe. We store all the reply messages from these listservs in a single email folder. This serves as a reminder of when we wish to remove ourselves from the list. It is simple, yet effective. Given the amount of time that can pass between when we subscribe to a list and when we want to get off the list, it is handy to have a single, unambiguous place on our desktop to go to for this information. We describe how to set up folders in Chapter 2.

Standards Implementation Scorecard

So far we have discussed what the various products do in terms of helping to send messages. Before we move on to talk about the future, we should first consider the past and how well these products have fared in terms of implementing the various standards mentioned earlier.

Why is this important? Failure to properly implement standards is perhaps the biggest reason why email doesn't get reliably delivered: We have all seen attachments that wouldn't attach (or detach, depending on which end we are on), garbled messages and mail that was refused to be delivered. The way each product implements Internet standards has a direct bearing on this behavior.

Let's take Microsoft Outlook Express as an example. Outlook Express was developed with several subtle quirks. For instance, it always uses the iso-8859-1 character set, even if the message you compose is entirely in ASCII text. As you may recall from our discussion on standards, the program should choose the more restrictive character set when appropriate. Outlook Express doesn't. Adding insult to injury, Outlook Express also encodes text messages in Base64 MIME encoding when it is invoked from another program. As we mentioned in our section on MAPI, this can be done from the Windows desktop with a simple right-mouse click.

And the beta version of Outlook 98 has another problem, too. Outlook 98 includes both the Sender: and From: addresses in its replies to messages when these two addresses are different. This doesn't sound like much of a problem, except that many mailing list programs put something different in the Sender: address. Again, the standards state quite carefully that the Sender: address isn't to be used for assembling replies.

We're quick to point out that Microsoft isn't the only culprit—each of the products we discuss throughout the book is guilty of various infractions. The trick is minimizing the number of errors prior to mass distribution of the software. Sadly, we suspect that many companies in the Internet space do not differentiate between alpha, beta and first customer ship.

FUTURES

Perhaps the most successful incremental upgrade of Internet technology is the introduction of multimedia capabilities to Internet messaging. Starting with a decades old text-only messaging system, the MIME standard made it possible for a wide variety of Internet multimedia products to be developed and deployed.

A Universal Mechanism for Data Representation

In a sense, MIME represents an interesting compromise in the standards/ product space. MIME is an agreement between sending and receiving software with respect to tagging messages sent by mail. It doesn't tell the sending software how to generate the files, nor the receiving software how to interpret them. This provides maximum flexibility to the product developer.

Initially, the poorest MIME implementations where those associated with email gateways. The implementations of MIME for actual users tend to be pretty good. As email gateways disappear (owing to 100% pure Internet clients), the overall MIME "IQ" is improving.

So, our first prediction is rather simple: Just as IP is the ubiquitous language of the network layer, so MIME shall become the ubiquitous language of the application layer. The ramifications of this are far reaching. Right now, many applications use their own syntax for conveying data. In the Internet family of protocols alone, it is difficult to find more than two applications that use the same representation for data and method for exchanging it. This must change as tremendous growth can be realized with a common framework for data representation and exchange. MIME has proven itself worthy to provide that framework.

Faithful Implementations Remain Elusive

SMTP, more than a decade older than MIME, has already achieved the same ubiquity as IP. Although extensibility mechanisms were added to SMTP, it is difficult to gauge whether they have provided a real addition in functionality to a substantive part of the Internet. However, the real issue comes down to how faithfully products implement SMTP along with the other Internet messaging standards.

While things have improved considerably over the past five years, there is still a significant amount of work to go. (Just look back to the previous page to see examples of commercial software released in 1997 with very basic errors in behavior.) In fact, as Chapter 2 discusses, few programs (old or new) generate Bcc: messages correctly. This is particularly ironic, because the correct way to do it is very simple (we explained it earlier in this chapter), and the consequences of doing it wrong are potentially quite damaging.

At this point, we are at a loss to suggest a second prediction. Although it seems obvious that implementers need to start writing correct products, the market has still not brought enough pressure to bear on the situation. Perhaps because manual intervention is possible when dealing with so many of these problems, there is a lack of urgency. But the lack of urgency helped create the year 2000 problem.

Endnotes

1. In addition to ubiquity, people's desktops and enterprise security perimeters, by default, are programmed to receive incoming email: In the former case, no new desktop software need be installed; and, in the latter case, no changes to firewall configurations are typically needed to accommodate messaging.

2. In practice, there is not much reason to be optimistic. Automated error recovery in many mail-enabled applications is quite poor. Current practice is perhaps best described as "bump anything you don't understand to a person." While not particularly scalable, it is somewhat better than "dump core on anything you don't understand." Of course, all points of this spectrum assume that the application is doing thorough checking of the incoming message before acting on it.

3. A different application that has some similarity to push is the use of Internet newsgroups to send messages to a group of users. This is outside the scope of this book.

4. A notable exception is Eudora. Qualcomm started using a spell-checker plug-in for Eudora a few versions ago, and now there are several plug-ins that are available for the product. Luckily, getting them set up is a lot easier than trying to install browser plug-ins, and many of them come bundled with the main Eudora software itself, so you don't have to try to install them separately.

5. A good example of this is Intermind's Communicator, one of the earliest push players. For those who publish their own channel, Communicator stores a series of pointers to various Web pages on your hard disk. The database format for the early version couldn't be used for the next version, and even after the company got behind a single format, you still couldn't move this database from one machine to another without a great deal of effort.

6. For more information on mailing list issues and how to diagnose problems with them, see *The Email Companion*, by John S. Quarterman and Smoot Carl-Mitchell, 1994, Addison Wesley Publishing.

7. For example, some listservs require the subscribe command to appear by itself in the Subject:. Others require that the word subscribe be followed by the actual email address and separated by spaces. Others require the word "subscribe" to appear on the first line of the message body. Some use another command word, such as join instead of subscribe. And these commands are supposed to be sent to the listserv processor address, rather than to a separate address that is used as the actual broadcast address for the group. This makes for annoying situations when users trying to join the list mistakenly send their email containing the sign-up commands as broadcast messages to the entire list.

8. In systems that aren't 100% pure Internet, there are proprietary techniques for email submission. As a rule, these are highly suboptimal, since they tend to introduce the same sort of problems that one sees with messaging gateways.

9. Of course, there is still plenty of room for user error when sending attachments. In Chapter 7, we talk about the kinds of errors than can crop up and how to resolve them.

10. MIME provides for non-ASCII information to be encoded in headers, typically the Subject: header. This topic is rather esoteric and won't be discussed further. Presumably, if your mail sending software allows you to specify character sets for various headers, it uses MIME's mechanisms for doing so.

11. For example, as discussed in Chapter 2, the message might have an empty To: header or an empty Bcc: header.

12. You also need to go to Accounts | Directory Service | Properties and click on the box to enable checking email addresses against your specified directory server. Outlook Express, along with other products we'll discuss in Chapter 6, comes with several directories already specified, such as the Four11.com directory.

13. This procedure is described in Eudora's documentation, but you first need to set up a text file with the following format. Each nickname (or group of names) is on a separate line. The line begins with the word alias, and the nickname follows, separated by a space. If there is more than one email address, each address is separated from the other by a comma. The entire file must be saved to a special directory, and this directory entry must be placed in the eudora.ini configuration file that can be found in the c:\eudora directory or wherever you have installed it. It might be easier just to type the stuff in from scratch!

4

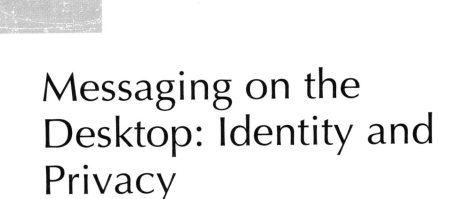

Messaging on the Desktop: Identity and Privacy

In this chapter, we consider two central issues for desktop email: how to manage separate messaging identities and how to secure messaging-based communications.

These two topics are actually two sides of the same coin: Facilities exist to obscure one's identity or to become anonymous; and facilities exist to ensure both the authenticity of the communicating parties and to make private their communications.

INTRODUCTION

To begin, let's ask ourselves what binds a messaging identity and the actual messaging user.

As a first step, we might ask what exactly comprises a messaging identity. From the perspective of the Internet messaging infrastructure, there are really only addresses and routes. Addresses refer to mailbox identities, and routes are used to direct messages to a particular mailbox. There is no concept of an email name, although the term "name" is sometimes used loosely to refer to a messaging identity (i.e., a mailbox address).

Hence, for our purposes, messaging identities and mailbox addresses are identical. What, then, is the significance of a mailbox address to the real world? In brief, the answer is one of convention and not of protocol. The domain "strom.com" refers to "David Strom, Inc." solely because one of the authors pays for its yearly registration; there is no algorithmic mapping from "strom" the domain to "Strom" the company, though it pleases both authors to think there is.[1]

What this teaches us is that, in the absence of out-of-band communication, the only assurance we have of the user identity binding is how the mailbox "behaves." If a colleague hands you a business card containing an email address, then it is highly likely that the asserted binding is meaningful. Otherwise, if you receive an unsolicited message from a mailbox claiming to belong to one of the authors, each successive communication you have with the user of that mailbox will affect your confidence in that binding.

There are many legitimate reasons why you might want several messaging identities. The simplest is that you might want different mailboxes for personal and business use. In the business context, you also might want different identities, for example one for internal use and another for anonymous use outside the corporation. In the latter case, you are likely to subscribe to an online service provider for a new account without a corporate affiliation. Some corporate policies require that any mail sent to discussion groups be sent using such accounts, both as a means of obscuring the affiliation of the sender and as a means of preventing "leakage" of corporate addresses to the outside world (e.g., to prevent unsolicited commercial email).

At the other extreme, secure messaging focuses on two related themes: certification of the originator's identity (typically by one or more third parties) and privatization of the originator's messages so that they can be deciphered only by the intended recipients.

Although there are numerous technical algorithms that may be applied to achieve these goals, the security of the communication ultimately relies on two factors: the security worthiness of the systems and software used by the originator and recipient; and the validity of the binding between messaging identities and actual users.

It is beyond our scope to discuss the security worthiness of Internet systems and software. However, it is within our scope to note that, in general, the security worthiness of these systems and software is quite poor. Few systems (Internet or not) or software packages (messaging or not) are written with security as an important goal. Furthermore, given the pressures of Internet development cycles, the authors are grateful that at least some basic testing is done before code is shipped.[2]

As such, our focus is on validity of the bindings. Although largely a nontechnical issue, emerging standards and products allow us to automate some parts of this task.

Finally, there is some interesting work being done in the area of integrating security functions into desktop messaging software. Although this is technically a matter of implementation and not standardization (another example of where products can not rely on standards to provide solutions), the market is beginning to converge in this area.

So, let us now consider these issues in greater detail, along with aspects of the legacy systems that cause them.

PROBLEMS

As email becomes popular, the need to have more than one email identity becomes more pressing. We have seen individuals go from being timid new users to establishing multiple personalities literally overnight. Business users want separation from their business domain names, as mentioned in our introduction. And some forward-thinking individuals, such as one of the authors, want simple mechanisms that can be used to filter and track incoming messages, and to organize their correspondents.

This expansion isn't limited to just corporate usage, as email has spread among every family member wanting his or her own identity. AOL was the first major online service provider to handle this quite elegantly and easily with up to five mailboxes per account, and now some ISPs offer something similar. For example, it is common practice in Sweden to offer five mailboxes per account, and Demon (*www.demon.net*), a British ISP, offers an unlimited number of email identities per account.

But just as managing multiple human personalities can cause some stress, handling multiple email personalities is a huge task. Keeping track of these different identities can take some effort to remember who is attached to a particular mailbox. You also have to choose which software program will work best and go through the extra work to make sure it is set up properly to collect messages from each mailbox. An extra complication is that many email programs didn't implement support for more than a single identity until relatively recently, making them somewhat useless in handling multiple mailboxes on a single desktop.[3]

Having more than one email identity raises other issues: How do you decide what your domain name should be, and who shall control this domain? What happens when you need to change your identity?

Master of Your Domain

The growth of the Internet over the past few years has proven that domain names matter. Witness the number of lawsuits over one company purchasing the domain name of its competitor, or cases where someone operates with a domain name that is slightly different from what you'd expect to try to draw traffic away to their own site.[4] And just because a corporation has a brand name or registered trademark in one country doesn't guarantee that someone in another country can establish a domain name with the same name. This promises to be a very active area for lawyers for the foreseeable future.[5]

The whole domain name situation has the feeling of a mid-1800s land grab. Savvy corporations quickly snapped up domain names relevant to their own names some time ago. For those unfamiliar with the process, we offer a brief diversion and explanation.

Every domain name is registered with a particular organization responsible for the corresponding top-level domain. In the United States, the organization is Network Solutions (*rs.internic.net*), which sets up domains for the .com, .net, .gov, .mil, .edu and .org top-level domains. This means that anyone who wants a domain ending in one of these suffixes needs to pay Network Solutions a yearly fee, provided that someone hasn't taken the name already. The fee guarantees that you will have rights to use the domain for the coming year, but nothing more: You still need to find someone to host your domain and maintain it.

Outside of these special three-character suffixes, each country is assigned its own domain suffix, such as .uk for Great Britain,[6] .mx for Mexico, .ca for Canada and so forth[7]. This means that if we wish to have a domain strom.co.uk, we need to contact the British equivalent of Network Solutions, called Nominet (*www.nic.uk*), to register our domain name.

There are various guidelines for each kind of organization and for certain kinds of domain names, and it varies by country and by registrar. For example, if we aren't a government organization, we can't make use of the .gov suffix.

Having a single registrar for each top-level domain has both advantages and disadvantages. When a new domain is registered, the owner is asked to provide different contacts for technical and administrative issues relating to maintaining the registration. There is a great deal of debate whether this is fair, just or even desirable, and some have called to make additional top-level domains.[8] But that digresses from our focus, which is how to control the domain itself with respect to email identities.

Seinfeld episodes notwithstanding, we all want to be masters of our own domain, at least in the Internet sense of the word. For some of us, this means that ideally we'd like to own our domain name if we could afford it and have the time and energy to make use of it. If the name is not yet taken, all well and good.

But mastery of the domain also means parceling out various email addresses as part of that domain. This could be done automatically, with a series of computer programs, or it could be done manually, after a person vets a request for a new email identity. This request sounds technically simple, but in practice could turn out to become a major undertaking for all sorts of nontechnical reasons. It depends on whether or not the request comes from inside the corporation that owns the domain or outside.

For example, let's say we, as presidents of the Example Corporation, own the example.com domain. Our IS manager is responsible for day-to-day matters of administering this domain and keeps track of newly hired employees, newly departing employees and other administrative matters. The corporation has an overall email naming policy set up, perhaps with first initial and last name as the default email identity of choice. As our company grows and adds employees who need email access, we can make changes to this naming structure—perhaps expand it to include the first two initial letters of the first name, or perhaps some other scheme.

So far, so good. Now let's introduce our friend Sidney Example, who just happens to have a surname with the same name as our company. He wants to have the obvious email identity of *sidney@example.com*. Sidney has no other place to go besides us to obtain this identity, unless he wishes to have another suffix besides the popular .com address. If we have complete freedom to configure mailboxes on this domain name and have the technical wherewithal to do so, Sidney's request will be satisfied. But that is often not the case, as several factors could get in the way.

First, the IS manager at the Example Corporation could just be mean-spirited and not want to be bothered with dealing with maintaining this mailbox. Or, we may not have the freedom to grant his request: We may have been told it is against corporate policy of the Example Corporation to grant new mailboxes on our system to anyone not employed by the Example Corporation. Our IS manager might be worried about the potential security issues of having outsiders on our email system, something that would be entirely reasonable and justified. Or, we may not want to maintain the physical disk storage on our email server for Sydney.

These really are not technical issues; they are strictly political ones.

But they aren't the only obstacles. Our domain server hosting example.com may not be completely under our control, or even located on the corporate premises. In fact, many corporations don't even own the host computers that run their domain services. Instead, corporations delegate this task to their Internet service provider (ISP). The staff of the ISP handles the registration process and the renewal of the fees to maintain your name with the appropriate authorities.[9] This has the advantage of not having to deal with the day-to-day mechanics and responsibility of keeping your servers properly running; but it also means that if your ISP doesn't do a very good job, you won't have a very reliable connection and identity on the Internet.

But it also means that the staff of your ISP may not be able to add a mailbox without charging Sydney or us for the privilege.

All of these situations are more than possible. We've seen them first hand. Then our friend Sidney would be out of luck and would have to find some other place in cyberspace to hang his hat.

Sometimes being master of your domain isn't always possible, or even desirable. For example, if you have an account with AOL, you will have to accept that you'll be *somebody@aol.com*. You can't choose your domain name: You have to abide by the fact that AOL owns it and gives you one or more mailboxes on its domain. If you don't like to be a party to the AOL domain, you are better off looking elsewhere for your email.

Sometimes mastery of your domain is difficult because your corporate email system isn't 100% pure Internet. While we will discuss this matter further in Chapter 7, for now the main issue is that your email gateway might require additional host names in the domain name part, such as *someone@ccmail.example.com* instead of just purely *some-*

one@example.com. This is yet another reason to despise gateways and steer clear of them whenever possible.[10]

Moving Day

The Internet is a chaotic and dynamic place, as we've said before. That means that corporations come and go. Internet providers certainly come and go. We've seen our share of mergers, bankruptcies and changes. What happens, however, when these changes mean it is time for you to move your domain?

Again, we've seen this first hand. A few years ago, the service provider that maintained our domain name decided to exit the Internet business. We were given plenty of notice—several months—but still we had to take the time to find a new provider and make the arrangements with Network Solutions to transfer the administrative details of our domain to the new location.

It sounds easy, but it took effort and skill to not only make the decision but to implement it in such as way as to maintain service during the transition.

Here the Internet is less capable than our physical world. In America, your local post office will forward your physical mail to a new address for up to six months. They are usually pretty good about doing this, and while mail may take a bit longer to reach you, it generally does get to your new address. One day, mail is going to your old address. The next day, forwarding begins and your mail goes to the new address.

On the Internet, though, these changes take several days to be recognized by the various routers, servers and hosts. It is a big world out there, and there are many machines that require the new information. Sometimes the owners of these machines don't make frequent updates to their domain databases, in which case email will continue to flow to your old address. This means that you end up having to check mail in two different places for a few days until all the changes percolate around the globe.

Remember, this is a best-case situation, where we had plenty of time to implement these changes. Often you aren't so fortunate and have to act quickly to replace your existing ISP, which quickly shuttered its doors and went out of business.

The analogy in the physical world would be if your local post office went out of business tomorrow. All the letters and packages that were en route were held captive in whatever location they landed at the time, never to be found. Luckily, email isn't usually lost in transit: It either makes it to the intended destination or it doesn't, and you get an error message indicating such.

But unlike the U.S. Postal Service, Internet providers are under no obligation to forward mail when you change your address, and many have the attitude that once you leave that is the last they'll see of you. As a result, none of your email gets forwarded and your correspondents are stuck trying to figure out where you've gone. As we discussed in Chapter 2, these moves and changes are the source of many error reports returned to your mailbox.[11]

Some ISPs offer email forwarding as part of their normal package of services: As long as you continue to pay their fees and they continue to stay in business, you can automatically forward email from their address. In Chapter 5, we'll show you how one national provider, MindSpring, makes this relatively easy to accomplish with a series of forms that you can access from your Web browser.

But whether you forward your email or not, there are other issues. First, you have to remember to turn forwarding on and off, depending on where you want your email to be forwarded. And you may want your messages to be forwarded to different places, depending on their contents and origins. (Chapter 5 covers how to set up filters and folders to automate these processes.) Complicating this is that your email address may change frequently, meaning that you'll have to adjust the forwarding address when these changes happen. At least in the physical world, we generally stay put for a few months at one address. This means that it is likely that some of your messages stored in your electronic files are out of date. You'll find out soon enough when you try to use these addresses and get errors!

There is a way around these moving blues that gets you back to owning your own domain and taking it with you when you change circumstances, ISPs or jobs. For example, we know many friends that have their own domain names and use an alias to point it to whatever corporate identity they are housed that particular year. In the meantime, their friends and business associates don't have to even know what job they currently occupy; the name remains the same.

But that is the rare case for the general public. Many people don't necessarily want to pay the yearly fees to keep up their domain on top of the fees they have to pay for Internet access. Anyway, this is something we don't necessarily want to encourage as the number of available domain names continues to shrink.[12]

Another option is to maintain just an email address at some ISP without dealing with the domain name ownership issues. This may be your "permanent" address, one that anyone can always send mail to you despite where you might be working at the time.

Mailboxes Are for Tasks, Not People

There is another reason for multiple mailboxes and that has to do with maintaining different mailboxes for particular tasks and projects, rather than for any particular person. We have touched on this earlier in Chapter 2, but the example is worth repeating here of having one mailbox for, say, project X and another one for project Y.

Many of the popular email products, including the ones we have chosen for this book, have never been designed for this situation. They assume, rightly or not, that for every mailbox there is a corresponding carbon life form handling that mailbox. Getting them set up to do otherwise is either difficult or impossible. It usually involves making use of some form of scripting language to automate the right behavior and organize your message processing.

The problem here is that you need to have some expertise in order not only to design the appropriate systems and responses but also to keep them running and keep track of all this email. There is a wide variety of alternatives here, including consulting services and packaged software, and we'll describe the choices in more detail in Chapter 5, along with how you can make use of one product to handle various email identities (such as *info@example.com*) for corporate support correspondence.

Having programs reply to messages can also create some confusion as well, if these programs are poorly designed or if the resulting reply looks too human. For example, not too long ago we received a message that looked like it came from a living person. It had his email address in the header, and it seemed to be addressed to us personally. However, it was machine-generated and really had no personal element at all.

```
Subject: Spread The Word!
From: rayb@netopia.com

Now that your office is open it's time to let
everyone know!
Netopia has created an automated system that
allows you to
send electronic invitations to your colleagues,
customers,
friends, family members... anyone you want to
communicate and
collaborate with you!
```

Proving Who You Are

The problems around having more than a single email identity are certainly not trivial. But they are just one half of our discussion in this chapter. The remaining half is concerned with proving your identity to your correspondents and securing the contents of your messages so that others can't view them readily.

Proving your identity is called authentication. In the physical world, this is accomplished in several ways: with photo identification, such as a driver's license or passport, or a corporate identity card. When the time comes to prove who you are, like before a major purchase, you show your card. Your appearance and signature hopefully matches the photo and signature on your card.

But on the Internet, things aren't as easy. Does email from *sidney@example.com* really originate from our friend Sidney? Maybe it was from someone else, who just happens to be using Sidney's machine when he was out to lunch? Or, worse, someone trying to impersonate Sidney illicitly? And even if the message actually was from the "real" Sidney, how can we be sure: Is there an electronic analog to a signature?

Most of us are trusting souls: We tend to want to believe that someone says who they are unless we have particular reasons to doubt someone's identity. But on the Internet, we have to look beyond face value. And proving that someone indeed did send a particular message gets to be a very difficult problem.

This may be one of the biggest reasons why corporations employ Lotus Notes and other non-100% pure Internet-based messaging systems. They want to ensure that all messages carry the appropriate authentication with them at all times. In order for any new user of Notes to start using the software, he or she must first obtain an electronic certificate that authenticates him or her to the system. The certificate is created by the Notes system administrator, which works in conjunction with that particular Notes server owned by that particular corporation.

Indeed, the problem of authentication goes beyond messaging and can involve other Internet applications. For example, how can you be sure that someone's Web site is truly authentic? Maybe during the night a group of impostors has diverted all traffic from the real site to their own, or put up their own pages on the authentic site, unbeknownst to the site's Webmaster? It has happened in the past, and it probably will continue to happen.

There are plenty of examples of Web sites that are from start to finish complete frauds. They range from the benign, such as the parody site dole96.org (the "real" site from the presidential candidate was at dole96.com) to much less obvious ones such as *stopbiopeep.com*.[13]

It helps to be skeptical, but you need more than just a doubting personality to prove authenticity. Part of the challenge is that the tools and techniques are relatively unknown and infrequently used by the general public.

Cryptography

In order to provide for authentication and privacy, we need to introduce the concept of cryptography. As we mentioned in Chapter 2, all messages sent over the Internet, unless otherwise protected, are sent in clear ASCII text. If you have the tools, the time, and the technical know-how, you can capture this traffic and read anyone's correspondence. It isn't simple, but it is quite possible to do so.

Some people feel that their correspondence doesn't present much of a target. They aren't famous, or their businesses aren't well known and don't handle very sensitive matters. But anyone can benefit from encrypting their messages: You may wish to discuss a confidential personnel matter, or you might want to communicate with your salespeople about prices that you don't necessarily wish to see in the hands of your competitors.

Besides being sent as clear text, email can also be intercepted and its contents changed between when the sender composes the message and the recipient reads it. Again, this isn't likely nor a simple task, but it can be accomplished if someone is determined enough to do so. This means that a sender can't either prove or deny that he sent a particular message to you; it could be a forgery or real.

If you are worried about these issues, then you'll need to encrypt your messages and protect them from attackers.

Once you make the decision to encrypt your messages, you have to deal with all sorts of issues: choosing the right technologies, maintaining your keys and passphrases, and actually performing the appropriate operations on your messages so you can read and respond to them.

But first you may have to deal with the notion that encryption carries with it the image of some cloak and dagger business. Your correspondents may ask you what you are trying to hide, and why you have to use it. We disagree: Encryption can be for fairly mundane reasons, and as the saying goes, just because you are paranoid doesn't mean someone isn't after you. Better to protect yourself prior to any real reason.

The problem is that you and all of your correspondents need to implement the same encryption scheme in order for this to work. You can't just decide to encrypt your email without getting others involved. It is a two-way street. You all need to add this technology to your messaging environments and to continue to use it in order to be protected.

Making use of encryption isn't a simple task. There are several complicating issues: First, cryptographic algorithms have gradually evolved over time, as computers have gotten better at cracking them. The U.S. government has muddied the waters by placing restrictions on what kinds of algorithms could be exported outside of the U.S., and as a result products have had to offer different versions: one for domestic use and one for non-U.S. use. Second, all government agencies aren't necessarily singing the same tune when it comes to cryptography, having differing points of view on how to properly encrypt messages. Some agencies feel it is their natural right to be able to read their citizens' messages, encrypted or not. Third, messages are no longer simply text and contain graphics, HTML markup tags and video that can complicate how they get encoded and decoded. Finally, encrypted signatures that pass through email gateways may get mangled because the gateway doesn't understand the encoding and tries to convert the signature into something else, inadvertently corrupting the signature and making it indecipherable by the recipient.

These issues mean that encrypting messages is often met with some degree of experimentation to establish a working path between sender and recipient. To get set up for encryption, you first have to decide on the appropriate technology that you wish to use for encrypting and decrypting your messages. As we'll see in our next sections on standards and solutions, there are at least two major methods used today for this, and even within each method there are variations and incompatible products. So, you'll want to do some fairly extensive testing, sending noncritical messages back and forth between you and your correspondents before you really roll any scheme into production use.

The encryption techniques we'll discuss in the remainder of this chapter are called public key methods. They make use of two electronic files, also called keys or certificates. One is public and freely available to anyone who knows you, or who can locate your key on a public key server. The other key is private and used only by you. You need both keys to encrypt and decrypt any messages sent or received.

In order for these keys to work, you need to be able to trust each other's keys and determine whether or not they are valid. Of course, there are different mechanisms for establishing this trust relationship. One way is to use an independent certificate authority such as VeriSign and Thawte. The latest browsers from Netscape and Microsoft come with special routines that will take you to VeriSign's Web site and allow you to purchase a certificate. You can obtain certificates from them and they will verify that you are who you say you are. We have had mixed success with both routines. In one case, we never were able to get the certificate to work properly from within our browser, although the software said it worked successfully and our credit card was charged the requisite $9.95![14]

Another way is to set up your own certificate server inside your company. While this doesn't work for verifying certificates outside your organization, it could be useful if you intend to get involved in encryption for more than a few users. This method is the most secure but also most expensive in terms of machine and staff resources. And while having your own certificate server makes sense for maintaining your entire enterprise's keys, it doesn't help when the time comes to trust keys obtained from other corporations.

And you can create your own key and store it locally on your own machine. This is simple but has the potential problem that if your disk crashes, your key may be lost. With local keys, you also need to make use of what is called a Web of trust, meaning that you keep track of others' certificates that you trust, and they keep track of others and so on down the chain. This quickly can get cumbersome if you communicate with a great many different people.

Sound complicated? We'll go into more details in our solutions section on how to implement these encryption techniques, but first we need to discuss the relevant encryption standards.

STANDARDS

(this space intentionally left blank)

Think we're kidding? We're not. The state of secure email standards for the Internet is best described as a sucking chest wound! Think that characterization is unprofessional? It is actually quite detached considering the amount of culpability enjoyed by the principals of the Internet's secure email debacle. Both of us would dearly love to write a few pages describing the high crimes and misdemeanors of these scoundrels, but that would only publicize the guilty, not punish them. So, instead we'll survey the horizon and see if we can make sense of what little terrain there is.

In brief, there are no technologies for secure email in the Internet that meet all of these criteria:

- Multivendor
- Interoperable
- Approved or endorsed by the Internet's standardization body

There are two competing technologies, each of which satisfy at most one of these criteria. The authors claim that any 100% pure Internet solution must be based on technologies that satisfy all three. We hope you agree!

Basic Concepts

In order to understand secure email, there are only three concepts you need to know:

- Data encryption (privacy)
- Message integrity (authentication)
- Key management

Everything else is a matter of data formats.

Data Encryption

When the contents of a message are to be protected from third-party disclosure, it is necessary to agree upon an encryption algorithm. Because cryptographic algorithms are constantly being scrutinized, a secure email standard must be extensible with respect to the algorithms that it allows.

Historically, *symmetric* encryption algorithms are used for this purpose. A symmetric algorithm is one in which the same key is used to both encrypt and decrypt the data. The choice of symmetric algorithms is due to the fact that they are computationally less burdensome (read: "faster to execute") than *asymmetric* algorithms.

As such, each time a message is to be encrypted a new *session key* is generated for that purpose. Although one could send the session key via some secure path, it is easier to include the session key along in the message, but encrypted so that only the intended recipient can decipher it. Upon deciphering the session key, the recipient will be able to apply the encryption algorithm and retrieve the original contents.

For example, Network Associates' Pretty Good Privacy (PGP), one of the two technologies we'll examine, uses an asymmetric algorithm to encrypt the session key and a symmetric algorithm to encrypt the user's data.

Message Integrity

When the contents of a message are to be verified as authored by a particular user and unaltered by any other user, it is necessary to agree upon a *signature* and *hash* algorithm. The former is used to verify the authenticity of the message, and the latter is used to verify the integrity of the message. Again, any secure email standard must be extensible with respect to the algorithms that it uses for these purposes.

For signature algorithms, asymmetric algorithms are typically used. These algorithms utilize a public key and a secret key. A signature algorithm combined with a secret key allows someone to generate a digital signature for the contents of a message. A signature algorithm combined with a public key allows someone to verify the digital signature for a message. As you might expect, signature algorithms are one-way functions: You can't reconstruct the input to a signature function by looking at its output.

Hash algorithms are often called message digest algorithms. These simply compute a checksum on their input. No keys are involved. Hash algorithms are also one-way functions, and a good hash algorithm is one in which very similar inputs produce dramatically different outputs. Hence, if even a single bit is altered or corrupted in transit, the hash value will be different.

Key Management

All discussion now hinges on how keys are used for asymmetric algorithms. Specifically, how do you trust the identity of the secret key used to make a digital signature? To start, we have to introduce the notion of a public key certificate. Although the actual formats vary, at its heart a certificate contains three things:

- The identity of the "owner" of the certificate
- A public key
- Zero or more guarantees to the validity of the binding between the identity contained in the key and the owner in the "real world"

So, the next step is to ask what do these identities and guarantees look like? Unfortunately, we now enter the realm of sociology rather than technology. The only theoretical limitation on an identity is that you have to be able to represent it digitally. It could be a name (e.g., "Jim Bidzos") or an email address (e.g., *prz@pgp.com*) or a key in some database (e.g., the name of an object in a directory). More interesting examples could include a series of assertions (e.g., your driver's license number is this, your passport number is that, and so on).

Fortunately, the guarantees are a bit simpler to describe—they are digital signatures from other public keys that vouch for the veracity of the binding. For example, if you encountered a public key certificate in which the identity was someone's passport number, it would be natural to expect that the certificate contains a digital signature from the government entity (or its agent) that issued the passport. However, this begs another question: Why should you trust the entities that have signed someone's public key? It turns out that our two contending technologies have different answers for that question.

As you might expect, certificates have some additional properties, such as a date the certificate becomes valid, the date the certificate expires and a "fingerprint." The fingerprint is simply a hash of the identity and public key so you can tell if it's been altered in transit.

Finally, there are things called certificate revocation lists that identify certificates that are no longer valid. For example, if the secret key associated with a certificate is accidentally disclosed, then the corresponding certificate is revoked.

Pretty Good Privacy

It is difficult to separate "PGP the soap opera" from "PGP the technology." In the interests of brevity (but not of levity) we won't discuss the former here. Instead, we'll just state the obvious: Pretty Good Privacy (PGP) is encryption for the masses. Despite the fact that it required a couple of complete rewrites in order to achieve stability, it gets the job done.

As of late 1997, an effort is underway to provide a "standards-based" version of the PGP technology. This is termed "OpenPGP." The "pre-standards" version of PGP uses the RSA algorithm for signatures and the IDEA algorithm for encryption. The version being developed is more flexible with respect to the algorithms it supports.

The Web of Trust

The most remarkable thing about PGP is its trust model. Remember the earlier question: How do you know whether you should believe the identity in a public key certificate? To answer this in the context of PGP, each user assigns two attributes to the PGP certificates that they encounter: trust and validity. Trust is a measure as to how accurate the certificate's owner is with respect to signing other certificates. Validity indicates as to whether you think the identity in the certificate refers to the certificate's owner.

So, initially your local collection of certificates starts out with one—your own PGP certificate. You then sign your friend's certificate and he or she signs yours. Because you trust yourself when signing those certificates, your friends' certificates are automatically considered valid. Then, based on your judgment of your friends' abilities to sign other certificates accurately, you assign a level of trust to their PGP certificates. As you receive messages containing other people's certificates, if they are signed by you, or any of your trustworthy friends, they are automatically deemed valid. This organic, highly decentralized approach toward validating public key certificates is termed the web of trust.

There are also key servers available that are repository of PGP certificates. If you need to send email to someone, but don't have his or her certificate, you can query a server to see if a copy is there. Of course, the usual rules apply with respect to assigning trust and validity—it's up to you! Key servers also help when you receive email from someone new. Although the message will contain a copy of someone's PGP certificate, you may not know about any of the signatories. So, you can go to a key server and fetch the certificates for the signatories. You might decide to trust them after seeing who signed their certificates.

We've left out the details as to how you really know who sent you the certificate and that no tampering was involved. When you receive a certificate for signing, you run a program to calculate the signature and then contact the owner (usually on the phone), and the two of you compare signatures. If they match, you know that the PGP certificate wasn't altered in transit, and it's now up to you as to whether you believe that the identity in the certificate matches the certificate's owner.

We've also simplified the web of trust in that validity isn't "all or nothing" as we implied above. Rather, PGP offers a flexibility spectrum of possibilities, for example requiring two trustworthy signatories before considering a certificate to be valid. But the one thing that should be clear is that trust and validity are different. You will probably have many keys in your local collection of certificates that are considered valid, but only a few of those will probably be considered authorized to vouch for others.

Secure MIME

There is an interesting concept in advertising called "ambush marketing." The basic idea is that your advertising campaign leverages off the brand and promotion of a competitor. Secure MIME, or S/MIME, is an example of ambush marketing in the Internet. Although MIME is an Internet

standard, which has been implemented by hundreds of vendors and provisioned in tens of thousands of networks, S/MIME is the product of a
closed vendor consortium.[15]

There are two versions of S/MIME: version 2 and version 3. As of
this writing, products that claim to implement S/MIME implement version 2. They use the RSA algorithm for signatures and a weak algorithm
for encryption (RC2 with 40-bit keys). In late 1997, an effort was put
underway to provide a "standards-based" version of the S/MIME technology; this is version 3. The version being developed is more flexible
with respect to the algorithms it supports.

The Hierarchy of Trust

S/MIME uses a hierarchical model for establishing trust. For example, if
your employer assigns you an S/MIME certificate, then your employer will
act as a certification authority and sign that certificate. As a consequence,
trust is established on the basis of a hierarchical relationship between the *subject* of a certificate (the identity) and the *issuer* of a certificate (the signatory).

There are some strengths to this model in that users rely on the certification authorities implicitly. However, there is still a bootstrapping
problem: How do you know to trust the issuer? The answer is that your
local collection of certificates also has some "top-level" certificate authorities, and it is these authorities that sign the public key certificates of the
issuers. Providing that the hierarchy of trust can be kept to one or two
levels—this is manageable in practice.

The web and hierarchical models of trust share many attributes in
common. For example, when you receive a message, it contains a copy of
the certificate that was used to make the digital signature. If you aren't
familiar with the signatories, you can look in a remote repository of keys.
The only difference between the two models here is that the hierarchical
model needs key servers to make its key infrastructure work. Because of
this, keys are usually stored in a directory service accessed via Lightweight
Directory Access Protocol (LDAP) (which Chapter 6 discusses).

Data Formats

The multipart/encrypted and multipart/signed contents are used to convey secure email. Fortunately, they are both very simple content types.

A multipart/signed content has two subordinate body parts. The first
contains the data that is being authenticated and can be any MIME content
type (text/html, multipart/mixed, and so on). The second contains the digital signature used to authenticate the content. The multipart/signed content
has two mandatory parameters. The protocol parameter defines the tech-

nology used to generate the digital signature, and the micalg parameter defines the hashing algorithm used (for "MIC" read message integrity check). The value of the protocol parameter is also the content type used for the second body part. The only tricky part is that the digital signature is calculated on the data before a transfer encoding, if any, is applied.

Let's make this a little more concrete. If we assume that the Open-PGP effort produces an Internet standard based on the current draft (a reasonable assumption at 50,000 feet), then the structure of a multipart/signed message created using PGP technology would look like this:

- The protocol parameter would be application/pgp-signature
- The micalg parameter would be pgp-md5
- The first body part would be labeled as whatever you wanted to sign
- The second body part would be labeled as application/pgp-signature

The second body part is a data structure defined by the OpenPGP document and contains the digital signature along with any supporting material (e.g., a copy of the sender's PGP certificate).

Note that you don't encrypt the first body part in a multipart/signed content. In this way, if only some of your recipients have secure email, but you still want to sign it for those who do, everyone can still read the first body part.

A multipart/encrypted content has two subordinate body parts. The first contains whatever information is needed in order to decipher the encrypted data (e.g., the encrypted session key along with an indication as to the certificate needed to decipher the session key). The second contains the encrypted data, labeled as application/octet-stream. The multipart/encrypted content has one mandatory parameter, protocol, which defines the technology used to encrypt the data. The value of the protocol parameter is also the content type used for the first body part.

Let's also make this a little more concrete. Again, if we use OpenPGP as the basis for a hypothetical example, then the structure of a multipart/encrypted would look like this:

- The protocol parameter would be application/pgp-encrypted
- The first body part would be labeled as application/pgp-encrypted
- The second body part would be labeled as application/octet-stream

In practice, the input to the encryption algorithm would be multi-part/signed.

Finally, there may be one or more MIME content types defined for sending certificates, certificate revocation lists, and so on. These are all specific to the particular secure email technology being used.

SOLUTIONS

Let's get to the details of setting up your email software to handle multiple identities, along with discussing the various methods of applying encryption "standards" to protect your messages.

Setting Up Multiple Identities

Each email program has somewhat different ways of handling multiple identities. Before you jump in and start changing things, first make sure you have a working configuration for a single account. Take note of the names of incoming and outgoing mail servers, your user name and a password if you store it in the program. You'll need at least this information for each new email account you intend to set up with whatever software program you choose.

Sometimes the server names differ from incoming and outgoing machines. This is because of the way your ISP has set up its email system. Generally, when you establish a new account with your provider, you get this information. If you are lucky and have kept track of this particular piece of paper, you should have everything you need to get set up now. If not, you can either call the technical support line or look around on the provider's Web site support pages for this information.

Keep in mind you can set up each identity to have the same "reply to" address, if you so desire. Sometimes you want to have all of your email replies back to a single place. Of course, you can always have different replies to addresses.

Not all programs make it easy for you to maintain more than a single email identity. The two most capable are Outlook Express and Eudora: You can check email from all or some of your accounts readily, and with a single series of keystrokes. With the others, it is more cumbersome.

In Outlook Express, you go to Tools | Accounts | Mail | Add | Mail to create a new email address. This brings up a wizard that walks you through the process. One caveat here is that once you specify whether the mail server is running POP or IMAP protocols, you can't change it without deleting this account and starting from scratch.

Once you have your account specified, you can choose to just send and receive messages on all of your accounts (by pressing Control-M) or by selecting only one account (by going to Tools | Send and Receive and then highlighting the name of the account as shown in Figure 4.1).

You can import existing settings for your email accounts from either previous version of Microsoft email products, from Netscape Messenger or from Eudora. Go to File | Import | Mail Account Settings and follow the wizard's instructions.

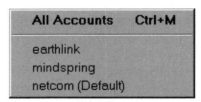

Figure 4.1   **Multiple identities in Outlook Express**

One further option in Outlook Express is that you can specify accounts that won't have their messages checked as part of the overall send and receive operation. To do this, you go to Tools | Account | Properties | General and uncheck the box at the bottom of the window that says "Include this account when doing a full send and receive."

In Messenger, to create another email account you need to use the User Profile Manager, which is run from the Windows Start menu. Before you can run this program, you need to exit out of all other Netscape programs running on your desktop. This also means that if you want to check more than one email account, you'll first have to exit all your Netscape programs and then reload Messenger, choosing this new identity, as shown in Figure 4.2.

Click on New and you'll go through a series of windows asking for your user name and server names, and whether the server is IMAP or POP. Once you complete this information, Netscape Communicator will launch, and you can then go to Messenger and read your mail. You can also make changes to the configuration by going into Edit | Preferences | Mail and changing the various user and server names, as well as switching back and forth from IMAP to POP.

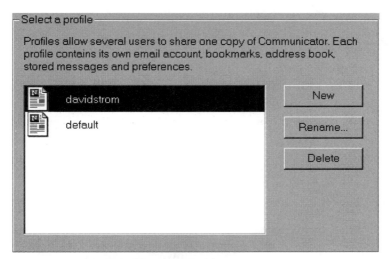

Figure 4.2   Multiple identities in Messenger

While creating and modifying new profiles is relatively easy, you can only run one at a time. In order to collect mail from multiple accounts, you first need to exit all of your Netscape software, including any browser windows, and then rerun the User Profile Manager and select one of your other profiles. This quickly gets cumbersome. Netscape sets up a default account that will be used unless you specify otherwise.

In Eudora, you need to first go to the left-hand windowpane and click on the tab at the bottom of this window to go to Personalities. You set up new accounts by right-clicking anywhere in this window and choosing New. You'll then have a series of windows to set up your account, and you can choose to import settings from older Eudora software or from Netscape or Outlook Express. You can only import a single email account at a time. When you have typed in your user and server names, your Personalities screen will look like the one shown in Figure 4.3.

Persona	Account
🧑 <Domina...	dstrom1@popd.ix.netcom
🧑 GrandCe...	dstrom@mail.grand-centr
🧑 Test	davidstrom@mindspring.c

Figure 4.3   Multiple identities in Eudora

As with Netscape, you have a dominant or default personality that will run unless you specify otherwise. As with Outlook Express, you can send and receive messages for all of your accounts in one operation by using Control-M. If you only want to check your mail for some of your accounts, type Shift-Control-M and you'll get a list of options to choose before checking your mail. Eudora also will automatically select the appropriate address to use in the From: portion of the header based on how the message was addressed to you, which is helpful.

It can get a bit confusing remembering who you are and which account does what. Say you wish to choose which identity you want to use when replying to a particular message. First, make sure this message is displayed in one of your windows. Then go to the left-hand windowpane, and right-click on one of your email addresses that you want to use. Then go to Message | Reply As, as shown in Figure 4.4. This address will be inserted into your reply message.

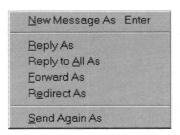

Figure 4.4   **Eudora reply options**

Eudora has many other options that you can change. For example, each account can have its own signature file and a default stationery file as well, so you really can change the look and feel of each of your email identities.

In WinCIM, you can set up as many different accounts as you wish by going into Access | Preferences | Connection. Choose the Add button and you'll bring up a small window and be asked to name your new connection. But only one account can be active at any given time, and if you wish to collect your email from all your accounts you'll have to go choose the particular connection first, then dial up CompuServe and get your mail from that account. In this window, as shown in Figure 4.5, you can also specify that WinCIM use a local area network connection to connect to CompuServe instead of a dialup modem.

Figure 4.5   WinCIM account options

cc:Mail also only works with one email account at a time. In order to add new accounts, you need to type in a new account name at the initial login screen. You'll then bring up a series of windows asking for the user and server name information, as shown in Figure 4.6. You need to specify whether your messages will be stored on your local hard disk (mobile) or on a network server (network).

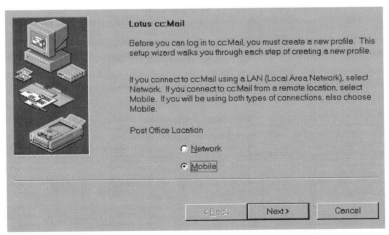

Figure 4.6   cc:Mail wizard for setting up a new identity

With AOL, you set up each new email identity (what AOL calls screen names), but need to disconnect and redial AOL in order to collect email for each one. You can automate this using AOL's FlashSession, but it still takes time to do all that dialing.

Mailboxes for Rent

So far we have just concerned ourselves with setting up our software. But that is just one part of the story. We also need to consider how we will implement multiple mailboxes.

If you run your own email system, then obtaining new mailboxes is a matter of requesting them from your systems manager. But if you have your own account with a service provider, then you might not have this much flexibility. Some providers only allow a single email identity per account, while others charge more to host your entire domain name. It may be time to check around.

If you are looking to purchase an additional email identity separate from your business or other, there are several providers that will do this for you. EarthLink Network, Delphi and Best are examples of three ISPs that provide additional email addresses for about $5 per month. And, as we mentioned earlier, British ISP Demon will provide an unlimited number of addresses per account.[16]

But you may wish to just have your own domain name that matches your own surname, perhaps as something akin to a vanity license plate. You'll find that a Vancouver, Canada-based company called MailBank (*www.mailbank.com*) has already taken many of them. They will resell you a single mailbox for about $5 a year. As an exercise, we looked up the surname domain names of a group of 30 randomly selected people. All but six were already taken, and some of the surnames were (we thought) quite obscure. MailBank already owned many of these surname domains.

Encrypting Your Messages[17]

Of the six products that we feature in this book, three of them come with built-in technology to encrypt messages. Both Microsoft's Outlook Express and Netscape Messenger include support for S/MIME, although we'll see in a moment that the two have radically different capabilities. And the Eudora Pro package comes with an add-on module for supporting PGP, which you may or may not have installed when you installed the software.[18]

A word of warning, however: None of these three products is simple to use, and we feel the overall software quality with respect to encryption is lower than we'd like to see with regards to a version 4 email product. You'll soon see what we mean and be reminded of our earlier "sucking chest wound" description.

If you use AOL or CompuServe, you'll need to purchase a standalone encryption product and use it before you prepare your messages in the AOL and WinCIM software. Or, if all of your sensitive correspondence is wholly contained within the AOL or CompuServe network, you may feel that you don't need encryption products because these messages don't travel over the public Internet.

cc:Mail has its own built-in encryption as part of its messaging infrastructure. It is entirely proprietary, and it is transparent to its users. Indeed, you don't have any choice when it comes to using it or not: All cc:Mail messages are encrypted.

Before you get started with the various technology choices, we should mention some political and personnel issues. While this chapter focuses on desktop issues of privacy, choosing encryption can quickly become an enterprise issue. Does your boss know that your email is encrypted? Should you be required to send a copy of all of your messages to someone else in your corporation, just in case you either leave or forget or damage your encryption setup and can't read your messages anymore? Does your enterprise have a particular security policy that may or may not work well with encrypted email? These aren't easy questions to answer, and in some cases you may be the first one to ask them in your corporation.

If your corporation has a security officer that is technology savvy, there is some hope that you'll be able to implement an encryption policy through this person. But chances are the security officer is someone coming from the law-enforcement arena, or this person may be a true technophobe. In this case, you will have a very hard time getting any enterprise encryption strategy off the ground. The problem here is that deploying encryption means also coordinating how everyone's keys are managed, whether they be digital files or physical ones.

In order to encrypt a message, you'll need to go through the following process:

1. Choose which of the two competing technologies (and specific email software) you wish to use for your encrypted correspondence. There are advantages and disadvantages to both methods.

2. Choose whether you want to just digitally sign your messages or encrypt their entire contents, or both.

3. Choose either an enterprise certificate authority and set up the appropriate server software, or obtain a certificate from a public authority. There are advantages and disadvantages to both methods.

4. Enroll with this certificate authority and obtain an encryption certificate or key for a particular machine and a single email address.

5. Exchange keys with your correspondents, and manage where these keys are stored on your machine.

6. Encrypt and decrypt messages.

If this seems rather involved and complex, it is. The process is nowhere near where it should be to enable encryption to be useful by the vast majority of email users, and won't be for some time. If all of this seems overwhelming to you, we certainly understand.[19] It is to us, too! But let's go through these six steps in more detail.

PGP vs. S/MIME

Our discussion in the standards section might have convinced you that encryption technology is still very much a work in progress, and once you begin to use the encryption features of Messenger, Outlook Express and Eudora, you'll be further convinced. Nevertheless, unless you plan on testing lots of different software products, you should first decide on which product and which encryption technology you intend to use. You definitely want to limit yourself to as small a universe, because running more than one email software product will only make your encryption life miserable. So which to choose?

PGP (*www.pgp.com*) is everyman's product. It was designed for single individuals to use and still remains the easiest method to set up and get going, although it is far from simple. The version of PGP that comes with the Eudora Pro box is the individual version: There is a separate and more capable version for workgroups, or businesses, called PGP for Business Security version 5.5. This is available from Network Associates for $119. This business version is the one we recommend you use, even if you are the only person in your corporation that will use encryption. You'll find that once you start, others will follow, and you might as well start off with the more capable version.

PGP at the moment isn't part of any email software, unlike S/MIME, although Novell was talking\ about including a version of it with a future version of GroupWise. If you want to use PGP, you will need to run a separate piece of software to encrypt and decrypt your messages. If you already use Messenger or Outlook Express, that is certainly more cumbersome than using the built-in S/MIME features of those two products.

Since early 1988, PGP is more capable than S/MIME when it comes to setting up an enterprise encryption policy and putting it into practice on a daily basis. For example, with PGP you can establish that all outgoing and incoming encrypted messages are first copied to a special archive. And all outgoing messages are encrypted with a special administrator's key that can be used in an emergency to read the message if the sender forgets his key or leaves the company. S/MIME doesn't have this ability yet, although it is something that is being worked on for the future.

PGP is a single-vendor solution: All of your software must eventually come from Network Associates to run the various certificate servers and encryption modules. With S/MIME, you'll have some degree of choice, although we found that in practice you probably want to make use of the same email product when exchanging encrypted messages if you want them to be read with a minimum of fuss and bother. Not all S/MIME packages can exchange encrypted messages with each other, owing to differences in their implementations. When Dan Backman of *Network Computing* magazine tested five different products, he found several that couldn't read messages sent by others, along with a bug in Outlook Express that prevented it from recognizing opaque signatures.[20]

Part of the problem with S/MIME is the various choices of "strength" of cryptographic algorithms that are in use in today's browsers and email software. This is more a debate about politics than technology, as the U.S. government places restrictions on various algorithms as we mentioned earlier. There are two different parameters that are of interest: the length of the key itself used in any certificate and the type of encryption technology used. Netscape software supports key lengths ranging from 512 bits to 1,024 bits, for example. There are several choices for encryption technology as well, which go by the labels RC2 (which can either be 40-bit encryption, the only one allowed for export by the U.S. government, or more complex encryption of 64, 128 or even 255 bits), and DES. RC2 was developed by RSA, Inc. On the other hand, DES was done by the U.S. government, and there is plenty of debate there about which is better or more or less proprietary technology. Details of these are outside of the scope of this book,[21] but you should know that the larger the key size and encryption algorithm, the harder it is for someone to decode an intercepted message.

We recommend using Messenger if you intend on receiving messages from many different recipients. In our tests, Messenger turned out to be the universal "recipient" and was able to decrypt messages coming from many other products. We recommend Outlook Express if you intend to be on the other side of the fence: It turned out to be the universal "donor" and was able to send messages to many other products.

Digital Signature Required?

Your next choice is to consider whether to just make use of a digital signature or to encrypt the entire message, or to make use of both technologies. All encryption products can do both, but in somewhat different ways.

Digital signatures guarantee that your recipients have received your message without any tampering and that they can trust the message came from you. The actual message body, and any attachments, arrive without any encryption, meaning that someone could still capture this traffic and read your correspondence. You might want to use a digital signature without encrypting the message, if you care that your message was received intact and that your correspondents can know that you sent it.

The notion of a digital signature is still far from being widely used, and you might find that the work involved in preparing a digital signature is almost as much as what is involved in encrypting the entire message. Please note that the concept of a digital signature is different from the "signature" block that appears at the end of your email messages. This kind of signature consists of several lines of text that are added automatically by the email software and can be read by anyone.

There are two different types of signed messages: clear and opaque. With clear-signed messages, you can still read the message text even if you don't have any encryption functions in your email software. The signature is carried along with the message in a separate MIME portion of the message from the message body, which remains untouched and still readable. That can be handy, especially if you correspond with many people and they probably haven't adopted any particular encryption product, or if they are using older versions of email software that don't support encryption.[22] Clear signing is also useful in the circumstances where your encryption technology isn't compatible with your correspondents' technology. PGP only supports clear signing in its products.

One problem with clear signing is email gateways. They often will break the encryption of the signature, either because they will add or remove characters from the message, and that sloppiness could invalidate the signature block. After all, part of the role of the signature is to ensure that the message was delivered intact and unaltered!

Opaque signing means that your recipients will get a blank message if they aren't running any encryption software, or if their encryption software doesn't work with yours. Opaque signing wraps the entire message in a Base64 encoding, which is usually left alone by most email gateways. This then gets transmitted and then decoded by the S/MIME recipient. Our tests revealed a bug in Outlook Express, and it can't decode opaque-signed messages. However, it does have an option to send either clear or opaque-signed messages. To specify this option, go to Tools | Options | Security | Advanced Settings | Digitally Signed Messages, and check the box marked Send messages using opaque signatures, as Figure 4.7 illustrates. (Messenger can only send clear signed messages, although it can receive both kinds.)

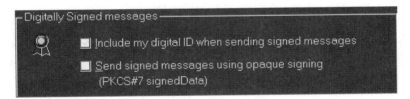

Figure 4.7   Outlook Express encryption options

PGP places its signature inside the encrypted envelope when it sends messages: This makes it difficult to determine the signature of such a message until you first decrypt it. The PGP producers claim this is a feature, offering extra protection in case the message is compromised or copied en route. Newer versions of PGP offer a MIME option that places the signature outside the encrypted envelope. This is how S/MIME products work, making it easier to determine who sent it. To set PGP for this option, go to the PGP Keys program and choose Edit | Preferences. You'll see something like Figure 4.8, and you want to check the option labeled Use PGP/MIME when sending email.

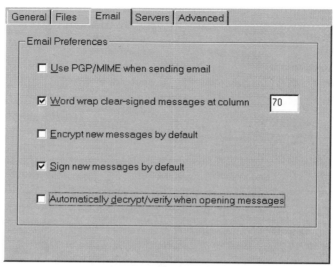

Figure 4.8   PGP encryption options

This screen, by the way, is also where you choose to automatically encrypt messages and decrypt messages, and if you are going to do a lot of this, you might want to check these boxes now.

Choose Your Certificate Authority

Now you have another decision to face, and that is how to set up what is called the certificate authority (CA) for your enterprise. This is a piece of software that runs on a UNIX or NT server and manages the keys or certificates of everyone in your corporation. It serves as a central place of trust and signs all of your user's certificates. If you trust your CA, in theory you should be able to trust the certificates that are signed by the CA, called inherited trust.[23]

The problem is that there isn't any "central" CA for the entire universe of email users. While there are several public CAs that anyone can use, either for free or for a fee, they don't necessarily trust each other nor should they. What happens if an employee of VeriSign turns bad and starts issuing bad certificates? There should be checks and audits to ensure that problems such as this can't undermine the entire CA system, just as there are checks and audits to prevent rogue banking employees from crediting their own accounts.

Setting up a CA is the beginning of setting up a very complex security infrastructure for your enterprise. Your CA needs to establish a link of trust from all of your users to the administrator or operator of the CA itself, and from your CA to other CAs with which you communicate.

There are two different kinds of CAs: One uses software that you install on your own server inside your enterprise and that you maintain; the other are public servers. Having your own places the burden on creating and revoking certificates on your security administrator, or whomever is going to operate the CA server. For S/MIME CAs, there are several products to choose from, including Netscape's Certificate Server and Xcert's Sentry CA. In both cases, these products can be administered from a web browser once they are installed. Each product can handle certificates from a wide variety of S/MIME products, which is one of the few shining spots on the interoperability scene at the moment.

PGP for Business comes with its own version of a certificate server. It runs on a Windows desktop machine and typically is used by the administrator of the entire security apparatus to handle certificates. It can handle only PGP certificates.

If you are the only one testing or using encryption products in your corporation, you probably don't need to install any certificate authority software initially. In this case, you can make use of one of the public certificate authorities such as VeriSign or Thawte. Both Netscape and Microsoft browsers come with links to these as well as other authorities. The public authorities are useful for single individuals, and they are a good place to start, particularly if you just want to test how the process works. However, once several people begin to use encryption, you will definitely want to install your own CA. See the table below for references to these products.

Certificate Servers

Vendor, URL	Product	Platform, Price
Enterprise CAs		
Netscape, *www.netscape.com*	Certificate Server	NT, UNIX; $525
Xcert, *www.xcert.com*	Sentry CA	NT, UNIX; $1495
Public CAs		
VeriSign, *www.verisign.com*	Secure Server ID	Pricing varies
Thawte, *www.thawte.com*	Public CA	Pricing varies

CAs are useful for more than just email encryption certificates. They also can be used to provide security for Web servers. But that is outside the scope of this book.

Enroll and Acquire Your Certificate

Once you have your certificate authority either in mind or installed, you next have to set up how you want to acquire your own certificate.

You have two broad methods: by Web or by email. Actually, you don't have any choice: If you have picked your email product and CA at this point in the process, you have to use whatever method comes with that choice.

Messenger and Outlook Express make use of their related Web browsers to enroll certificates, as you might suspect. Everyone else makes use of email to send and enroll certificates. For example, Xcert's Sentry CA sends you a message telling you that your certificate has been granted, but in the email it has URLs for both Communicator and Internet Explorer where you can download the certificate and place it inside the appropriate software. Why two different links? Because each product supports a different way of acquiring certificates, of course. So much for standards.

The process is cumbersome, and unfortunately not well-specified in any of the product documentation. Let's walk through what you do in Messenger. Click on the Security icon at the top or bottom of the screen and choose Messenger on the menu at the left, and you'll see something like Figure 4.9.

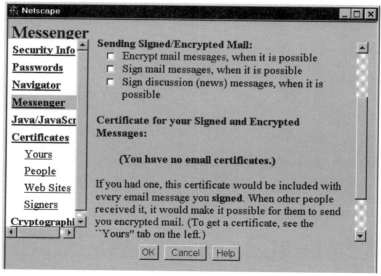

Figure 4.9   Messenger security options

Notice here you have several choices. You can automatically choose to encrypt and/or digitally sign your messages. This control panel shows you that you don't currently have any certificates, and you'll need to get one in a moment. You also can decide on the various encryption options for your certificate. You can choose the strength of the encryption algorithm, for example.

To get your certificate, bring up Netscape Communicator and go to Help | Security. You'll next go to Netscape's Web site and see something like Figure 4.10.

CERTIFICATES

Certificates are digital documents that are provided by a Certificate Authority to give assurances of a person's identity. They verify that a given public key belongs to a given individual. You can learn about certificates by visiting the following pages:

- Netscape Certificate Server
- Certificate Authority Program
- Netscape Certificate Download Specification: Navigator or Communicator
- Netscape Certificate Extensions: Navigator or Communicator
- Netscape Extensions for User Key Generation: Navigator or Communicator
- Sample Netscape X.509 Test Certificate
- Sample RSA X.509 Server Certificate
- Sample RSA X.509 Commercial Certificate

Figure 4.10   Netscape Web site information on certificates

This is more of an information page, and you might want to check out some of the links to various resources to learn more about the security options in Netscape products. On the frame to the left of this window is a menu of choices. Go to Partners and you'll see a list of public CAs that Netscape supports. Choose one of these, or, if you are running your own CA, you should connect to the URL of your CA server and fill out the form there to apply for a certificate.

In Outlook Express you begin the process by going to Tools | Options | Security and click on the button labeled Get Digital ID. This will bring up Internet Explorer and connect to the Microsoft Web page as shown in Figure 4.11. If you are just going to get a certificate from a public CA, then you can follow these instructions. If you have installed your own CA, then you need to point your browser to the

URL of your CA and follow the instructions on the screen to apply for a certificate.

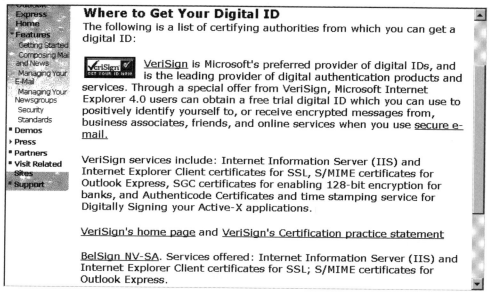

Figure 4.11　Microsoft Web site information on certificates

You can add certificates automatically whenever you reply to a user. Go to Tools | Options | General and click on the box labeled Automatically put people I reply to in my Address Book.

With either Netscape or Microsoft's products, after you apply you should receive an email message telling you the URL to go to collect your certificate. Make sure at this point you are running from the very same machine where you applied for the certificate, otherwise all this effort will be for naught. Cut and paste the URL from your email into your browser, and you should be led through the process to grab the certificate and place it inside your program. You'll need to do this twice: First for the certificate of the root authority of the CA, and then for your own certificate.

In Eudora, you first need to install the PGP plug-in. There are several software modules for PGP, including PGP Keys, which is the main desktop software piece. You first need to create your own certificate, which PGP calls a key. Go to the PGP Keys program and choose Keys | New Key. You'll go through a series of steps via a wizard that will create a key and store it in a file on your hard disk. You then need to exchange this file with your correspondents (via an email message) as part of the next step.

As you can see, there are many places for things to not go as planned, and we even experienced the situation where Netscape told us that our certificate was installed fine, but it wasn't the case. There is much room for improvement here.

Exchange and Manage Certificates

So far we have just covered creating your own certificate, and we assume that you have installed one satisfactorily on your own machine. Now comes the hard part—dealing with the certificates of your correspondents, and managing both theirs as well as other certificates around your corporation.

As we mentioned in our standards section, you first need to exchange certificates with your correspondents before you can begin to exchange encrypted email. And that means sending your public key to them, and sending their public keys to you, before you can exchange actual encrypted messages. If you are corresponding with someone who doesn't have the same CA in common, you'll first need to establish a trust relationship and exchange root CA certificates before you can exchange the individual certificates. This is somewhat painful, but once you get the hang of it, it isn't that difficult.

Once you begin to exchange more than a few of these certificates, you might think that this is a job for a directory server, and, thankfully, the vendors are already there. The CA server can set up entries in an LDAP directory to keep track of who is issued a certificate, and you can query this LDAP server to find who has them. That is the good news, and indeed the PGP product makes use of its own LDAP server to keep track of its certificates. However, the LDAP server is only used by PGP: If you want a general-purpose LDAP server to keep track of your users, you'll have to install something else.

As a challenge for open systems and interoperability, we installed the Xcert Sentry CA and Netscape's Directory Server on a test network. The Xcert was used to create and manage our certificates for our test corporation, and the entries were placed in the Netscape LDAP directory. We created the certificates using the Netscape browser and stored the information in our Messenger email software. After going through the process described above, we had a valid certificate and could see it in the Security | Messenger settings. While the Sentry CA couldn't automatically deposit a certificate in the Netscape LDAP server, we (operating as the security administrator) could do so with a few simple Web forms and keystrokes. So far, so good.

The challenge was trying to pry these certificates loose using other products, such as Outlook Express. There we ran into trouble, mainly because the Netscape software creates the certificate in a nonstandard place in the LDAP directory. According to the standards documents, the certificate should be placed in a particular spot in the LDAP directory schema, called usercertificate. Netscape, for whatever reason, places them at a location called usersmimecertificate.[24] This meant that non-Netscape products couldn't view the certificates in our directory, because they were looking in the wrong place.

This brings up a very good point: The connection between a user and his or her certificate is tenuous at best. Just because you know that *david@strom.com* is the email address of David Strom and you have his certificate, it doesn't mean that any of your expensive software tools can make this connection either. This will create all sorts of headaches for your security administrators, and it means that you need to maintain at least two directories on your own machine—one for users and one for certificates.

It would be nice if the address books of our email software could handle this automatically, but they don't. The closest that any product comes is Outlook Express. Each entry in its address book can also store information on the location of the certificate you receive from your correspondents. You can't add them automatically, unlike adding an email address. To add the certificate of your correspondents, you first need to go to the message and click on the certificate icon, then click on View Security Properties and check Add digital ID to address book. It is cumbersome, and the folks at Microsoft claim that this is a feature rather than a bug. They say that you wouldn't automatically want to add certificates from spam mail, right? We think this is a weak claim, given that this is rare.

As an example, let's look at what you have to go through with Netscape products to keep track of your certificates. First, you'll want to make sure that the LDAP server that is managing your certificates is available from within the Netscape browser. Go to Edit|Preferences|Mail|Directory and add the location of your LDAP server. Then go to Communicator's Address Book and search for yourself on this server to make sure your name and email address are actually listed. If you have entered the information correctly, you should see a listing of your name in the search query results screen. If you click on the icon to display the details, you'll get something like Figure 4.12.

david

Object Class	**top**	**person organizationalPerson inetOrgPerson**
First Name	**Strom**	
Last Name	**David**	
Name	**David Strom**	
uid	**david**	
Email	**david@cousteau.nwc.syr.edu**	
creatorsname	**cn=Dan Backman,ou=Editorial,o=NWC,c=US**	
createtimestamp	**19980307161407Z**	

User E-mail Certificate

This Certificate belongs to:
David Strom
david@cousteau.nwc.syr.edu
Editorial
Strom, Inc.
Port Washington, NY, US

This Certificate was issued by:
NWC Syracuse Lab
cert@nwc.syr.edu
Editorial
Network Computing Magazine
Syracuse, NY, US

Serial Number: 35:01:70:4E
This Certificate is valid from Sat Mar 07, 1998 to Sun Mar 07, 1999
Certificate Fingerprint:
82:77:E5:43:D8:4D:97:42:EC:19:E4:0D:BF:A0:56:A5

Phone Number	**516 944 3407**

Figure 4.12   **LDAP query of Netscape Directory Server**

Notice on this screen you can see all sorts of information about the certificate and its user. For example, you have a phone number and other fields that aren't shown on the screen shot, such as fax and address. This could be an issue if you want to protect your privacy, and certainly you should consider what information you supply a CA when you fill out your application. You can also see who created the certificate and the period during which it is valid.

Next, you'll go to Security | Certificates | Yours and make sure that your certificate is displayed in the menu. Finally, go to Security | Messenger | Certificates for your signed and encrypted users, and select the particular certificate you want to use for your correspondence.

Now, that is a lot of effort, and we still haven't established the trust relationship between ourselves and our CA yet!

As you can see, there is a great deal more work that needs to happen here. What if someone leaves the company? Or changes his or her email address? Or if you want to use the same certificate, but on several different machines? Most certificates are tied to a particular machine and a particular email address, meaning that any new address will require a new certificate. Again, this is a pretty sad situation, and we aren't happy with the state of these products.

Encrypt and Decrypt Messages

Now you can finally go and encrypt your messages. It seems like a long road to get here, and it was. You first need to set up your default operations in Messenger, Eudora or Outlook Express. You have seen the screens to do this as part of our earlier discussions. If you aren't going to be sending lots of encrypted mail, we recommend you leave the encryption options off and then just encrypt individual messages.

To do this in Messenger, click on the Security icon at either the top or bottom of the screen. You'll get a menu that will tell you whether or not you have a certificate to send encrypted mail to your recipient. If not, you click on the button to search for a certificate and Messenger will lead you to the LDAP query screen for that email address and perform a search on one of your LDAP servers that you have specified. (Chapter 6 goes into more details on how to set up various LDAP servers in Messenger.)

If you do have a certificate, you can also choose to sign the message as well, with a check box that is further down on this screen. Once you choose this option and close the menu window, a small icon appears on the bottom of your screen next to the lock icon, indicating that the message has been signed.

In Outlook Express, there are two icons at the right-hand side of the toolbar when you are composing a message: The first one (with a ribbon on the upper left-hand corner) is to digitally sign your message. The second (with a stamp on the lower right-hand corner) is to encrypt the message, as shown in Figure 4.13:

Figure 4.13   Outlook Express toolbar

If you click on either icon, the header area of the message will display the appropriate icon, indicating that it is either signed or encrypted.

In Eudora, you'll first compose your message. You'll want to press either of the last two buttons at the right-hand side of the toolbar, as shown in Figure 4.14.

Figure 4.14   Eudora toolbar

The envelope with the lock is for encrypting the message, while the paper and quill is for a digital signature. If your correspondent is in your

PGP directory, you are in good shape, and you'll next see the PGP Keys screen with a list of all of your correspondents' certificates. If your correspondent isn't in the directory, his or her email address will be displayed with a line through the address, and you'll have to first exchange certificates before going any further.

Eudora has an annoying operation: When you send an encrypted message, the message gets turned into an attachment before being sent. This attachment isn't saved, so if you keep copies of your outgoing messages, you won't be able to refer back to them—all you will see is an empty message with a broken link to the attachment.

That is the encryption portion. What about the decryption side of things? If you have done your homework and exchanged certificates as we discussed earlier, then when you receive your encrypted message, it should automatically decrypt and display in plain text. You shouldn't have to do anything else—unless the encryption system is broken by a gateway or product incompatibility.

That's it. You should be well on your way toward exchanging encrypted messages.

Whew! What a process! Was it worth it? We guess so. But we look forward to when users of these products don't have to have such intimate knowledge of their security infrastructure, and when sending an encrypted message is almost as easy as sending a plain text one.

Futures

The obvious question when concluding this chapter is whether the Internet needs two standards for secure email.

Proponents for either side can make superficially compelling arguments. On the PGP side, one can point to a grassroots constituency and a huge installed base of legacy systems. PGP emphasizes privacy for individuals. On the S/MIME side, one can point to some major vendors and an emphasis on nonrepudiation.

If history is any judge, the PGP side will win because it requires less infrastructure to make it work. S/MIME has to solve all the problems that PGP has to solve, plus a few more. However, these things aren't decided overnight. So, our prediction is rather straightforward: The two sides will slug it out in the Internet marketplace for a couple of years, but ultimately the game is PGP's to lose. It requires less infrastructure and fewer broad agreements to achieve ubiquity.

Endnotes

1. At the risk of foreshadowing Chapter 6, it is a quaint Internet custom to view the lack of an all-encompassing directory service as justification for pretending that domain naming provides such a facility.

2. As an Internet security guru explained: "If you were an Internet engineer, would you rather ship your product now, have the stock go up and buy a nice car, or would you rather take an extra three months to test your code thoroughly, giving your competitor an opportunity to ship before you and driving your stock price down?"

3. Eudora and Messenger, for example, only included such support with the release of version 4 of their respective software. Prior versions could only handle multiple personalities by constantly changing the user parameters within the software, or by having to install separate copies of the program for each identity. And most LAN-based email products such as cc:Mail still can't handle multiple identities.

4. One example of this is the site *whitehouse.com*. No, it is far from being the home of the president, which has always been located at *whitehouse.gov*. Another extreme example is the Martinside Marketing company, who has registered hundreds of domain names that are variation on common Web destinations: *ny-times.com*, instead of the *nytimes.com* site that is maintained by the newspaper. Martinside then sells these typo-domains to vendors who hope that poor typists will find their sites and stick around—a dubious assumption at best.

5. If you are in these circumstances and need to find a good domain name lawyer, check out Jeff Sengstack's list in *New Media* magazine *at newmedia.com/new-media/98/03/tradecraft/Sourcefile_Domain_ Name.html.*

6. Great Britain actually has two country codes: .uk (which includes Northern Ireland) and .gb (which doesn't).

7. A complete list of the two-letter codes for each country can be found at several places around the net, including the site *www.rtw.com.au/internet/suffixes.html.* The site *alldomains.com* has not only the country codes but links to each country's registrar, along with the fees associated with registering the domain in that country. The United States has its own two-letter code, .us. And if you are interested in finding out more about registering domains in other countries, go to Yahoo, under Computers and Internet:Internet:Domain Registration:Network Information Centers, or *www.uninett.no/navn/ domreg.html.*

8. Some of these suffixes are quite ridiculous, such as .store and .web, but we'll leave that discussion for some other forum. And adding suffixes may only worsen the trademark problem and make it harder to figure out whether example.com, example.firm or example.web is the appropriate site for the Example Corporation.

9. This certainly does happen, and indeed is the situation for one of the authors. But this means that you depend on your ISP and Network Solutions to notify you about when it is time to renew your registration. In the past, Network Solutions has most notably been somewhat lax about keeping track of renewals of domain ownership. Indeed, there was the celebrated and somewhat embarrassing case where Microsoft Network was disconnected from the Internet for a few hours for supposed nonpay-

ment of its renewal fee. The mistake was Network Solutions', but still the damage was done for many users who couldn't get access to the MSN Web site.

10. Gateways can serve a useful purpose. For example, if a person's name changes or if he or she transfers from one department to another, a gateway can hide these changes and maintain the same email address to the outside world.

11. It is certainly ironic that when the inventor of the Domain Name System—the Internet service that keeps track of services and hosts—changed jobs, his previous employer was unable to forward his email to his new address!

12. A good explanation of what is involved in establishing a new domain name, in the context of creating a Web server, may be found in *Poor Richard's Web Site*, by Peter Kent, Top Floor Publishing, 1998. There is a good discussion of resources available for you to search for new names, along with the pros and cons of having your site hosted on someone else's server.

13. This latter site was part of an elaborate hoax by professional media trickster Joey Skaggs. The site, which looks like it was assembled by a disgruntled employee from a genetic research facility, warns about the potential dangers of genetic engineering. Skaggs was successful at duping several members of the daily press into believing his cause was a real one. The Dole site was assembled by Brooks Talley, a computer trade newspaper editor, and featured pictures of the candidate against a background of labels taken from canned fruit of the same name. It contained obvious parody, including saying "Bob Dole is often mixed up with the Dole fruit company. He is a big fan of tropical fruits, especially slightly over-ripe bananas...." Both the real site and the parody site are no longer maintained.

14. And to add insult to injury, VeriSign will continue to charge us $9.95 each year, unless we can get this certificate canceled. Revoking a certificate isn't a simple process, as you can see if you go to *digitialid.verisign.com*.

15. You know you're not in Kansas anymore when you go to the "S/MIME Central" Web site and find that it carries banner advertisements.

16. Go to EarthLink at *www.earthlink.com/company/getmailbox.html*; Best at *www.best.com/services /pop*; Delphi can be found at *www.delphi.com/dir-html/ benefits/register.html*; and UK-based Demon is available at *www.demon.net/ser-vices/mail/pop3.html*.

17. Our thanks to Dan Backman of *Network Computing* magazine for his help in sharing his lab and providing lots of valuable insights in the preparation of this section.

18. PGP also makes a plug-in for Outlook 97. However, it has a lot of problems and we would not recommend its use, and Outlook already comes with support for S/MIME anyway.

19. There is an alternative to this process. The United Parcel Service has produced a file transfer utility called NetDox, available at *www.netdox.com*. It requires special software to be installed on each computer, and it simplifies the certificate and encryption process somewhat. But this is yet another proprietary solution to the encrypted email problem—something we think goes in the wrong direction.

20. The article has more in-depth examination of testing MIME interoperability and features of Messenger, Outlook Express, Baltimore's MailSecure, OpenSoft's ExpressMail and two Worldtalk plug-ins for Eudora and Outlook Express. See "Secure E-Mail Clients: Not Quite Ready for S/MIME Prime Time. Stay Tuned." *Network Computing*, Feb. 1, 1998, *techweb.cmp.com/nc/902/902r2.html*.

21. There are many sources of cryptography information. Here are just a few to get you started. For a simple explanation of public key issues, see Anita Karve's Lesson 104 in the April 1997 *LAN Magazine*, at *www.networkmagazine.com/tutors/9704tut.htm*. For a 10-part series that goes into more depth and information on algorithms, vendors, and issues, visit *www.cis.ohio-state.edu/hypertext/faq/usenet/cryptography.faq/top.html*.

22. Non-S/MIME users, for example, will receive the signature block, but as an attached file called *smime.p7s*. This file can be deleted, since it won't do these users any good!

23. We say "in theory" because there are cases where trust is a complicated thing, just like in the physical world. What happens if an employee leaves the company, or does untrustworthy things? Then his certificate has to be revoked. The converse is also troubling: You can't automatically check the validity of any certificate you receive. There are CAs that can operate in real time to see if the certificate has been revoked, so in theory your email reader could query these servers and determine the status of the certificate. This is a very complicated issue, and so far we haven't seen any products that really do a completely satisfactory job here.

24. Ironically, the author of the relevant LDAP standard is now employed by Netscape. When we asked our friends at Netscape why they did this, here is their response: "The missing information is which cryptosystems we can use, and what key length we can use. We might, for example, use the strong-crypto U.S. version of the client and want to use 128-bit encryption. The trouble is this: When the certificate server publishes your certificate to the directory, it just publishes our basic certificate. It does not have any knowledge of our S/MIME capabilities. So, if you want to send us email, you fetch our certificate from the directory. But you don't know what key length to use. So, you send us an email using the lowest common denominator, which is 40 bits. We get your email, and send a signed reply. With that reply we're sending our certificate and the fact that you should be using 128-bit encryption. Now, on your next email to us, you'll be using 128 bits of encryption. But it does not make sense to have to send email three times to establish the stronger encryption." We agree entirely.

Messaging in the Enterprise: Receiving

In this chapter, we consider two central issues of receiving mail throughout the enterprise: how to manage remote access to messaging services and how to use messaging to enhance customer support. These two topics are a good place to begin for enterprise issues. First, the problems associated with remote access provide a good road map for examining how enterprise-level email is provisioned; and, second, email provides a useful mechanism for automating many support features for an enterprise, both for internal use and external consumption.

INTRODUCTION

To begin, it is important to understand something of the origins of email in order to understand the present state of affairs.

As quaint as it seems now, the original Internet messaging infrastructure had no formal notion of a separation between the processes that accepted email on behalf of a user, and the processes that the user employed to access that email. The interface between the final messaging relay was unspecified. In fairness, at that time, desktops were little more than extensions of a timesharing system. However, this situation didn't last long, and soon a mailbox access protocol was added to the infrastructure.

Of course, providing a mailbox access interface between the desktop and the server raises several issues. First, is the whole notion of authentication and authorization. How should users of a mailbox access service identify themselves, and, having done so, what level of access should they be provided to the mailboxes available? Second, other security issues come into play. At the risk of repeating many of the issues discussed in Chapter 4, the network traffic to the mailbox access service must be secured. Ideally, it should not be subject to third-party interception[1] or masquerade.

However, the issues associated with remote access become considerably more general once access is allowed from outside the enterprise. Although security issues typically are given greater importance, as one moves further from the enterprise infrastructure and into public Internet or network access, connectivity issues become more focused. Within the enterprise, it is a straightforward issue to analyze user quality of service requirements and provision an internal internetworking infrastructure accordingly. Outside the enterprise, the ability to control throughput and latency becomes tenuous. This argues for control at the messaging level to help mitigate the twin issues of slow access and transient access.

There are many solutions to the problem of slow access. At the lowest level, the network may provide compression to reduce the amount of bandwidth required. The effectiveness of link-layer compression is highly variable, depending on whether the email itself contains attachments that are already compressed. (Notably, this is a weakness of existing Internet standards. There is no standardized set of compression encodings for Internet messaging—something we will discuss in more detail in Chapter 7.) A more interesting solution is to provide a filtering mechanism within the mailbox access service. This allows the user to prioritize the order in which messages are downloaded to the remote desktop.

In practice, solutions to the problem of slow access are also applicable for transient access. Filtering is a good example of this. Of course, the true challenge in providing these mechanisms is balancing the flexibility needed by the remote desktop in order to optimize access with the resource requirements on the mailbox access service to allow for scalability.

Another powerful trend in enterprise messaging deals with the use of email to automate "customer service" capabilities. From our perspective, there is little difference between who and where the "user" resides, whether he or she is an employee or a customer, or either inside the organization or otherwise.

Although rewarding, there are many challenges in provisioning these capabilities with messaging. First, as noted earlier in Chapter 3, reliability is not guaranteed by the underlying messaging infrastructure—only a best effort is made. As such, reliable service must be layered on top of the messaging infrastructure. This explains why many such systems are tied to a trouble ticketing system of some sort, so that the user gets "immediate" feedback indicating that the original message was received.

A second problem deals with the ability to understand incoming messages and route them accordingly. Although unique email addresses can be used for first line management, there is a fundamental weakness with such an approach—the limit to the amount of meaningful triage that can be performed by the user. This suggests that second line management techniques, such as automated routing based on message content becomes increasingly important.

Finally, we are faced with the myriad issues that arise when automated processes inadvertently communicate with other automated processes. Although discussed earlier in Chapters 2 and 3, we'll take a slightly different look at these issues. It simply isn't good customer service to inadvertently deliver several hundred acknowledgments to someone who asked a simple question exactly once.

So, let us now consider these issues in greater detail, along with aspects of the systems that cause them.

PROBLEMS

Let's continue with our story of the day of a typical email user. It is now 9:30 p.m. and you have just gotten off the plane in Omaha for an all-day business meeting tomorrow. You have to find your rental car, collect your wits and bags, and get to your hotel.

On The Road Again...

This trip is a regular one for you, and you return back to the same hotel because you like the familiarity on the road. But, more important, you like being able to make use of your laptop to get your email, and you know that this hotel has the right set of phones, wall jacks, power outlets and rates. By the time you check in and unpack, it is close to 11 p.m. local time. You don't even want to think about what time it is back home.

You plug in and proceed to reconfigure your laptop to dial the number of IBM's Global Network. You've found over the years of traveling that IBM has the largest amount of local phone numbers in the most cities that you end up visiting, and the cost for this access is around $20 a month. Since you travel so often, you have gotten the company to pick up the charges. And, because this isn't your first trip to Omaha, you have an icon in your dialup networking folder for the local IBM Omaha number. So far, so good.

But when you connect, you see that you have 76 messages waiting for you. Groan. This could take a while and you really want to get to bed. What to do? It would be nice if you could just preview the messages and see their subjects or who sent them, but you don't have the ability to do that with your setup, which is running Eudora. You do set up your email software so that you don't download any messages larger than 50 kilobytes. Hopefully, that will cut down on the time involved in the overall download and weed out a few huge files that you could do without for the time being. So, you let your laptop chug away while you listen to David Letterman's quips and try to relax. It is going to be a while before you get to sleep.

Our typical day on the road had some advantages over what most business travelers experience. First off, our prototypical traveler was using an Internet service provider (ISP) that has nearly global reach for dialup access. This cuts the cost of phone calls down tremendously, especially when you consider the near-obscene surcharges many hotels add for long distance telephone calls. IBM is fairly unusual among most ISPs in offering such wide access and a choice of cities.[2] Most providers are strictly local shops, with just a few access points beyond your home metropolitan area. Some have slightly wider reach, but they still don't go very far afield. Others have toll-free 800/888 access numbers, but charge a premium for using them.

And even some nationwide providers have pretty spotty coverage overseas or in certain states. Others, like Netcom, tack on hefty surcharges for users going abroad. It pays to check this out before you sign up with any provider, and have a good idea of where you intend to travel with your laptop, too.

Part of the issue here is that corporate IS managers don't usually have the time to evaluate providers in terms of where they provide local access. Usually they are busy looking at other factors, such as what they will charge for internal Web hosting or ordering another high-speed circuit for headquarters. It may be faster, not to mention prudent, for you to do some of your own research. Try to find a provider that has the right set of cities with access numbers where you yourself travel on business, and just write off the monthly expense as part of your other travel expenses. Or, better yet, pick an ISP for your travels and use it for making connections from your home as well.

Our scenario painted a very rosy picture for the traveling user in other areas. Our traveler was comfortable making changes to his laptop computer and being able to figure out the dialing strings required for his connection software. This isn't always the case, as we'll get to in a moment. Our example pointed to the use of filters to limit the size of incoming messages—again, something that you might not realize how to do.

We demonstrated in Chapter 2 how you can begin using filters in each of the various email programs. We'll also get into more specifics on setting up filters later on in the chapter. This feature is one of the most important yet least used of any email product. Part of the problem with filters is that you don't necessarily become motivated to use the filtering feature until it is too late and you are stuck downloading some monster file over a slow-speed modem. And part of the problem is that you have to have a clear picture in your mind of what kind of mail you get and what you want to do with it before you can set up the appropriate filter.

Filters aren't the only solution, however. We'll see in our discussion on standards how a new series of email standards can help in terms of previewing messages and manage where and how you'll download your mail.

Sometimes you want to be able to do more than just reject messages above a certain size. You'd like to be able to act on particular messages automatically, such as when one of your customers requests a catalog. Ideally, you should send him or her email saying the catalog is on its way almost immediately upon receiving the request. This is a lot more work than it should be, and requires some careful reading of the software help screens and trial-and-error testing.

Dialing Up Is Hard to Do

In our example, our traveling user was able to use Eudora and the Windows dialup protocols to get access to his email account. There are two parts to this: making changes to your dialup configuration and making changes to your desktop configuration. The dialing configuration can be easy or difficult, depending on many factors. First, you have to find the local phone number for your Internet connection. If you had enough presence of mind to remember to search for this before you left town, give yourself a gold star. Most of us don't remember until we are on the plane. Many ISPs have Web pages where you can search for the local access number by country and city name or area code, and we'll go into more detail about other ways to access this information later on in this chapter.

Once you find the correct number, you then have to enter it into the right place in your dialing software. You also have to remember to add the right digits to obtain an outside line. Some hotels require you to dial an 8 or 9 for an outside line, some overseas hotels use a 0, and other times you'll be dialing direct and won't need any prefix. If you don't travel enough to remember how to do this, you may be stuck in a strange city late at night and have no one to call to guide you through the process. We've been there, many times, and it is a lonely place.

But finding your local access number is just the beginning of the fight for remote access. Your next obstacle is the hotel room itself. Is the phone configured for modems, or does it sit on a digital telephone switch, making any modem call impossible? Is the phone located far away from any power outlets, making your laptop cords stretch across the room? Or maybe you didn't bring any extension cords to make the connection of power and phone cables work. You don't know until it is too late, and you are already at the room, unpacked, and ready to get down to work.

Furthermore, your phone may present a problem. Not all hotels use the RJ11 modular phone plugs that are found in most American homes. Your hotel phone may be hard-wired to the wall, making any connection to your computer's modem difficult. We've taken along various tools, including screwdrivers, pliers, electrical clips, and so forth—all in the crusade against taking apart our phones and finding the right set of wires to attach to our modems. This is still a problem in the late 1990s, amazingly enough.

Even if you can plug in your modem, you may not be happy with the kind of telephone line quality you get in your hotel. We've been in plenty where our fast modem had to be throttled down to a puny 9,600 or 2,400 bits per second because the phone connection couldn't handle anything faster. Trying to figure this out is mostly trial and error. You may try several times to make a high-speed connection, and if that doesn't work, then you may try a slower speed and see what happens. You have to be an expert in interpreting the various squeaks and squawks that your modem makes to understand what is happening.

This is one of the reasons our weary traveler decided to stay in the same hotel from one trip to another: If connectivity is important, then familiarity breeds success. Stick with hotels in which you or your colleagues have stayed and have been able to communicate.

It is amazing to us that business travelers can make reservations at hotels and request the type of bed, bathroom and even in some cases the brand of shampoo, but when it comes to finding a room with an RJ11 jack, it is still something left to chance![3]

Our dance with the dialing configuration is just the first act. We may have more work to do before our laptop is communicating properly.

We often have to make other changes to our desktop software. And finding out exactly what is required and understanding how to configure this software is a challenge, even for very experienced computer users.

Let's take as an example Marshall Rose's situation. Although his story is complex, it is depressingly typical. In the office, his laptop sits on a LAN behind a firewall (requiring a connection to his proxy server); at home, his laptop sits on another LAN (connected to a cable ISP). Moving this laptop from work to home requires making changes to its IP address, default gateway address, name server addresses and deleting the reference to the proxy server. It isn't a lot of work, but it is tedious.

Now, what happens when he takes this laptop on the road? Yet a third configuration. Here he connects to the Internet via a dialup connection—luckily the various IP addresses are assigned dynamically, but if he has been using his office proxy server, he has to delete the reference there.

Notice that these changes aren't in a single place in Rose's Windows95 computer: They are spread through several different programs (his Web browser for the proxy server entry, the Dialup Networking parameters, the IP networking parameters in the Control Panel). The optimal situation would be for Rose to be able to select one of his three configurations by clicking on one icon. No such luck. He has to enter the information for each configuration he wants to go to, whenever he wants to switch to it. (And then, to add insult to injury, he has to reboot his system. Marketing types may claim that Windows is easier to use than UNIX, we suspect that their lips are moving.)

Rose isn't alone in wanting a simpler solution. Some email programs, such as Outlook Express and Eudora, incorporate the dialup networking piece directly, so when you launch the software you can also initiate a call and download your messages. But this isn't always a time-saver when you are on the road and have to first make changes to your dialup configuration. Some ISPs install their own dialing software on your disk, while others make use of the Windows Dialup Networking application. You would think that just changing the dialup number wouldn't be so hard, but it can be.

Who Are You, Really?

The issues surrounding changes to the dialing configuration and applications is just one part of dealing with access to remote email. There is another problem relating to how users prove who they are and how they receive their authentication from the network. In many cases, corporations have placed their email servers behind firewalls, making it impossible to collect mail over the public Internet by using any ISP's dialup ports. In those circumstances, you'll need a special piece of software to authenticate your identity and also dial up your server via your own network. That can result in expensive phone charges, especially if you travel overseas. Or, you might be using cc:Mail or some other mail system that is less than 100% pure Internet, requiring a special product for remote access.

Sometimes there isn't any outward sign that something has been done to block your access. After all, it isn't like driving down the freeway and seeing an onramp closed for construction. This is much more subtle, and sometimes things can go wrong in odd ways.

As we were writing this section, we were using a borrowed office that had good Internet connectivity and all the software we needed. However, the corporate IS manager had decided, for whatever reason, to block access for sending email out via the Internet, even though we could collect our email just fine. First we thought there was something wrong with the configuration we had typed into the Netscape Messenger software we were using. But that wasn't the problem: It was the way the firewall was set up.

Now, we have lots of experience with getting our mail remotely. And it still took us several attempts and a few times examining the various parameters in Messenger before we realized that something wasn't quite right. This news isn't very encouraging, but it serves to highlight that you can always expect the unexpected on the road.

In short, dialup access and authentication become issues for remote users. Your corporation may not feel comfortable using an ISP to provide the authentication and access, and it may want to do it instead. One solution is to establish your own private network, bypassing the public Internet and making use of telecommunications lines and equipment that are wholly owned by your corporation. While expensive to set up and costly to maintain, your enterprise retains complete control over its communications. No information goes out over the public Internet until it leaves the firewall. This is what most corporations did 10 years ago with dedicated IBM Systems Network Architecture (SNA) networks. Many still use their own networks, but today they are running IP protocols as well.

However, building your own network may not be your cup of tea. You need to pay the staff to maintain this network, and that gets pricey over time. Keeping all this gear up and running is several full-time jobs, and you'll also need staff that is either willing to travel or else located in branch offices where you have large departments.

A second alternative is to outsource this network to a service provider that runs it for you. You still have a private network, you just leave the dirty work of running it to someone else. This still can be quite costly, however.

What is becoming more popular is a third alternative. You could establish a separate private network that is only available to users at your corporation. You do this using the public Internet infrastructure and a series of products to create what is called a virtual private network (VPN). The VPN extends the Internet protocols and standards with a set of secure pathways from your remote users to your corporate computing resources. You don't have to pay for expensive private lines, and your staffing needs are minimal, since you rely on the public ISPs to provide remote access connections to your corporate network.

There are various VPN implementations, and we'll cover them later in this chapter. However, VPNs bring an extra layer of complexity to both how the remote computer and server are configured. Some require special hardware, some require a mixture of hardware and software. Some encrypt the entire data conversation, others only encrypt the IP packet contents and leave the header in the clear. This means that someone snooping on the conversation couldn't read the contents but could see the source and destination of the conversation.

Email as a Corporate Support Tool

All of these issues relate more to access. There is a second set of enterprise issues when it comes to receiving email, and that concerns how corporations handle email as a mechanism for technical and customer support. As email becomes more pervasive outside the computing and engineering world, more and more companies are finding they can connect to their customers with email. Many are offering email access for questions about their products, for complaints about their service and for sales inquiries. The challenge is to keep up with this flow of mail, and handle the responses in a timely manner.

Email has also become popular as a means of providing contact information on corporate web sites. But just putting an email address on every Web page—or even on one's home page—isn't sufficient. There have to be procedures in place to route these queries to the right person or program inside your corporation and respond quickly. All too often, corporations treat the Internet as a simple, one-way communications stream. They think that publishing via the Web is a broadcast activity. This is plainly wrong. Even if you don't list an email address on your web site, people will send you email. It is simply amazing how many companies gain a Web presence but forget to build an email infrastructure.

The trade publication *Network World*[4] took an interesting approach and assembled a short list of vendors that provide various computerized solutions to this problem. The reporter then used the address on each vendor's Web site and timed how long it took before he received a response, either from a program or from a human, to his query. Interestingly, most took at least an hour to respond and one took more than 18 hours. A similar tactic for general consumer products companies was tried by the trade publication *Computerworld*,[5] with even more dismal results: Vendors there took anywhere from an hour to days to send a reply. And that's not counting several vendors that didn't even reply, such as U.S. Airways and Mobil Oil. Clearly, there is some room for improvement here.[6]

The notion of providing inbound support via email is still undergoing change, and there seems to be more questions than answers yet in this arena. Consider:

Who answers email that is sent to these addresses? Is it a human, a program, or some combination of the two? Do you send an immediate reply that is obviously machine-generated to confirm that you got the question and then follow up with something more thoughtful, or just route the message to the right carbon-based life form to begin with? This could create an entire cottage industry, with web sites and books devoted to sample email responses, just as there are books devoted to sample business letters for various situations.

Do you have a single address for all inquiries, or separate addresses for different kinds of communication and departments? Do you publish the actual email addresses of key employees, say, the vice president of sales and head of investor relations? What about publishing the CEO's address?

And there are plenty of other issues. What constitutes "timely" responses to this kind of email—especially if you need to have staff available around the clock to answer questions from around the world? Most of us expect to see a reply within 24 hours of sending a message and get annoyed when it takes longer.[7] Finally, how do you keep track of your company's performance here?

This amounts to a lot of questions in an area that didn't even exist a few years ago. And that shows exactly how important email has become as a tool for dealing with customer support.

General Mills' Ask Betty (Crocker) email box for cooking inquires gets email from about 100 consumers daily. All the customer service representatives who answer these queries are trained by a single supervisor to ensure consistency and a similar style and wit. And General Electric, which pioneered the concept of a 24-hour-a-day telephone customer response center, gets more than 1,000 email messages a month. The same staffers who man the phones take shifts answering the email.

An Example

When we ordered some paper goods from one Web site, we got the following reply almost within minutes of our order:

```
From: WebBot

Greetings,

It's very hot here in Arizona and we're all relieved
that paper doesn't melt. (Speaking of paper melting,
have you ever tried to run coated stuff through your
laser printer? For this very situation we carry
LaserCast(TM), a glossy colored paper that's
engineered specifically to work in lasers without
melting as it goes through. Our favorite color is Hot
Cocoa because it reminds us of skiing on the cool
slopes of Northern Arizona which is just a few hours
up the road.)

Say, thanks for your interest in us. Now that we're
up on the www, please feel free to send us your
comments and questions through our email page. We'll
respond as quickly as possible.

And, don't forget, you can still call us at 1-800-000-
0000 if you wish to place your order over the phone.

Bye for now. We've got orders to fill and we've got to
come up with some more clever conversation to use on
the FedEx guy while he waits for us to finish those
last few shipments.
```

This email shows several good and bad things about customer support. First, it clearly comes from a computer program, and indeed the return address was something like *WebBot@example.com*. Second, the company tries to do an upsell in the course of telling you that it got your inquiry. That is a nice touch, but it isn't why you wanted to communicate in the first place. The tone of the message is a bit too folksy for our taste, but it is memorable and somewhat comforting that the company received our order. And, finally, the company mentions both the phone number and the Web site (although the actual URL for the site wasn't supplied, and we might have misplaced it).

We'll have more to say about this topic later in this chapter when we discuss solutions. But, first, let's look at some of the standards that are relevant to receiving email in the enterprise.

STANDARDS

There are two enterprise-specific standards for receiving mail: the Post Office Protocol (POP) and the Internet Message Access Protocol (IMAP). For historical (some say hysterical) reasons, there is a kind of imagined rivalry going on between the supporters of each protocol.[8] In addition to these two standards, there are others that relate to VPNs, which we will also examine.

The Post Office Protocol

The original POP was developed and deployed back in 1988. Since that time, there have been some minor embellishments to the protocol, but nothing that would prevent a client implementing the latest version of POP from interacting with a vintage server (or vice-versa). This is both a strength and a weakness. While its stability has made it attractive to implement POP in a wide range of products, it has not evolved to meet new needs.

The design goals of POP are two-fold:

1. Minimize resource requirements on the server by supplying only very simple access methods to messages stored in the user's mailbox.

2. Minimize implementation complexity on the client by supply only the smallest sufficient functionality for the majority of environments.

Hence, in addition to stability, an important design goal is that of scalability. A modest server can handle hundreds of simultaneous clients—delays are due to network latency, not server bottleneck. Furthermore, because it is often easier to install, configure and maintain a single POP server than to do the same for full messaging servers on multiple workstations, this design trade-off can work for everyone from enterprise managers to ISPs.

It is important to appreciate that neither POP nor IMAP are replacements for, or subsets of, Simple Mail Transfer Protocol (SMTP). As Chapter 3 discusses, SMTP is responsible for sending messages, POP and IMAP are responsible for retrieving them. It is also important to understand that message envelope information is not available from either POP or IMAP. That is, when an SMTP server makes final delivery to a mailbox, the SMTP envelope is not placed in the mailbox—only the message being delivered is.

Protocol Interactions

There are four parts to a POP session:

1. Exchange greetings
2. Examine the mailbox
3. Retrieve and (usually) delete messages
4. Release the session

The actual commands used in POP aren't particularly interesting. However, the minimalist functionality they provide is. POP is also somewhat unique in that its command syntax is even simpler than SMTP—rather than using the three digit reply codes from Chapter 2, if a POP server likes what it sees it says "+OK," otherwise it says "-ERR." Any text that follows (on the same line) is meant for human consumption. So, by simply looking at the first character of a response, the client can decide whether things are working or not. This minimalist syntax works because the protocol operations are very simple.

The exchange of greetings is used primarily to authenticate the user to the server. Unlike SMTP, in which no authentication occurs when relaying messages, access to a particular mailbox requires some kind of authentication. At present, there are four different authentication schemes of varying cryptographic complexity. (Indeed, the addition of these schemes is really the only change made to POP over the past decade.) The original scheme, PASS, uses plain text passwords (and, obviously, has no cryptographic complexity). Other authentication schemes include the exchange of cryptographic hashes based on shared secrets (APOP and AUTH), and Kerberos.

Mailbox examination allows a client to determine how many messages are in the mailbox and the size of each message. This provides a basic functionality for clients that wish to filter based on size of message (e.g., "don't download anything over 50 kilobytes"). Messages are identified by positive integers (e.g., 1, 2, and so on), and sizes are expressed in octets, although they may be approximations to reduce the complexity of the server.

Message retrieval and deletion is straightforward. The client tells the server to send back an entire message. Typically, once a message is downloaded, the server is told to mark the message for deletion. Some servers may also support a "top N lines" command, in which the headers of the message and the first N lines of the body are returned. This is provided to clients that wish to filter based on values in the headers.

Session release tells the POP server to remove all messages marked for deletion (typically every message retrieved).

Limitations

Although POP has enjoyed much success over the past decade, its short-comings are also evident. These typically fall into two areas:

• Inefficient use of the network

• Inability to cope with decentralized operations

Let's look at each.

Although POP is highly optimized to allow for efficient implementations on host systems, its use of the network is suboptimal with respect to latency. The typical POP session consists of at least 4+2N round-trip interactions, where N is the number of messages retrieved (three round-trips to exchange greetings, one round-trip interaction to release the session, and two round-trips for each message). Although the data carried in each round-trip may be very small, latency can be when accessing the Internet via a dialup connection or across several networks. If the POP client decides to filter messages (because they are large), the number of round-trip interactions may climb to as high as three per message (although this may be offset by not downloading large messages). In order to remedy this situation, the server would need to somehow apply the user's filters to the mailbox and then blast the selected messages down the network toward the client.

The issue of decentralized operations is considerably trickier, as its roots come from a different style of user interaction. The POP model is that a single mailbox is split between the server and the client. The server's job is to put messages into the mailbox for later retrieval by the client. The client's job is to retrieve the messages and then let the user process them. Implicit in this shared contract is the notion that the client deletes messages on the server after they are retrieved. For users who utilize a single machine to process their mail, the POP model is usually adequate.

However, some users may decide to utilize multiple machines to process their mail. For example, they might use a desktop system at the office, a laptop system on the road and another system at home—all to process messages addressed to the same recipient. For those users, the POP model of centralized operations (all processing done on a single client system) is inadequate. Throughout the history of POP, there have been some attempts to support this additional model, but they have proven largely unsatisfactory. For example, some clients are able to talk to multiple POP servers and manage multiple mailboxes. This really doesn't provide for decentralized operations, but it does allow users with multiple mailboxes a centralized mechanism for managing their mail. To deal with the decentralized model, we need to look at a different protocol.

The Interactive Message Access Protocol

The original IMAP (IMAP2) was developed and deployed back in 1988. Since that time, the protocol has undergone substantive changes. As of this writing, the current version is termed IMAP4rev1. Although the continued development and refinement of IMAP can be viewed as a strength, its lack of stability has certainly hindered its deployment in operational systems. (The fact that there are no fewer than 10 documents in the IMAP standards suite doesn't help either.[9])

The design goal of IMAP is to deal with the decentralized model.[10] To do so, three new building blocks are present:

- Servers maintain multiple mailboxes for a client

- Message properties are available for retrieval and storage

- Message transfer is at the body part level

Let's look at each.

By allowing a client to manage multiple mailboxes, the client can use the server as a bona fide replacement for its own message store. This means that users can decide how to organize messages and then have the client tell IMAP how to carry out the necessary operations (e.g., moving messages from one mailbox to another) on the server. This is a powerful feature provided by nearly all desktop email software, so by providing it as a protocol service, IMAP goes a long way toward usability as an access protocol. The difficult part, unfortunately, is that both the IMAP client and server have to agree on naming conventions—the

IMAP standards provide little guidance in this area. As a consequence, interoperability suffers.

The second building block needed by the user's email software is the ability to associate properties or attributes with each message. Although a "deleted" attribute first comes to mind, there is actually a much more important one: a unique, persistent identifier for the message at the server. If messages can be uniquely identified, then it is possible for multiple clients to synchronize their behavior if they become disconnected from the server. In addition, entire messages can be uploaded back to the server.

For example, an IMAP client might connect to a server, download some messages, possibly delete them, and then release the IMAP session. Later, when the client reconnects to the server, it can determine which of those messages are still on the server—even if some other program accessed the mailbox and "did things" in the interim. It may decide to upload the message back to a different mailbox, and so on.

The final concept allows for more efficient use of network resources. IMAP provides a mechanism that allows a client to send search criteria to the server to select messages within a mailbox. The client can also examine the structure of a message in order to select different parts of the message for download (e.g., "send me the 1-kilobyte text part, but skip the 50-megabyte video clip").

Protocol Interactions

There are four parts to an IMAP session:

1. Exchange greetings
2. Select and manage a mailbox
3. Manage and process messages
4. Release the session

However, unlike the typical POP session, the client may choose to iterate between steps 2 and 3, managing the messages in different mailboxes.

As might be expected, IMAP has a considerably richer command set than POP. What is unexpected, however, is that IMAP's syntax is considerably more complicated than either POP or SMTP (or just about any other Internet application protocol). There are two reasons for this:

- To allow the client to have multiple IMAP commands in flight simultaneously
- To allow the server to send unsolicited information to the client (e.g., new messages have arrived)

With respect to the first reason, both SMTP and POP operate in lock step: The client sends a command and awaits a response before issuing another command. IMAP allows the client to send multiple commands, and hence requires a mechanism for correlating responses with the original requests. While an interesting concept in theory, the practice is another story. First, if the server isn't multithreaded, it will process the requests serially. Second, clients have to be particularly clever in order to use such a feature. As a result, the overall protocol is considerably more complex, with dubious benefit in the field. With respect to the second reason, this is a useful feature of IMAP. It allows the server to tell the client when new messages have arrived without the client having to continuously poll for this information.

However, setting aside this feature, the IMAP command syntax is simply baroque (read: "broke"). It mixes syntactic features from LISP (parenthesized lists), pre-MIME encodings (character counts), and so on. As a consequence, IMAP parsers are rather complex.

The exchange of greetings serves the same function as with POP—it allows the client to authenticate itself to the server. Like POP, different authentication mechanisms are possible. (In fact, the only time POP gets changed these days is when someone invents a new authentication scheme for IMAP and then decides to fit it onto POP!)

Mailbox selection allows the client to access whatever mailboxes are provisioned for the user. There is one hard-coded mailbox, termed INBOX, which is where incoming mail is received. Beyond that, the client is free to issue commands to create new mailboxes or rename or delete existing ones. Mailboxes can be nested, which requires the client to ask the server what separation characters it uses (a.k.a. the server's "hierarchy separator," such as the backslash character for the Windows directory structure). As you might expect, IMAP provides a mechanism for the client to determine its list of available mailboxes. And, consistent with the IMAP philosophy of letting the server filter information before sending it to the client, the list can be a subset based on user-supplied search criteria.

Message management revolves primarily around searching for messages that meet a certain criteria, fetching them across the network and then updating the message's properties back on the server (e.g., to set the \Deleted flag). Both searching and fetching allow for considerable flexibility. Rather than treating each message as a single unit, IMAP provides access to the headers, body parts and several IMAP-specific attributes, such as:

- An internal date in which the message was created on the server
- Internal flags, managed by either the server (e.g., \Recent) or the client
- A unique identifier for the message on this server
- The MIME structure of the body
- The "envelope"

This final attribute shouldn't be confused with the SMTP envelope described in Chapter 3. Rather, in IMAP, an "envelope" is a collection of certain headers from the message structured as a parenthesized, nested list. Presumably the purpose of this encoding is to minimize the cost of sending the headers over the network. In practice, it isn't particularly clear if this results in a latency reduction. It is clear, however, that the client has to implement yet another parser in addition to the header parser.

Finally, session release closes the selected mailbox (if any) and terminates the session.

Virtual Private Networking[11]

Email transactions can be made more secure by exchanging mail protocols such as POP and IMAP over a VPN. Depending on your perspective, there are either no stable standards for VPNs, or many different and sometimes contradictory standards. Part of the problem is that there isn't any generally accepted definition of the term virtual private network. As VPNs have become popular, vendors have twisted and stretched the acronym to fit product offerings.

Certainly the goal of all VPN products is to enable deployment of logical networks, independent of physical topology. That's the virtual part—allowing a geographically distributed group of hosts to interact and be managed as a single network, extending the end-user dynamics of a LAN or workgroup without regarding the true location of hosts within the VPN.

And private? Within the VPN market, this is generally interpreted as a provision of security characteristics such as privacy, integrity and trust among hosts participating in a virtual network. VPNs provide security by establishing a virtual connection called a "tunnel" over all or part of the network. For example, a roaming laptop may use a tunnel to obtain secure access to an enterprise mail server over the public Internet. Access controls ensure that tunnels are set up only between authorized endpoints, and data sent through the tunnel can be encrypted to protect it from prying eyes.

But every VPN product takes a different approach and supports a unique mixture of proprietary and (draft) standard protocols and algorithms. This makes interoperability between products difficult, if not impossible, until stable standards emerge. This means that any corporation contemplating VPN solutions may want to purchase products from a single vendor or search carefully for complementary products that operate at different layers.

Layer 2 tunnels (named after the layer in the protocol stack with which they are associated) provide point-to-point data link connections between tunnel endpoints. Several competing approaches have been defined to support layer 2 tunnels, including Cisco's Layer 2 Forwarding (L2F) protocol and Microsoft's Point-to-Point Tunnel Protocol (PPTP). PPTP is included in Microsoft's Windows NT and Windows95 operating systems, and it is catching on with vendors that sell access servers to ISPs. But PPTP is far from being a standard, and, like anything else from Microsoft, is subject to change whenever the company releases a new operating system version.[12] Consequently, vendors in this market are working together to produce a common, interoperable Layer 2 Tunneling Protocol (L2TP) standard.

Layer 3 tunnels provide IP-based virtual connections—in this approach, normal IP packets are routed between tunnel endpoints that lie anywhere, separated by any intervening network. Encapsulated within tunneled IP packets are headers that provide packet-level authentication and/or data integrity and confidentiality, all covered by a variety of draft international standards that are too technical for us to be concerned with here. These standards, which go under the umbrella name of IPsec (secure) are still under construction. This means that IPsec vendors' products may implement different versions of these standards and therefore may not work together.

Finally, there are *layer 5 tunnels*, supported by circuit-level proxies that sit between client and server applications. In this approach, a proxy server permits secure UDP or TCP-based access to network resources. This means that traffic from clients outside the VPN must go through the proxy, which blocks unauthorized access to servers inside the VPN on a per-application and per-user basis. Many products in this market use the SOCKS v5 protocol for authenticated firewall traversal.

Of course, as you might expect, combining these approaches is rather popular—and to satisfy some security policies, absolutely necessary. For example, the TIS Gauntlet firewall supports IPsec tunnel protocols as well as application-level filters and content scanning. And VPN products can be layered on top of each other, complementing one vendor's authentication product with another vendor's encryption product, for example. We'll have more to say on specific VPN implementations and limitations in our next section.

SOLUTIONS

There are various ways to help reduce the burdens of traveling email users. They range from relatively simple solutions to reconfigure your existing software to more complex changes that require new and still-emerging technologies of VPNs. Let's start with the former and work our way toward the latter.

Scheduling Connections

One suggestion that is easy for remote users to implement is to make sure any scheduled checking of your email software is turned off, and understand how to compose messages and save them in a queue for later delivery. After you compose a single message, you don't necessarily want your software to automatically dial up the server when you are on the road. Instead, to make best use of your time, you want to explicitly make these connections on your own, after you are ready to receive a batch of messages and perhaps have composed a series of messages and saved them in a queue. Each product has different ways of doing this.

Eudora has a series of screens that contains configuration options for traveling users. Under Tools | Options | Checking Mail, there is a box for checking mail every few minutes. Make sure that "0" is filled in here, otherwise it will try to dial your modem when you are on the road. (See Figure 5.1.) You also have a switch to send messages that are in your outbox whenever you check for incoming mail. We like to leave that box checked all the time. Also under Tools | Options | Sending Mail, make sure that the check box next to immediate send is blank, otherwise every time you compose a message it will try to send it.

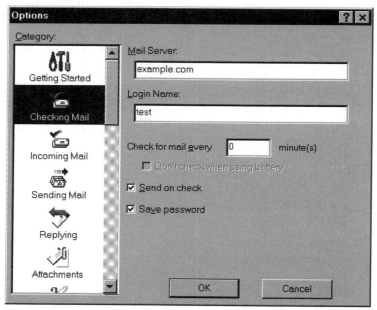

Figure 5.1   Eudora checking mail options

AOL has a nice feature called the FlashSession, which is designed just to sign on to AOL, collect your mail and send any queued messages, and log off. This way you avoid most (but not all) of their annoying advertising and downloading of updated graphics messages. And while you are composing your messages, both AOL and CompuServe let you choose to either send them immediately or save them in a queue for later delivery.

cc:Mail has several ways to schedule connections in the Action | Location series of menus. You can tell it to use a local area network connection, a particular dialup connection and even wireless modems! And while you are connected, you can just receive messages, just send or do both. There is a series of screens and forms to fill out, providing a very confusing array for first-time mobile users. The screen that specifies how you set up your location is shown in Figure 5.2.

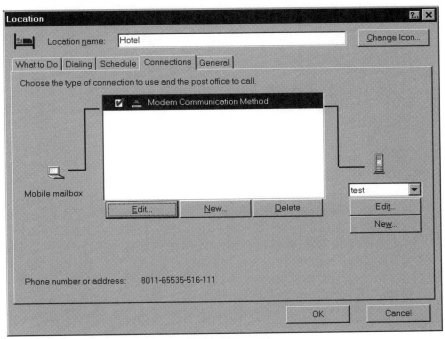

Figure 5.2   cc:Mail location management options

Netscape Messenger Edit | Preferences | Mail | Mail Server | More Options has a special checkbox to automatically check for mail every designated number of minutes. Leave this box blank to not have it automatically look for new mail.

But changing the scheduling behavior is just a small step toward managing your remote email. You can also set up your connection profile to help ease the remote retrieval of email. Products such as Outlook Express and Eudora have the ability to automatically dial up an ISP and check your mail. You can store the login information for your ISP as part of your user profile for the mail.

If you use Microsoft Network (MSN) as your ISP, you'll be faced with a slightly different option. MSN sets up the Dialup Networking parameters so that any application making use of IP automatically will bring up its own dialing software and connect to the Internet. This is fine if you want to use MSN in this fashion, but if you want to make use of another ISP for dialup connections, you'll need to go to your Start | Settings | Control Panel | Internet | Connections and uncheck the top box labeled Connect to the Internet as needed.

There is one caveat: If you do decide to store this information, realize that anyone who has access to your machine can now retrieve and send email, posing as you. If your desktop or laptop can be secured by other means, such as a power-on password or password to turn off the screen saver and resume operations, and if you diligently use these protections, you are in good shape. But if you don't have this protection, we recommend leaving the password field blank and entering it each time you need to check your email.

In Eudora, go to Tools | Options | Advanced Network, and check the boxes next to Automatically dialup this connection and save password. Your password isn't shown but will be stored by Eudora, so that every time you check your email it will bring up the appropriate dialup-networking configuration and connect you to the Internet. Of course, this means that you must first set up an appropriate configuration, including your user name, password and, most important, the phone number that you need to dial. See Figure 5.3.

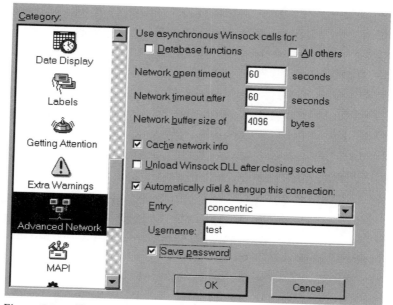

Figure 5.3   Eudora dialup options

Outlook Express has a similar setup to Eudora: Go to Tools | Accounts and highlight the name of your email account. Then go to Properties | Connection and check the box next to Connect using my phone line, and then choose the particular dialup networking configuration from the scroll bar. See Figure 5.4 for an example.

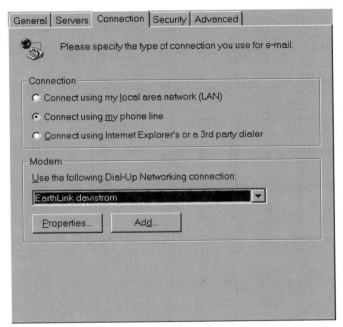

Figure 5.4   Outlook Express dialup options

How can you find out about these local access numbers, especially as you travel to a new city? The easiest method is to check your ISP's Web site. The better providers have put the lists of their access numbers on either their support or member information pages, and usually you can search them by area code, state, or country or city name, or just display the entire list.

CompuServe has the best tools for tracking down its access numbers, and that makes sense, given how long CompuServe has been in the marketplace. You can search its Web pages (see Figure 5.5); you can use Win-CIM (or MacCIM) and type GO PHONES; and you can dial an 800 number and key in your own phone number to find the closest access number to you. As we mentioned earlier in the chapter, it is a good idea to first check these resources before heading out on your next business trip and setting up your laptop ahead of time.

COMPUSERVE *Access Numbers*

Search for Global Access Numbers by **City Name** or by
Area Code/City Code

| New York | City Name FIND IT |

| | Area Code/City Code FIND IT |

| | Country FIND IT |

<u>Hot off the Press!</u>, newly released 56K (analog) access
numbers. Check for more to come!

Figure 5.5   Searching for the nearest CompuServe access phone number

Making Copies

Setting up these schedules and dialup connections is helpful, to be sure,
but you can do much more to manage your email when on the road.
Before we discuss filters, there is the ability to make copies of your messages and leave them on your POP server.[13]

All POP servers have this ability, and figuring out how to use it will
take some concentration and organization. First you need to understand
how you will go about your daily email life. Do you read your email in
the early morning at home and then want to save some of these messages
for later resolution once you get to work? Or do you need to download
some of them now, and leave others to deal with later?

If it's the former, you can make use of the "leave copies on your
server" feature of your email software. This means that you first download all your messages at home, say, and then download a second copy of
them at your machine at work. If you want to be more selective, you'll
need to implement an IMAP server, as we'll discuss later in this chapter.

Let's show you how to use the "leave copies" feature.

Eudora has several places where you can specify the behavior for how you download messages from your server. Go to Tools | Options | Incoming Mail Options, and check the box next to Leave mail on server if you want to save a copy of your messages for later retrieval. There is also an option to delete mail from the server after a specified number of days.

Another way you can control Eudora is by holding down the Shift key when you choose File | Check Mail (or hold down Shift when you click on the icon in the Eudora toolbar). You'll see something similar to Figure 5.6, showing Mail Transfer Options. You just can collect your waiting inbound messages, or just send outgoing ones. There is also a feature at the bottom of this screen called Fetch all message headers to In mailbox, which will retrieve the header and the first few lines of every new message. If you select this option, your messages don't go through your filters. After reading the first few lines, you can then reconnect to your server and either download the remainder of the message or mark them for deletion.

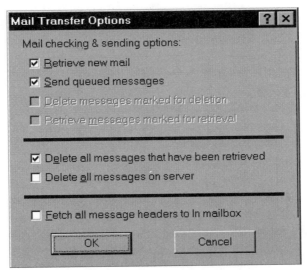

Figure 5.6   Eudora mail transfer options

Messenger has a single option to make copies of messages and leave them on the server. You can find this on the Edit | Preferences | Mail | Mail Server screen. With Outlook Express, go to Tools | Options | Advanced and you'll see something similar to Figure 5.7 for local message options. You can delete messages from the server after a specified number of days, like in Eudora, or you can keep copies on the server.

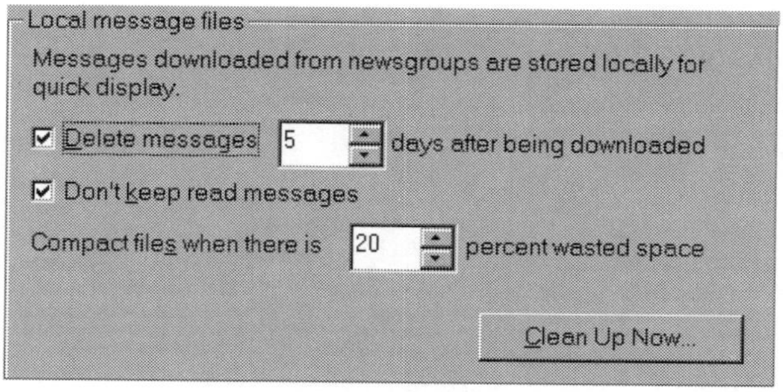

Figure 5.7   Eudora local message options

Filtering Messages

Making copies of your messages is fine, but a more powerful feature is the ability to skip downloading large messages that can take 15 minutes or more to collect over a slow modem connection. To do this and other tasks, you need to be able to set up filters and folders.

We discussed in Chapter 2 how each of the featured email products enables you to filter your messages. Let's get more specific as to how to restrict the size of all your messages that you download. We'll also go into more detail on how to create a very complex filter.

Restricting the size of your downloads is your security blanket when you are on the road and at the end of a thin pipe and a long day of travel. You never know if someone has decided to send you megabytes of graphics just as you were walking out your door and heading for the plane. (This has happened many times to us: Your colleagues' timing may be equally impeccable!) And, as we said earlier, these megabytes take loads of time. We recommend setting a limit around 40 kilobytes; anything larger than this is probably too large to download over a slow connection. And most text-only messages are under 10 kilobytes.

The best product to do this job is Eudora. Under Tools | Options | Incoming Mail, you can specify that you don't want to receive messages larger than a certain size in kilobytes (where you specify the size). If you don't check the box next to the skipping messages of a certain size, it will download everything.

In Netscape Messenger, go to Edit | Preferences | Advanced | Disk Space.

You should see a check box next to a line that says Do not download any messages larger than __ K, and you can put "40" in the blank to prevent large messages from being downloaded. In previous versions of Netscape's email program, this option was somewhat easier to find: In Messenger version 3, it was located in Options | Mail and News Preferences | Servers.

In Outlook Express, you have to use the Inbox Assistant and set up a new rule to limit the size of your message downloads. Click on the Add button, and then on the properties sheet click next to the Larger Than box and type in the size restriction you wish.

Once you set up your size restrictions, you'll know the next time you attempt to download a message that is bigger than your limit. If you are running Eudora, you'll get something like the following message:

```
WARNING: The remainder of this message has not been
transferred.
The estimated size of this message is 113133 bytes.
Click on the server retrieve icon above and check
mail again to get the whole thing. If the server
retrieve icon is not showing, then this message is
no longer on the server.
```

If you are running Messenger, your screen will look like Figure 5.8:

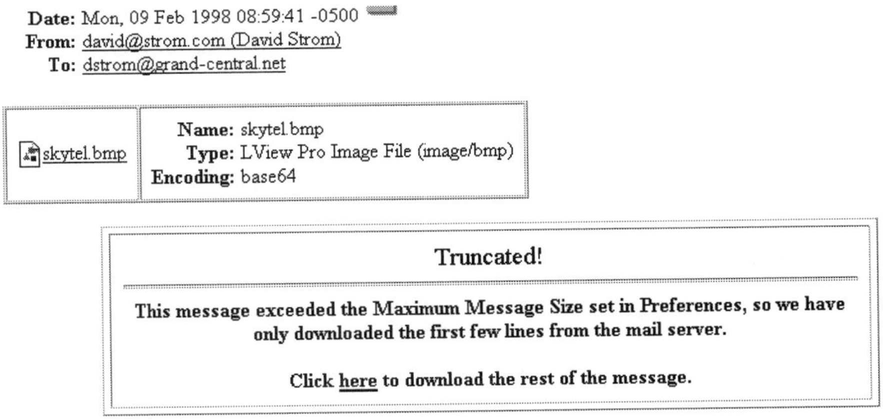

Date: Mon, 09 Feb 1998 08:59:41 -0500
From: david@strom.com (David Strom)
To: dstrom@grand-central.net

	Name: skytel.bmp
skytel.bmp	**Type:** LView Pro Image File (image/bmp)
	Encoding: base64

Truncated!

This message exceeded the Maximum Message Size set in Preferences, so we have only downloaded the first few lines from the mail server.

Click here to download the rest of the message.

Figure 5.8   Messenger truncated message notice

And if you are running Outlook Express, you'll get a rather cryptic error message report that will look like what is shown in Figure 5.9 after you try to collect your email:

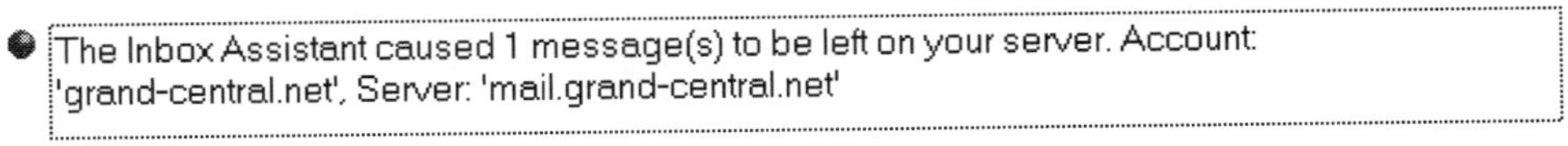

The Inbox Assistant caused 1 message(s) to be left on your server. Account: 'grand-central.net', Server: 'mail.grand-central.net'

Figure 5.9   Outlook Express truncated message notice

Say we want to retrieve this message. Using Eudora, there is a small button with an arrow that appears next to the BLAHBLAHBLAH button at the top of the message. When you click this button, the next time you go to collect your messages the entire message will be downloaded. Note that this will download a second copy of your message—the only difference is that this copy will contain the complete message. You will have to delete the truncated copy of the message on your own. It is somewhat confusing, especially the first time you attempt this.

In Outlook Express, we have to turn off the rule that prevents large messages from being downloaded. In Messenger, we click on the phrase Click here (as in the message displayed above) while we are connected to the Internet and the complete message will be downloaded. As we mentioned earlier in our standards section, this large message remains on the server until we successfully download it and disconnect from the server, at which point it will be deleted.

But setting size restrictions is just one of many ways to organize your received messages. A much more powerful method is to use filters and folders to automatically place these messages in appropriate containers, where you can read them when you have the time and can deal with urgent messages first.

Some products, such as Eudora, have the ability to filter on both incoming and outgoing messages. Others, such as Outlook Express, can only filter on incoming messages. Most of us will probably only use the incoming filters, and let's use Eudora as an example to see how you can set up a few different filters.[14]

Before you can set up any filters, you should have created some folders to organize your messages. Folders group messages together so you can find them easily. As we mentioned in Chapter 2, you can have folders within folders for better organization. We generally create a folder for a new project, a new client, a new discussion or something that has already generated many messages and has no place yet to call home. But you may work differently. The important thing to keep in mind with folders is to make them somewhat mutually exclusive, so you don't have to go searching through several places when it is time to locate a message.

In Eudora, create a folder by right-clicking on the left-hand window pane that displays the folders, or choose Mailbox | New from the menus. As we mentioned in Chapter 2, you need to decide when you create a new folder, whether it will just be a container for your messages (which Eudora calls a mailbox) or be a container for several other containers (which Eudora calls a folder).

First, you need to go to an actual message that you have received, which will serve as the model for constructing the filter. Open this message and go to Special | Make Filter. You'll then have to specify the particular conditions and actions you desire.

This window, as shown in Figure 5.10, is for creating simple filters, with single match conditions and a single operation. Let's say we want to take any incoming messages from our friend at *test@example.com* and move to a new mailbox, called Test Messages.

In our case, we are filtering on an incoming message, so we'll want to check that box. This means that every time Eudora receives a message, it will automatically run the filter and perform whatever operations are specified here. Notice that there is also a check box for Manual operations. This means you can also perform the same filter by choosing Special | Filter Messages command on your own.

We then click on the button next to From and type in the address of the sender, in our case, *test@example.com*. We then choose the button under Action to Transfer to New Mailbox, and then type Test Messages in the dialogue box to name the mailbox. Finally, we click on the button Create Filter to save this filter and have Eudora begin to use it on our received messages.

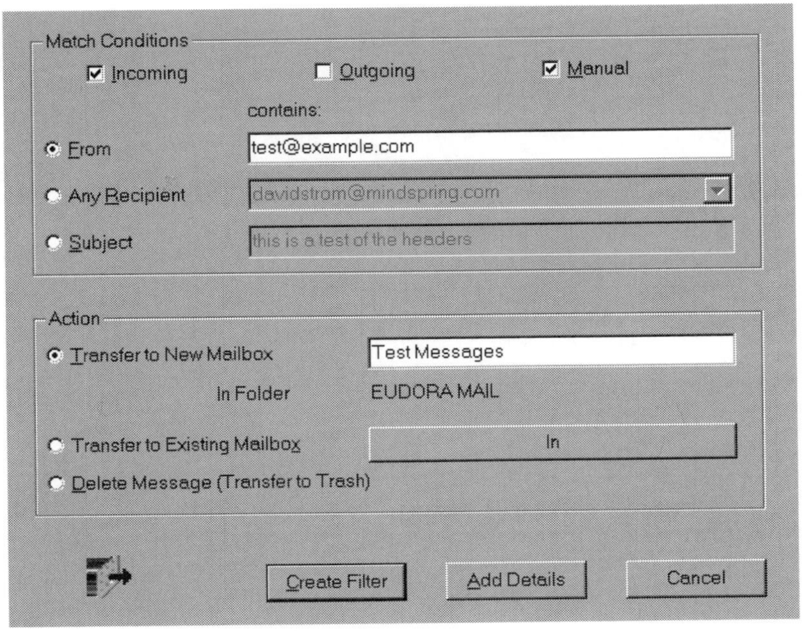

Figure 5.10   Eudora simple filter creation

Now, let's create a relatively complex filter that will scan incoming messages for two particular items (being sent to a user at either the domains file.com or files.com), play an alert sound and then transfer the message to another email user. You'll see the complete filter assembled in Figure 5.11.

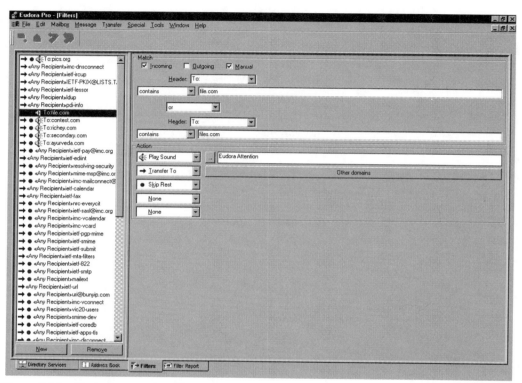

Figure 5.11   Eudora complex filter example

Again, we begin by opening a message that we want to use as a template and creating a new filter. This time we go directly to the bottom of that screen and choose the button marked Add Details to bring up a more complex filter specification form.

Next we specify the particular conditions to check when we receive the message. In our example, we want to search the To: header for any reference for the domain file.com, so we choose the To: choice in the pull-down menu under Header, then choose the contains choice in the pull-down directly below for the type of search. Finally, we type in the words file.com in the box next to the action.

Our particular filter has a second condition—check for the text files.com—so we choose the or condition and fill out the rest of the information as before, only this time typing in the words files.com.

This sounds more difficult than it actually is. Our next task is to choose the appropriate action for any message meeting this particular description. We choose the Play Sound option in the pull-down menu, and then hit the "..." box to browse through our hard disk to find a particular sound file that we should play to alert us when a message such as this is received. We can choose other actions as well, including transferring this message to other domains.

We are now finished. Once we leave this screen, the filter automatically is saved, and Eudora begins to use it whenever incoming messages are received.

Automatic Replies

There is another method to set up automatic replies for dealing with receiving messages, and these go under the common name of email autoresponders. You can build them yourself, if you have access to a UNIX system. You can also make use of the services offered by your ISP or purchase specialized software for the autoresponder tasks.

In the case of UNIX systems, most run a program called sendmail that is responsible for relaying messages and delivering messages locally. When sendmail is ready to deliver a message to you, it looks for a file called .forward in your home directory. If this file contains email addresses, your messages are relayed to those addresses, rather than being delivered to your mailbox. But, if the file contains a UNIX command, then the incoming message is passed to that program for processing. Typically, the program is used to filter messages before doing local delivery. The most commonly used UNIX program for this purpose is called procmail, which provides the same functionality that we've already seen for Windows-based products, albeit without the graphical user interface (GUI).[15]

As an example, let's look at one ISP, MindSpring, and show you how it is done. Every user at MindSpring has the ability to perform two special automatic operations on all of his or her email: the user can forward email to another location (including any location accessible via the Internet) or send an automatic reply (such as when the user goes on vacation). To enable either option, you first go to MindSpring's Web page and click on Manage Account. You'll next select one of the options on the left-hand side of the screen. You'll then get another Web page where you enter your user name and password, and choose either the forwarding or vacation option in the list box.

Let's say you pick the forwarding option. Now you'll get an instructions screen, as shown below. At this point, you simply enter the forwarding email address. Click on the enable box below the instructions, and you should get a confirmation message that the forwarding has been enabled, as shown in Figure 5.12.

Step One:

Enter the email address to which you wish to have your mail forwarded:

put the email address you wish to have your mail forwarded to in the box below. (Example: mailboxname@mindspring.com).

DO NOT INCLUDE INSTRUCTIONS (Example: Please forward all mail from user@mindspring.com to user@aol.com) as this will forward your mail to:

Please@mindspring.com
forward@mindspring.com
all@mindspring.com
mail@mindspring.com
from@mindspring.com
user@mindspring.com
to@mindspring.com

as well as to the email address you really want it to be forwarded to:
user@aol.com.

```
david@strom.com
```

Figure 5.12   MindSpring forwarding option

But you may not have the ability to build your own, and you might want more flexibility that the simple "out of the office" or forwarding options provided by your ISP. In that case, you might want to look at the specialized software tools for autoresponders.

Some products, like Mailback (*www2.databack.com/mailback*), charge you a monthly fee that starts at $6 and goes up depending on the kind of services and the number of mailboxes. These services add your autoresponder name to their own domain name and maintain the configuration on their own mail server. The advantage here is that you don't have to maintain your own continuous connection to the Internet, but the downside is that you don't have as professional an appearance by having the autoresponder come from your own domain. Others, such as RSVP ($49), install on your Windows desktop and make use of your own email accounts and servers. The downside is that you'll need to install this on a machine that has continuous access to the Internet, and if you are hosting your domain at your ISP, the provider might not be willing to run the software for you.

There are many other products in this marketplace: We recommend you first check Yahoo under "autoresponders" and visit the various vendors' Web sites listed there for more information.[16]

Using Other Software to Read Your Email

As we said earlier, these adjustments are all relatively simple and don't require any new software to improve your remote access of email. But these aren't the only weapons at our disposal. You can make use of several other products and services as well. Let's talk about how you can use a browser and a character-mode email product when you are on the road.

Why would you want to do this? The Web is useful in those situations where you find yourself without your email software and need to check messages. For example, if you travel without a laptop or are visiting a colleague's office and don't want to have to reconfigure his or her own desktop software to read your mail. Or you might want to check your mail when you have a few minutes in between flights at a public terminal at an airport.

One of us has been using cybercafes and public terminals for checking email for years. Cybercafes can be very cost effective, since they offer better bandwidth at very reasonable prices. Many cafes have high-speed connections to the Internet, better than you would usually get using a 33-kilobits-per-second modem in your hotel room. And their charges typically are under $10 per hour of access, which is much less than most hotels charge even for local phone calls of any duration.[17]

You may not have to use a cybercafe or a library. The latest innovation in hotel connectivity is to provide direct Internet access, sometimes complete with an in-room computer. Sheraton has begun experimenting with direct access in a few of its hotels, including its Sydney Australia and Orlando properties. And the small chain managed by the Kimpton Group, including the Hotel Vintage Park in Seattle, began installing wireless laptops in all of its rooms. The laptops are connected to the hotel's Internet provider.

There are several products that you can use, depending on your circumstances. A good first choice is to use the built-in email software that comes as part of the browser package itself, such as Messenger. You can set up these products to download your messages, but keep copies on the server so you can later retrieve them when you return back home or to your office. If you do decide to borrow someone's machine and set up Messenger in this fashion, remember to remove this information before leaving the machine. We had a situation where we forgot to erase our user information after borrowing a friend's computer. When the friend tried to send email from Netscape, it went out under our identity!

A disadvantage with using some cybercafes and libraries is that they have turned off many of the configuration options mentioned here. For example, at one cybercafe we use in Palo Alto, you can only download copies of your messages, and you can't gain direct access to anything on the local hard disk.

There are other alternatives that don't involve setting up any software on a borrowed machine. They operate inside the browser window itself and connect to a special service via the Internet. Which one you use will depend on different circumstances.

If you need your own email account, separate from one that you maintain at work or at home, check out one of the several free email services available (searching Yahoo for "Free Email" will uncover more than a dozen). You don't need to subscribe or pay a fee to make use of these services. You simply go to the Web page and enter your mail server location, and your user name and password. A few of these vendors, such as RocketMail (*www.rocketmail.com*) and Hotmail (*www.hot mail.com*), offer email accounts that don't require any special client software. You merely connect to their sites with your Web browser, enter your user name and password, and proceed to your email activities.

If you don't need your own account, and your mail server is running POP and SMTP, then you can use either ReadMail (*www.readmail.com*) or MailStart (*www.mailstart.com*). Point your browser to either site, type in your email ID and password, and in a few seconds these sites will retrieve your mail from your server. You can delete, reply and save this mail just as you would any other POP account—the only difference is that these actions happen inside the browser's frame.

ReadMail has the better interface, and with both services you can leave your email on your server so you can download it to your desktop when you later return to the office. Both claim not to store any identifying information, such as your password, but it is also a good idea to clear the cache and exit the browser if you are accessing these systems on a shared or public machine.

Another service you also might want to check into is from e-Now (*www.enow.com*). You set up an account with the company and hear your email being read to you via a phone call. Call 1-888-HEAR-E-NOW for a demo.

A warning: Some of these services don't work if your SMTP server is behind a firewall, or if your ISP has turned off the ability to get mail from outside its network. And if you aren't using an Internet-based mail system, you are almost out of luck unless you can make use of a Web-based gateway to your LAN email system. cc:Mail, among other LAN-based email systems such as Novell's GroupWise and Microsoft Exchange, have such gateways. It takes your mailbox and converts the messages to HTML, which you then can view in your browser. The gateway runs on a separate machine alongside the cc:Mail post office and routers, and typically is installed on the same machine as your Web server.

Using these services has the advantage of not having to learn any new software—you just use your browser. But Web access isn't always a time-saver. Often it will take you longer to navigate around your inbox via a Web browser than just downloading the messages normally via your existing email software. That is because there is a limited number of screen navigation features available within most browsers: The browser is set up to move from page to page, not necessarily from message to message.

There are some caveats here. If you decide to use these services on the road, remember to clear your browser's cache and exit the program before leaving the computer. This is important when you are sharing a public machine, as some of these services can save your user information in memory, making it easy for the next person who uses this shared machine to gain access to your account.

If you do use these services, you might worry about compromising the security of your mailbox, since your password and user name are transmitted in clear text across the Internet. Of course, your user name and password for POP or IMAP mail are usually transmitted in clear text across the Internet even when you check your mail with your ordinary email software, so this may not be of much concern.

One of the strengths of Internet messaging is its flexibility. For example, you can even find implementations of POP and IMAP for handheld computing devices such as the 3Com PalmPilot. It is a glorious tribute to Internet technology that even a minimal IMAP client can be hosted on a device with such minimal resources.

There are other products for 100% pure Internet email systems that perform the same function. For example, Infinite Technologies' Inter-

Change runs on a Windows95 or NT machine and can act as a Web gateway from your email system. Strom uses this in conjunction with a special digital cell phone to read his email on the road.[18]

There is another strategy for remote users that also doesn't involve any installation of new software, and that is using terminal emulation and character-based email software such as Pine or Elm to read your mail. In this scenario, you would run a Telnet session and connect to your mail server over the Internet. Since Telnet comes included with Windows95 and most other modern desktop operating systems, you don't need to know anything other than the name of your mail server to connect to it. You'll also need to install the mail software on your server, and in most cases this is already done.

IMAP

We have discussed changes to your email software to make receiving mail easier. But there is another alternative—make changes on the server side. Instead of using POP mail servers to send your mail, you can replace them with IMAP servers.

As we mentioned in our earlier section on standards, IMAP provides for more control over your mailbox, especially for remote users. You can have specific disk quotas for each user's messages. And you can download just the header information rather than the entire message, which is helpful when traveling.

IMAP messages are stored on both the server and the local PC on which you are running your email software. This means that you can download some of your messages to your work machine, and then go home and download other messages to your home machine. With a POP mail account, you don't have this freedom. You either download all of your messages and remove them from the server, or keep them there, as we mentioned earlier in our section on keeping copies.

This also means that you can keep your messages on your server and have another person, such as your administrative assistant, download them, provided your assistant knows your email password. Netscape claims it will support the ability to delegate folders to be shared among several people, although we haven't seen this demonstrated yet.

Of course, just having the server isn't enough. You also need email software that can connect to the IMAP server. The latest versions of Messenger, Eudora and Outlook Express all support IMAP connections. Let's look at how these products work, since each is set up slightly differently.

With Eudora, the only real difference with IMAP is checking the IMAP button on the Tools | Options | Incoming Mail configuration screen. Once you check this button, the screen changes to what you see in Figure 5.13.

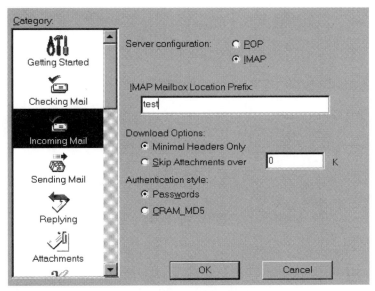

Figure 5.13   Eudora incoming mail options

Depending on where your personal mailboxes are located, you may also need to specify this location in this configuration screen. You can also choose to download just your email headers (which is the default) and whether you wish to skip attachments over a certain size. You can choose to download the entire message as a default as well.

IMAP messages are stored on the server as well as the client, and with Eudora you have to do two things to delete your message in both places. First, you have to mark the message for deletion in your mailbox. You can use the menus, type Control-D, or use the Delete key as you would with your POP messages. Then you need to go to Message | Remote Deleted Messages. This removes them from both places.

If you download selected messages to different machines, you probably will need to reorganize your messages. Eudora has additional commands to resynchronize your local mailbox with your IMAP server, and also to refresh your mailbox list. These can be found by going to your Mailbox window pane on the left-hand side of the screen, right-clicking with your mouse on one of your mailboxes and choosing the appropriate command.

With Messenger, you'll go to the Edit | Preferences | Mail | Mail Server screen, as shown in Figure 5.14. Once there, you'll check either POP3 or IMAP box. With IMAP, you have three choices. You can move deleted messages into the trash, you can connect to a server running a Secure Sockets Layer encryption scheme and you can set up new folders to download your messages. You need to click on the More Options button and type in the location of your IMAP mail directory.

Figure 5.14   **Messenger server choices**

Outlook Express has yet another twist on IMAP. To set up a new email server connection, you run the wizard (shown in Figure 5.15) at Tools | Accounts | Add | Mail. You specify the name of the server and pull down the IMAP choice for server type, as shown in the screen below. If you change your mind and want to switch your email server back to POP, you first have to delete this account and start over again with the wizard.

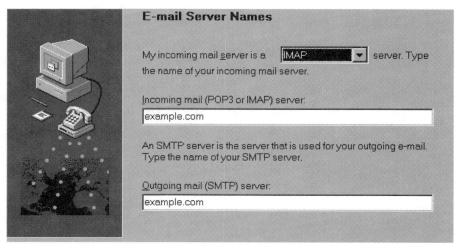

Figure 5.15   Outlook Express account wizard

But we have just touched the surface in our discussion of IMAP clients and servers. The trade publication *InfoWorld* did some extensive testing of several IMAP products and found that getting them set up and working together wasn't quite so easy. Some servers weren't compatible with some clients, and some combinations (such as Eudora with GroupWise) didn't work at all. The article ends by saying:

> IMAP4 remains a work in progress and, for the time being, many of these features remain only as promises. IMAP4 is certainly not a dismal failure, however, and there are some client/server combinations that work well. But if you want to deploy an IMAP4 server and plan to leave client choices up to your users, you can definitely expect less compatibility than with POP3-based clients.

We are still a long way off from seeing this protocol work as well as POP.[19]

VPN: Securing Your Messages[20]

So far, we have looked at products that help you get access to your email when you are on the road. As we mentioned earlier, access is only part of the problem. You must also prove that you are who you say you are—a process known as authentication.

All email systems require some form of authentication before they will deliver your messages to you. If you are using a 100% pure Internet email system, this authentication consists of a user name and a password that is sent from the mail client to the mail server. This information isn't encrypted: Anyone who is listening to your conversation using a packet sniffer can grab this if they are clever enough and lucky enough to capture it when you log in to your email system. Furthermore, email messages that you send or receive can also be sniffed if some form of encryption is not used to protect your privacy.

As corporations have become more dependent on their email systems, many feel sending email user login and message information "in the clear" is no longer adequate. Thus, virtual private networks were born. VPNs protect not only email transactions, but any network transaction that must be secured. There are several basic methods to implement VPNs:

- You can make use of VPN services provided by a commercial ISP[21] that will outsource your entire corporate network backbone.
- You can use VPN products to deploy private workgroups using LAN-to-LAN connections and offer Intranet services to a selected

series of authorized hosts—for example, allowing accounting to securely access payroll data without requiring a physically separate accounting LAN.

- You can implement a very low-cost, secure, remote dial access by using the public Internet as a means of connecting telecommuters and road warriors to the corporate Intranet, forming a virtual private dial network (VPDN). The same VPN technology can also be deployed to provide business partners and customers with economical access to Extranet services.

In each case, some form of VPN technology can be used to provide network-to-network, host-to-network or host-to-host through the use of secure tunnels—virtual point-to-point connections that offer authentication, encryption and access control between tunnel endpoints. Tunnels are supported by special software and perhaps hardware on both your own machine and that of various network servers, including email. These VPN products encrypt the conversation between the email client and server, so that someone listening in can't read the captured information easily.

There are several ways to implement a VPN. You could add special VPN hardware to your network. You could create a VPN entirely with software. You could augment your existing firewalls with special VPN capabilities. There are advantages and disadvantages to all of these methods. Here is a table that lists some of the VPN products available today.[22]

VPN Products

Company, Product Name	URL	Type of Product
Extended Systems ExtendNet VPN	www.extendsys.com/products/vpn/	VPN hardware
VPNet VSU-1010	www.vpnet.com/	VPN hardware
Fortress Technologies NetFortress VPN-1	www.fortresstech.com/index2.html	VPN hardware
Compatible Systems IntraPortl	www.compatible.com/vpn/intraport.htm	VPN hardware
RedCreek Ravlin	www.redcreek.com/products/rav10.html	VPN-enabled router

VPN Products (Continued)

Company, Product Name	URL	Type of Product
Timestep PERMIT Enterprise	www.timestep.com/products/ index.htm	VPN-enabled router
New Oak NOC 2000	www.newoak.com/solutions/ index.html	VPN remote access server hardware
RAScom RAServer 2000	www.rascom.com/home.html	VPN remote access server hardware
Microsoft Windows NT	www.microsoft.com	VPN remote access PPTP software
Aventail VPN	www.aventail.com/products.html	VPN gateway software
InfoExpress VTCP	www.infoexpress.com/vsec/von.htm	VPN gateway software
V-ONE SmartGate	www.v-one.com	VPN gateway software
Isolation Systems InfoCrypt Server NT	www.infocrypt.com	VPN gateway software
AXENT OmniGuard/PowerVPN	www.axent.com/product/vpn/ vpn.htm	VPN gateway software
Trusted Information Systems Gauntlet GVPN	www.tis.com/prodserv/gauntlet/vpn/ index.html	VPN-enabled firewall
CheckPoint FireWall-1	www.checkpoint.com/products/fire- wall-1/ descriptions/products.html	VPN-enabled firewall
Raptor Eagle Firewall	www.raptor.com/products/ datasheets/prodsheet.html	VPN-enabled firewall

To design your VPN, you'll need to carefully understand your network architecture and make sure you have all of your local networks behind some combination of firewall, screening router and VPN server. If not, then machines inside your network won't be protected and will be available to anyone with an Internet connection. You'll also want to pick a VPN server that can grow and handle the increased traffic. VPN servers require lots of RAM and a fast processor. You won't want to be stuck with something without enough horsepower when you begin to add mobile users, especially as they use the VPN for more of their network access.

These general issues aside, you also need to decide which of the various VPN implementation alternatives you wish to pursue. Let's take a look at some of the tradeoffs that should be considered.

Difficulty of Deployment: Layer 2 VPN products require access server upgrades, both at the corporate WAN access router and at your ISP. PPTP is already present in Windows NT and Windows95 desktops, but offers no solution for UNIX and other non-Microsoft operating systems. Layer 3 VPN products do not require ISP infrastructure upgrades, but may involve deployment of client software to every desktop. For this reason, take a good look at VPN vendor management tools for software download, network address assignment, key management and user administration. If you already have a firewall, check out add-on VPN products from your firewall vendor. Consider multiprotocol requirements—IPsec can only tunnel over IP, so you'll need another solution if you must tunnel over other protocols such as IPX. And don't forget network addressing—some VPN products permit use of private addresses, while others require public IP addresses.

Flexibility: PPTP supports only one of many payload encryption algorithms; IPsec is encryption algorithm-agnostic; products operating at higher layers may rely upon lower-layer encryption features. Review your corporate security policy before shopping for a VPN product, identify your algorithm requirements and don't forget to consider government restrictions on cryptography (a hurdle for global VPNs). It may be far more difficult to isolate your topology requirements. Expensive VPN products may support several methods of tunneling to enable flexible deployment in response to changing requirements, but how much flexibility are you willing to pay for? The best VPN product to provide low-cost telecommuter access may not be the right product for secure LAN-to-LAN or backbone connectivity.

Scalability: Despite vendor claims to the contrary, by its very nature, VPN technology introduces delay and reduces throughput. Obviously, VPN products are engineered to minimize the performance impact of authentication and encryption—for example, by using outboard cards to perform encryption without hogging the primary processor. VPN product prices vary widely in terms of throughput and number of concurrent tunnels supported. For example, the NetFortress claims 7 megabits per second and 44 megabits per second for its VPN-1 and VPN-3 products, respectively, with a maximum of 1,024 clients. It is common to price

VPN products based on the number of purchased client licenses. Remember this when estimating future costs.

Transparency and Ease-of-Use: VPN solutions only provide security if they're used! Products that require user intervention at the desktop are more likely to be subverted, even unintentionally, than VPN products that do their stuff transparently from the end-user perspective. Are specialized drivers, stacks or configuration required on the desktop? Will your VPN solution interfere with connectivity outside the VPN? For example, while layer 2 tunnels require exclusive use of a dial connection, the Compatible Systems IntraPort offers simultaneous tunneled access to VPN destinations and nontunneled access to the rest of the Internet.

By now, it should be clear—if you don't have any IP experience—that this isn't the place to start learning. Designing and deploying a VPN really is for experienced network planners and administrators.[23]

Providing Customer Support

While VPNs have received a great deal of interest lately, they aren't the only emerging market. We have also seen a great deal of activity and products surrounding using email to provide technical and customer support.

Just trying to sort out the issues surrounding support is tough enough, as we described earlier in this chapter. But before you go out and purchase anything new, consider your corporate policies for dealing with incoming email.

The biggest advantage cited by email advocates is how email can flatten corporate hierarchies and enable fast communications. But that can be a big disadvantage if there aren't any guidelines on how to respond to messages, particularly messages from paying customers.

First, does your corporation have any email guidelines in terms of usage, behavior and appropriate conduct? While you don't have to put everything down on paper, having some sort of guidelines is useful. And it helps to have the motivation to produce the guidelines because of looming customer support issues.

Second, is everyone in the corporation required to have at least one email identity? If not, what happens to those that don't? If you are going to support your customers, you first have to make sure that you'll be able to contact the appropriate person inside your organization.

A corporate email policy comes in very handy when more than one person shares a single email box, or if a program rather than an actual person answers the mailbox. It should deal with who is responsible for answering queries to this mailbox, as an example.

Your corporate email policy should extend beyond just mere usage of email. It should also specify how email addresses are published both internally and externally. We recommend that email addresses should be included on everyone's business cards and on corporate letterhead. And there should be various email addresses on a corporate Web site.[24]

We are constantly surprised and frustrated at the number of Web sites we visit that don't contain any email references. It is a sloppy practice, and we hope the maturing of the Web will change this for the better.

Specifically, you should match email addresses on your Web pages with the responsible person or department dealing with that content. If you are ordering something, then put the email address of the person who would normally handle inquiries about orders on that Web page. If you are designing a page that has press releases and investor information on your company, it should contain the email address of someone in your public relations department. This isn't difficult, just time consuming, since you will have to update these addresses as your staff changes.

One way around this updating effort is to create a series of email aliases and link them to particular people who will be responsible for receiving the messages. For example, you could have *info@example.com* for general inquiries, *corporate@example.com* for corporate inquiries, *support@example.com* for customer support issues, and so forth. Again, this should be spelled out in your email guidelines document.

Once you have your policies in place, it is then time to tackle the support issue. You can either build your own, using a series of scripts and programs, or buy something off the shelf. If you decide to buy a product, you'll have two different types: one that offers a turnkey solution, using packaged software that you need to install on your own network and work in conjunction with your existing email servers; and the other is more of a service than an actual product—what you are buying here is some very expensive consulting time.

Regardless of which route you take, we recommend that any customer support system should have the following three features.

First, it should automatically generate an immediate reply, acknowledging receipt of the message and taking ownership of the problem. This is handy because it reassures the customer that his query is being handled, and it puts a personal identity behind a faceless email box. We all like to know with whom we are dealing, especially when we have a problem with a vendor's product.

Second, it should work with your existing email system. Your users shouldn't have to run anything special to answer messages.

Third, it should track the messages sent to the system and produce reports on how many inquiries and what is the status of the corresponding responses. This is useful so you can monitor the operations of your support system.

The turnkey products and outsourced services come in various shapes and prices, ranging from $100 to more than $95,000. What you buy depends on your needs and how you address the questions mentioned earlier in the chapter. Here is a table with links to these products and services.[25]

Email Management Software

Company, Product Name	URL	Platform, Price
Select Response v2.0	www.aptex.com/products-select-response-facts.htm	NT, UNIX pricing varies
Brightware BrightResponse v 1.0	www.brightware.com	NT, $95,000
Mustang Software Web Essentials Internet Message Center v. 1.0	www.mustang.com/Products/WE/Default.asp	95 or NT, $1499
ErgoTech WebLeader E-Mailroom v 1.0	www.ergo-tech.com	NT, $100 Domino servers on either OS/2 or NT, $100
GFI Emailrobot for Exchange/SMTP	www.emailrobot.com	NT and 95, $349 and up
Adante v 1.0	www.adante.com/adante	NT, $35,000
Millennium Cybernetics EchoMail v. 1.0	www.interactive.com	NT, UNIX, pricing varies
MATRIXX CybeResponse E-Mail Management	www.matrixx.com/intserv/e-mail/e-mail.htm	Outsourced services
KANA Communications KANA CMS	www.kana.com	Outsourced services
Inference CasePoint WebServer	www.inference.com	Outsourced services
Castelle InfoPress Email-On-Demand	www.castelle.com/products	NT, $995

Let's examine how you would install one of these products from Mustang Software. You can download a free trial version of the product from the company's Web site (address above). The trial version works for 30 days.

Mustang's Web Essentials' Internet Message Center (IMC) processes incoming Internet email addressed to special mailboxes, such as *sales@example.com* and *support@example.com*, and provides an easy way to monitor and track customer messages and staff responses. IMC takes the place of aliases, rules and autoresponders that attempt to parse and forward incoming email. It allows immediate and automatic acknowledgment of each message received. It also provides a tracking number that customers can use for continued inquiries, and managers can use for monitoring and quality control.

Messages are distributed to "Pools" consisting of a group of "Agents," rather than to specific individuals. Agents log into the message pool, where each incoming message is forwarded to the next available agent, in much the same way as a telephone call center distributes incoming calls.

IMC prevents business-related email from being lost or delayed when staff call in sick or go on vacation, and protects the privacy of individuals' personal email. Optional features include filtering of return addresses so that only messages from a predefined list of customers will be accepted. Agents can work on or off site by running the IMC Agent tool to access message pools directly or through any POP3-compatible email client.

The software comes in several separate modules that need to be installed on your computer. There is the IMC Setup program, used to define agents, email accounts, status messages and templates. There is the IMC Service program, which works in conjunction with your existing SMTP/POP3 email server to process incoming and outgoing email messages. And there is the IMC Monitor program, which is used to administer the overall software. All of these programs can be run on the same computer. IMC Agent is a separate program that is the user portion of the software—this is what you'll run to review the incoming messages and compose your responses.

The server and user portions of IMC are all Windows-based. For the server, you'll need a fast Pentium PC with 48 megabytes of RAM, running either Windows95 or NT. You'll also need an Internet email server already set up. The IMC Agent runs on either Windows platform, or via a Web browser if you install a Web server on the same machine that runs the IMC Server.

The way IMC works is that you add the special email boxes to your existing email server. These should be new identities that aren't used by any actual person, otherwise email won't flow into the IMC system. Then you link these boxes to the IMC server, so that the IMC Agents will respond to this email.

How does a message get from a customer to an agent's mailbox?[26] Let's take a detailed look at what happens when a customer sends a message to the Example Corporation to inquire about technical support for his new Example Widget.

1. Customer Joe Pepsi sends a message to *support@example.com* with a subject of Help with Widget installation.

2. Example Corp.'s Internet email server receives and holds the message until IMC logs on as *support@example.com* and requests this message, in the same way as any other user would log on to request his or her mail.

3. Example Corp.'s IMC software connects to the mail server as *support@example.com* and retrieves all the mail addressed to this user name. It then assigns each new message a unique tracking number and records the messages into its own database. By scanning keywords in the SUBJECT: field, IMC can direct messages to a specific pool. In this example, it could be Support-Widgets, the pool designed to handle support questions for Example Corp.'s Widgets. This is useful because a company that has individuals trained as specialists in specific areas can break the messages down to some degree without having to provide a separate email address for each different support topic.

4. IMC immediately sends an acknowledgment email message back to Joe Pepsi using a customized form letter template. This template lets the customer know that his message was received by Example, discusses average response times and details Example Corp.'s hours of operation. The templates for Example Corp.'s support pools also include information such as how to access online knowledge bases, voice technical support options and costs, and newsgroup locations. The goal is to try to answer 25% of the most commonly asked questions in the template. For instance, Example Corp.'s *investors@example.com* pool might contain a link to its annual report and the *sales@example.com*

pool might explain how to get additional product literature online as well as online ordering options.

5. Kelly Jones, a support technician at Example, runs a small Windows program called IMC Agent. Jones clicks the "Get Next Message" button in the IMC Agent and the following chain of events occurs:

   a) IMC Agent tells the IMC server that agent Kelly Jones is ready for a new message from the pool (or pools) to which he is assigned. In this example, let's assume the next message is the one sent by Joe Pepsi.

   b) IMC changes the TO: field of the message to the agent's email address, *kelly.jones@example.com*, and changes the FROM: field to *Replies-Support-Widgets@example.com*.

   c) IMC Agent notifies Jones that the IMC server is sending a new message, and the server emails the message to Jones.

6. Kelly Jones receives the message using an Internet email product such as Microsoft Outlook Express or Eudora. The header of agent Kelly's email message looks like this:

   Sender : "Joe Pepsi" <joe.pepsi@mustang.com>
   Tracking Number : EDT2007199700000020
   Pool : Support-Widgets

7. This gives agent Kelly the sender's name, tracking number and the name of the message pool where the message resides. Jones answers Joe Pepsi's message, sending the reply back to Internet Message Center. In this case, the messages are sent back to *Replies-Support-Widgets@example.com*. Agent Kelly is careful not to change the tracking number in the subject file.

8. Once IMC receives the message from Jones, it looks up the tracking number, files the reply in its own database and forwards the reply to Joe Pepsi. By using this method of delivery, supervisors have a complete record and copy of every message coming in and out of a company message pool. If a customer never receives his or her response, due to an Internet failure or problem on the customer's end, it is easy to retrieve the original response and send it again, saving time.

FUTURES

Receiving mail in the enterprise is probably going to be a lot easier in the near future. There are two reasons for this: Remote connectivity to the enterprise network will become a lot easier, and access to mailboxes will, one way or another, become ubiquitous.

Remote Enterprise Networking

The VPN product landscape and supporting technologies are changing rapidly. High on the "wish list" for VPN product enhancements are improved multivendor interoperability, solutions for key management and distribution, and tools needed to administer this brave new world of virtual networks. L2TP and IPsec standards should stabilize within the coming year, bringing with them a new wave of VPN products. It remains to be seen, however, whether any two vendors' products will be able to work together, implementing the same standard.

Mailbox Access

It is difficult to predict which protocol will dominate in the area of mailbox access. There are two contenders: IMAP and the Web. As mentioned earlier in this chapter, IMAP provides flexible access to a collection of mailboxes, allowing a client to offload many of its functions to the message store. Interestingly enough, a Web-based interface to a mailbox can provide similar functionality with respect to remote access.

The key issue here is one of ease of configuration and use. In the case of IMAP, a client can be configured to know about multiple servers, each having one or more mailboxes. In the case of a Web-based mail reader, it can be configured to receive messages from multiple addresses to provide the same multi-mailbox paradigm. For example, a Web server could periodically poll different mailboxes (using either POP or IMAP) in order to provide a unified interface to the user. Several Web-based messaging services offer this now, in addition to the usual "here's an email address, go to this URL to read messages."

In the case of IMAP, messages may reside at the client or server, or both. In the case of the Web-based approach, messages always reside at the Web server. Either solves one part of the decentralized operations problem: Users can employ multiple computers from which to access their messages. The other part of the decentralized operations problem, allowing responsibility for the messages to be split between the client and server, is solved by IMAP, but not by the Web-based approach. That is, while IMAP implements both a decentralized message store and decentralized service, the Web-based approach implements a decentralized service by using a centralized message store. We find this rather clever.

So, our second prediction is that one of two things will happen: Either the market will enforce adult supervision on the process whereby IMAP technology is specified, standardized, productized and provisioned; or a huge opportunity will open up for Web-based email readers. Rather than just being the bailiwick of a few service providers, we'll start to see turnkey commercial products that enterprises can use. As noted in the closing of Chapter 2, companies that provide a mailbox concentration service are well positioned to offer these facilities.

Endnotes

1. One can reasonably argue that it makes no sense to encrypt messages retrieved from the mailbox service: If privacy is an issue, then the originator should have encrypted the messages prior to sending them. This illustrates the importance of end-to-end encryption: If encrypted by the originator, then using hop-by-hop encryption at any point of the message's transit is superfluous.

2. CompuServe is a close second in terms of number of cities served with local access numbers, although it really depends on the country and specific city involved. CompuServe does a far better job than IBM in terms of tools to use for searching for local phone numbers. You can search its Web site, call an interactive phone system, key in your local phone area code and inquire using the WinCIM product itself for the latest phone numbers.

3. This is slowly changing, as we'll discuss in our upcoming section on solutions. Some hotels have begun to offer high-speed Internet access, wiring their rooms with Ethernet cabling that any traveler can connect into (for a fee or not, depending on the chain).

4. September 22, 1997, p. 38 "Info@company.com Overload," by Paul McNamara. The article can be found at the publication's Web site, *www.nwfusion.com.*

5. September 15, 1997, p. 96 "Operators Are Standing Down," by Steve Ulfelder. The article, along with the results from their test queries, can be found at the publication's Web site, *www.computerworld.com.*

6. There is a lot of room for improvement, even in "the industry." The manufacturer of Rose's PC has a Web/email customer support system. Rose submitted a simple question about how to turn down the volume of his internal modem, got an automated reply acknowledging his email, and, several weeks later, has yet to receive any other response.

7. Actually, this is too easygoing. It is reasonable to expect a response during normal business hours. If you submit something at 3 a.m., then expect a response sometime later the next business morning. But if you submit something at 10 a.m. on a weekday, a response had better be returned by close of business that day.

8. In the interests of disclosure, one of the authors of this book is also the author of POP. Having said that, the treatment of both protocols in this book is ruthlessly brutal.

9. Before any readers cry "Foul!" because one of the authors wrote POP, remember what the real point here is: complexity costs. Sometimes the cost of the solution outweighs the cost of the problem. Besides, we're not even counting the deprecated work on IMSP or the newer ACAP standards in the count of IMAP-related standards. And the proof is in the products that implement IMAP: They are far from completely interoperable because of different and subtle interpretations to these standards.

10. In the IMAP framework, there are three models: offline, online and disconnected. Although one can cut the pie into three pieces, it is conceptually easier to consider the issue one of where message processing occurs: either in one environment (the centralized model supported by POP) or potentially in many environments.

11. This material is based on the report "VPNs: Virtually Anything?" by Lisa Phifer of Core Competence, available online at *www.corecom.com/html/vpn.html*.

12. More information on this protocol can be found at *www.microsoft.com/ntserver/ support/pptpfaq.asp*.

13. Note, however, that the administrator of your POP server might implement limits with respect to how much space can be taken up by your mailbox, or how long these copies can reside on your server!

14. Our thanks to Paul Hoffman for providing these examples.

15. More details on how to set up these command files, along with lots of helpful hints and plenty of references to other specialized software products to handle mailing lists, can be found in Chapter 15 of *Poor Richard's Web Site*, by Peter Kent, Top Floor Publishing, 1998.

16. There are many such vendors besides those listed on Yahoo. Go to *www.makura.com/auto/ autocomp.html* and see the descriptions of four different types of autoresponder products. They are: **one-to-one**, which allows a user to send a blank email message to a unique email address; **server**, where a user sends an email message to a non-unique email address; **web page links**, where a user selects a button on a Web page; and **dual response**, where a user receives an automatic follow-up message.

17. A good place to search for cybercafes is Ernst Larsen's Internet cafe guide at *www.netcafeguide.com/cafeindex.htm*.

18. More information on InterChange can be found at *www.ihub.com/products/interchange*. The cell phone makes use of AT&T's PocketNet services. For more information, see *www.attws.com/nohost/data/pocketnet*.

19. The article was written by Jeff Symoens and is entitled "IMAP4 Products Renege on Interoperability Protocol's Promises," and ran in the March 2, 1998, issue. You can check the publication's Web site at *www.inforworld.com* for more information.

20. This material is based on the report "VPNs: Virtually Anything?" by Lisa Phifer of Core Competence. Her report and links to the specific products mentioned here are available online at *www.corecom.com/html/vpn.html*.

21. For information about VPN services that commercial providers offer, we suggest visiting GTE/BBN at *www.bbn.com/products/security/sitepat.htm*; AT&T WorldNet at *www.att.com/worldnet/wmis/virtual.html*; and PSI at *www.psi.net/ intranet*.

22. Updated information to this table is available online at *www.corecom.com/html/vpn.html.*

23. For more information on selecting VPN products, we recommend *Virtual Private Networks*, by Charlie Scott (O'Reilly, 1998), and "Fortifying Your Firewall: Six Products That Reinforce Network Security," an article in the Feb. 15, 1997, issue of *Network Computing* magazine. Many VPN product reviews are also available on Core Competence's Web site at *www.corecom.com/html/technology_corner* and *Network Computing*'s Web site at *www.networkcomputing.com.*

24. In Chapter 2, we told you to remove any email references on your Web pages. This isn't contradictory advice: There the suggestion was to help eliminate spam messages. Here, we are talking in the context of helping your customers get in touch with you, and in any case the email identity you list on your Web site can be processed by a program and not necessarily a human. You can then set up the program to eliminate any unwanted spam.

25. We will have updated information to this table available on our Web site.

26. This information is from the IMC software documentation.

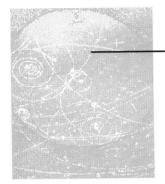

6

Messaging in the Enterprise: Sending

In this chapter, we consider two central issues of sending email throughout the enterprise: how to determine email addresses and how to integrate messaging with other telephony-based applications.

These two topics provide a good exposition of the power of email in the enterprise: First, they demonstrate the usefulness of integrating messaging with enterprise directories; and, second, they show how messaging can be integrated with other parts of an enterprise's communications infrastructure.

INTRODUCTION

To begin, let us consider an important point from Chapter 4: The mapping between real-world identities and email identities is a matter of convention.

Just as the Internet messaging infrastructure makes it easy for us to obtain multiple identities for various purposes, the lack of strong bindings becomes a burden when trying to contact someone for the first time via email.[1]

During the Internet's infancy, one could typically guess as to the correct mapping. For example, if the name of the company was "IBM," then it's domain name was probably ibm.com. Of course, "IBM" is an acronym for "International Business Machines," so another alternative might be some variation of "international-business-machines.com." (Fortunately, this particular company was an early entrant into the Internet, and registered its famous three-letter acronym as a domain name.) Continuing this example, if we were trying to locate someone named "Marshall Rose" at a given domain, we might try a variation of "mrose" or "marshall.rose."

The point of these two examples should be clear: There is sufficient flexibility in Internet messaging protocols and conventions, both with the naming of domains and mailboxes, that guessing, per se, isn't a particularly scalable solution. Furthermore, an important issue arises in these examples in that names and addresses have largely become indistinguishable. The Internet messaging infrastructure uses email addresses to deliver messages, but the users of that infrastructure treat addresses as names for the purpose of identifying other users.

This has led to the introduction of directory services that augment, but are largely independent of, Internet messaging. Although there have been several attempts to specify and provision an Internet-wide directory service, no such attempt has succeeded. The Internet community may be able to agree on a common infrastructure for many things, but directory service is not one of them.

Instead, there are numerous Internet directories, each having a different scope, and possibly competing, or perhaps differing, constituencies. In response, there has been some work in developing so-called metadirectories to provide a unifying interface. These, as we shall see, have met with only limited success.

Integrating the enterprise directory with messaging is an important challenge, but there are other enterprise resources that could also benefit from integrated messaging. For our purposes, let us consider paging and facsimile.

Both of these can be seen as early predecessors of electronic messaging. Despite some attempts to evolve, they remain simplex conduits for glyph-based messaging.[2] Having said that, there is a tremendous legacy investment in such systems, and, to a large extent, this drives significant usage of their corresponding infrastructures.

Fortunately, just as we have seen in Chapter 2 how application gateways can be used to connect different email systems, we can apply the same technological approach to achieve integrated messaging. Regrettably, the way is not entirely straightforward. First, there are many possible ways to construct the mappings between the two styles of messaging. Although addressing is a key concern, so also is the issue of content conversion. In addition, sometimes there may be duplex communications possible.

Finally, the largest practical concern is that existing email interfaces to these services tend to be highly proprietary and heavily legacy in nature. For our purposes, this means having to make do with suboptimal solutions simply because it isn't possible to make changes in the interface to the paging or facsimile networks.

So, let us now consider these issues in greater detail, along with aspects of the systems that cause them.

PROBLEMS

When it comes to finding someone's address in the physical world, we take a great many of the tools we use for granted. We keep files of printed business cards that may or may not be stored in some organized fashion. We look through printed phone directories, which we may or may not have handy. We have our own Rolodex and contact lists, which may be a combination of printed and electronic sources. We have the always-available directory services of various local, long distance and international phone companies, which may be able to provide a phone number but not any postal address. There are various Web sites that can track down anyone, and CD-ROMs that cover the entire United States' white pages. Any of these sources may, or may not, be up-to-date.

That's a lot of stuff to sort through, but the resources are available. Besides these resources, we have a search strategy in our own minds before we set out to find someone's information. We usually know where to begin and how to widen or narrow our search as we obtain results from one source. For example, we could start with our local community phone book if we know the kind of business (such as a dry cleaner) and don't want to page through the larger and longer listings of metropolitan-area phone books. But if we don't find any cleaners in our community book, we may have to move on to the metropolitan book, call directory assistance or use the Internet.

Addresses Change

But when it comes to doing the same tasks with finding out an email identity instead of a physical address, we aren't so lucky. Yes, there are many resources that catalog email addresses, but they aren't as complete, or as well known, or as useful as your average local telephone white pages. And ordering these resources and being effective in our searches is also a challenge.

When it comes to tracking down someone's email address, you have two choices. One is to use the last known address that you have for your correspondent. This may not be valid anymore, but usually that's where we start. Of course, you first have to find this address. That involves using the tools in your email program to find a message sent to that person, or looking up the address in one of your many electronic sources.

But the best tool for finding someone's email address is still the telephone: Call someone up and ask him or her to spell the email address slowly. You need to make sure you have transcribed the various punctuation and characters correctly. Finally, you hope that your correspondent (or the company's email system administrator) doesn't change this address anytime soon. That's a pretty grim situation, but it's the hard reality of email life these days.

There are several reasons for this. First, unlike a telephone number that is attached to a particular home or business, email addresses are easily changeable.[3] I may be dissatisfied with my ISP and move to another one. This may change my email identity from *joe@isp1.com* to *joe@isp2.com*, if indeed there isn't another Joe already with that identity on the new ISP and I have to now become *joe2@isp2.com*.[4] Any published directory quickly goes out of date, and even ones that can be automatically updated may still lag behind the actual changes.

Some of these problems are caused by the dynamics of the Internet marketplace itself. Say a new ISP comes on the block and becomes successful, gathering up thousands of customers. Then it goes broke, and overnight these customers have to fend for themselves, finding a new provider and a new identity. That's a lot of addresses to change and track down. It would be as if Cleveland got a new zip code, area code and renumbered half of its houses' street addresses all at once.

Or say a corporation decides to switch email gateways on its cc:Mail system, or move from cc:Mail to a 100% pure Internet email system. Overnight, all of its email addresses have now changed. And, depending on how the switch was made, the old ones may not work any longer. At least when a corporation changes its phone exchange or moves across town, the Phone Company usually can provide forwarding information.

But the real issue is that there can never be such a thing as a global directory for all email addresses. How do you get rid of out-of-date information from such a directory? How often do you collect information from local directories? What about dealing with people that wish to have unpublished addresses? If you want accurate information, you have to find someone who will take responsibility for maintaining this information. Will a service such as Four11 be so responsible? Hardly. It can barely keep up with tracking down new addresses (and we don't mean to pick on Four11; this is true for any global directory provider). It is a thorny problem.

Email Addresses Don't Have Any Physical Location

Our friend Einar Stefferud is fond of saying, "What is the first thing the telephone directory services operator asks you? 'What city, please?'" If you have ever tried to find a phone number without the right city, you know you are going to be in trouble. Often, operators can't help you without the city of the subscriber, or can't narrow down their search without at least some general notion of where this person lives or works.

But email addresses don't have cities, necessarily. Not everyone at *ibm.com* works in Armonk, New York, even though the corporate headquarters is located there. Indeed, you can probably state with some certainty that the majority of IBM employees do *not* work anywhere near Armonk. That brings up another important point in our search for email addresses: They may not really have a location in the sense that we think of city, state and country. We may use the same email address but move across the globe and set up shop elsewhere—and who will know? Indeed, one of us has had the same domain name for years but moved it from an ISP in New Jersey to one in Washington, D.C., to another in rural Virginia and then to New York City, all while working in the same office on Long Island, New York.

One reason why it is so difficult to find an email address is that it isn't tied to anything physical, apart from the server responsible for handling a particular domain name. Email addresses may or may not be easily portable, depending on what domain name is used and who "owns" the rights to use and move the domain name. If I use my ISP's domain as part of my email address, then (as our example above) if I switch ISPs, I have to leave that identity behind. But what if I have my own domain, such as *joe@example.com*? That is a trickier situation.

If ISP1 is presently serving the example.com domain name, then I should be able to move it to ISP2 if I don't like the service I receive at ISP1. It depends on how I have set up the account with InterNIC or whatever is the domain authority.

Email Addresses Are Difficult to Collate

Searching for a new address is a second issue. The protocol for looking up an address in the phone book is fairly well understood: It is called alphabetical order, and it is something we were taught in second grade. Addresses beginning with M come before N. There isn't any ambiguity here, and thankfully so. We scan the book looking for surnames first, and then when we find the right group of surnames, we look for the given (first) name we desire.

But when it comes to email, the alphabet isn't such a great system. If we were to print out a list of all our email addresses in alphabetical order, we wouldn't necessarily find it very useful. Many email addresses are a mixture of nonalphabetic characters, including numerals, punctuation, underscores and the ubiquitous @ sign. Trying to sort this melange in any order that two people might agree on is almost futile.

In addition, there isn't any single alphabet when it comes to email addresses. You may be in a country that doesn't use Roman characters, or has various accents and other characters not found in English. Our friend Robert Stanley writes about the growing Greek population in Canada and the Hispanic population in the U.S., both of which like to have names with accented letters and non-English characters. All of this makes collating addresses more difficult.

Even if everyone only used the characters from A to Z in an email address, we still have another problem—trying to usefully sort our addresses. This is because the email address may not be close to the actual user's name. For example *mrose@example.com* would come after *dstrom@example.com* in almost all of our lists. Yet, we might want to look for Rose before Strom in our list, based on a search for surnames. So, we'd have to establish two different sorting criteria: one for the overall email address and one for surnames that then map to the address.

Furthermore, we probably need a few other criteria, such as one that organizes business names and maps each name to a particular set of addresses, and one that organizes industry categories, products or something else that we might want to search.

Back in the early 1990s, there was a solution for this problem—X.400, named after the proposed standards. X.400 was, quite frankly, more of a problem than a solution: Various products that were supposed to be interoperable only did so after much pain and configuration on the part of their email administrators. Many of the popular email products at the time offered incomplete implementations. But the real reason that X.400 never went anywhere was that its addresses were monstrous. A typical user would have an address like:

```
c=US.a=sprint.o=company.ou=marketing.s=smith.g="Joe Smith"
```

Luckily for all of us who aren't fast or accurate typists, X.400 was easily overtaken by the Internet, and the @ sign came into vogue on everything from movie listings to bus shelters. Now the notion of separating a user name and the domain name with the @ sign is so popular that even grade school children can recite their own email address with little prompting.

Just as X.400 was dying of overwrought implementations, a series of standards called Lightweight Directory Access Protocol (LDAP) arose. We'll discuss these standards in our next section. LDAP is implemented in several current email products. And we'll also talk about ways that our suite of email products supports LDAP, enabling you to connect to a public directory server and search for a correspondent's email address.

Email Directories Are Incomplete

However, LDAP servers are just beginning to be established, and they aren't tremendously useful yet.[5] There are two basic problems. First, if you are searching for a relatively common name, such as John Smith, you probably aren't going to have much luck finding someone with these systems, unless you can uniquely locate John Smith by a particular town or business.

Think about searching the entire United States' white pages and imagine how many listings there are for John Smith. There must be thousands of them. Maybe the listing you are trying to find is J. Smith, or Johnny Smith, or J. D. Smith? Maybe John got tired of receiving telephone solicitations and now has an unlisted number, or he put his listing under his wife's name? Now add to this the problem of frequent moves and changes, and you see what you are up against with regard to searching through these LDAP directories.

A second issue is that the directories aren't very complete, since many of them just got started during 1997. Not all email systems have published LDAP information, and many won't for some time. No one is obligated to provide this information as part of maintaining a 100% pure Internet email system, and some of the email products don't yet work with LDAP. More to the point, some companies don't want to publish the list of all of their email users to the public for security or privacy reasons. This means that any directory effort, no matter how interoperable and flexible, might still fail if it doesn't have very many listings.

While X.400 was dying and LDAP was being created, the biggest online vendors such as CompuServe and AOL have tried to provide their own tools to help track down their own members. And given that both systems have millions of members, it is a worthy goal. CompuServe and AOL can provide whatever member directory tools they wish, since they are systems that are owned and operated by a single vendor.

However, neither vendor has been entirely successful in developing a system that is easy to use and returns accurate results of a search on member addresses. AOL doesn't require its members to provide actual billing names in its directory, so often your search may not find someone if they haven't bothered to add this information to their member profile.[6] And CompuServe's search tools are both too fine-grained and too broad, making it hard to locate someone. Some CompuServe users also elect to remain anonymous, or at least numerically identified, rather than attach their name to their account address.[7]

Both AOL and CompuServe's directories are only available to their own members for searching. This means if you aren't a member, you won't be able to use them. That isn't a very satisfactory solution, as those of you who have gotten error messages from the AOL or CompuServe postmaster have found out.

Part of the problem with any member directory is that you don't necessarily have the exact details about the member you want. Did the member list a postal address as the city he or she lives or works in? Was the user rigorous in using the actual city name, or did he or she use something else? So, the directory search tools need to incorporate some flexibility yet provide the right answer. That is a tall order.

Avoiding Spammers

Email users are becoming a more paranoid bunch. And many have taken to what Robert Stanley calls "paranoid aliases," using names like D. Duck or M. Mouse as their email identities. Many of these users don't have anything in particular to hide: They are just tired of getting spam mail or want to weed out the email equivalent of cold calls. (As we were writing this very sentence, we got two unsolicited phone calls: One from a telephone company representative trying to sell us long distance service, and one from a magazine publisher trying to sell us a subscription. Such timing!) And some corporate IS managers we know have taken to using Netcom or Metricom accounts so they can surf the net (including their competitors' pages) in private and not have to identify their corporate origins.

Spam is certainly a fact of email existence these days, as we mentioned before. And many people are afraid that listing their email addresses in some public directory will only encourage spammers to harvest these addresses and send more unsolicited emails.

The Case of Multiple Identities

All of these directory efforts have another problem when dealing with those of us who have more than one email identity. Just because we can find a listing of someone's email address doesn't necessarily mean that this is the best address for our purposes.

Think about how you search through your phone directory and what you do when you come across multiple phone numbers for a single name. What does this mean, other than a person has multiple phone lines coming into their home or business? To make sense of this, you have to have additional information. You must establish that all of these multiple phone numbers do indeed go to the same household; you could examine the street addresses, for example. Then you might not know which one is the person's fax line, which one is used exclusively for the teenage children, and which one just rings by the computer and is used primarily for outgoing modem calls. So, you end up calling each number in sequence, maybe getting a fax or modem tone when the phone is answered. Then perhaps you make a notation in your phone book with this information, so you don't call the fax line again.

The same situation awaits these email directories as more and more people establish multiple identities. Just finding out that *somebody@example.com* is the email address of your long, lost college roommate doesn't mean that she ever looks at this mailbox or even works for the Example company any longer. She may have several mailboxes, or the Example domain may now be owned and operated by someone else, or she may have gotten married or divorced and changed her name and mailbox identity along with it.[8]

Compounding this problem is that many of these email identities may have nothing to do with mailboxes of carbon-based life forms: They may be aliases for groups or departments. Or the address may point to a program that could be an autoresponder or some other process that manipulates this incoming message. Should these addresses be listed in any public directory? Well, it depends really on what the address does. Most corporations would probably shy away from publishing their departmental alias addresses in any public forum.

What a mess! Yes, it is easier to pick up the phone and just ask someone to send you a message so you can see how to reply to them. This argues for email addresses that are easily distinguishable over the phone. Longish mailbox and domain names or those with underscores or hyphens aren't easily transcribed.

Telephony Integration

Before we describe some of the standards efforts to resolve these directory and addressing issues, we should also talk about another issue facing senders of enterprise email—integrating telephony applications into your email working life. For those of us who spend a great deal of time in our email application, we'd like to be able to send email to a variety of non-email destinations, including most noticeably fax machines and pagers.

A typical scenario would be to mix email and non-email addresses in a single list of addresses: Perhaps one of your recipients is traveling that day and is away from his normal email access, but you happen to have a nearby fax number and want to keep him in the loop of your discussions.

One problem occurs, which we've experienced. If your discussion group gets carried away with replies, and the fax number was in all of their replies, your traveling colleague could become buried in faxes in no time.

Perhaps, to keep telephone costs down, you'd like to only authorize certain users of your email network to send faxes in this manner. Or perhaps you wish to provide a series of email aliases so that your users can page your support people without having to remember their actual pager numbers and who is on duty at any particular time.

Integrating email and faxing makes a great deal of sense, especially for people who are frequent travelers. It would be nice to make use of the store and forward capabilities of email along with the universal transmission of images and text of fax. We've seen situations where someone is trying to send a fax to our office when we are working in another city or country. How are we notified about this fax? Can we direct the fax to our email inbox so we can read it wherever we happen to be? Or how about setting up a local fax number in a distant city, giving the impression that we have a branch office there?

Sending faxes to our email inbox is also more secure than sending them to a public fax machine. We all know of faxes that mistakenly have been read at inopportune times, all because they were left on the fax machine too long. Sending these sensitive faxes to one's email address ensures privacy and avoids the need to have individual fax lines for key employees.

Finding and using Internet fax services isn't that difficult, as we'll show you in our upcoming section on solutions. But finding out prices and how the services go about collecting their fees can be a bit tricky.

And, as many paging companies have found out, it also makes sense to have pagers be Internet accessible. We can quickly receive notifications and status updates from our networks, telling us when a breakdown or break-in has happened. However, your pager may not have this feature, or you may only have it in your local metropolitan area, or you may have an older numeric-only pager that can't receive text.

But just attaching your pager to the Internet isn't going to always work. Even the fanciest and most expensive alphanumeric pager still has limits on how many characters can be received in a single message. This can result in messages with long headers, and carbon copy lists often get truncated before the actual body of the message is displayed on the pager. And by mistake we have set up endless loops where the pager forwards its message to our email inbox, which forwards it back to the pager, which forwards it back to the email box, until we remember to turn off one forwarding mechanism or another.

And, to make matters worse, there are all sorts of new cellular services that combine messaging and paging as part of the features of a new breed of digital wireless phones. While it is good to have choices, it all makes evaluating what to use when more difficult.

Speaking of phones, while we are traveling we'd also like the option of using our phones to collect our email and have our messages read over the phone. There are several products that can accomplish this, as we'll see shortly.

Given the confusion of just figuring out what your correspondent's email address might be, you may be suspicious of any real standards of integrating email with fax machines and pagers. And you would be correct. While there are several products that can send email to print out on a fax machine or display on a pager, they all make use of different address schemes and systems. But there is hope, as our next section will describe.

STANDARDS

Although the previous section covered many services available when sending messages in the enterprise, there are Internet standards for only one of those services: directory access. There are no Internet standards for services such as fax or paging gateways.[9] In fact, the standards dealing with directory access are silent with respect to communicating directory servers—the only topic provided for is how client software can talk to a directory. Other aspects of provisioning a directory service—for example, referrals among servers and replication of data between servers—are simply out of the scope of this book.

The Lightweight Directory Access Protocol

To understand the Lightweight Directory Access Protocol (LDAP), we need to understand the context in which LDAP was developed. The need for an Internet directory service was perceived as early as the mid 1980s. In 1988, the CCITT published the X.500 series of recommendations on directory service for telecommunications providers. For several reasons, some political, an effort was made to provision X.500 within the Internet.

Unfortunately, like most of the OSI protocol suite (of which X.500 was a member), the actual development and deployment of the technology proved problematic. The reasons for this are legion, and recounting the failure here does little good. However, two positive things did come out of experimenting with X.500 in the Internet. First, X.500 provided a framework, which, when the actual details are ignored, seems reasonable.

Second, while X.500 proved too difficult to provision as a whole, parts of it were salvaged.

The LDAP model is rather simple: It defines the packet formats for asking questions of a directory server. How that server chooses to answer those questions (e.g., what other servers it might talk to, where else it might find its data, and so on) is irrelevant. Thus, to understand LDAP, one need only understand how data is named. All other aspects of the directory are irrelevant!

There are three important kinds of data in LDAP:

1. Names of objects in the directory
2. Names of the attributes associated with each object
3. Values of each attribute associated with each object (there can be more than one)

Thus, at the coarsest level, the directory that LDAP talks to contains objects having one or more attributes, and for each attribute there may be one or more values. A breakthrough that LDAP made possible was recognizing that while X.500 provided for complex binary representations of different kinds of data, virtually all attributes values could be represented in textual form.

An object is named using a "distinguished name"—something that unambiguously identifies the object within the directory. Although there are many possible schemes for devising distinguished names, X.500 uses a hierarchical model. The namespace can be thought of as a tree—as one progresses from the root of the tree to a leaf, a distinguished name is built by concatenating the labels at each node. Because there is only one path from the root to any given node, each node has a unique, distinguishing name.

Although LDAP uses the X.500 approach to naming, it is unencumbered with the actual details (e.g., having to know which directory server holds which part of the tree). So, the only thing that LDAP cares about is how to represent a name as a string. Here's an example:

```
cn=Marshall Rose, o="Dover Beach Consulting, Inc.", c=US
```

This corresponds to a node with a label of cn=Marshall Rose, which is below a node with a label of o="Dover Beach Consulting, Inc.", which is below a node with a label of c=US, which is below the root of the naming tree. So, the rules are fairly simple: The least significant label appears on the left (just like with a domain name, e.g., mail.example.com), labels are separated by commas, and if a label value contains a special character, then double quotes can be used to delimit the label value. There are a few other nuances to the rules (e.g., if a label has two or more values), but since users rarely see or write these distinguished names, we won't bother describing them.

In X.500, an attribute type is named using an "object identifier,"[10] which is merely a unique sequence of integers. There are also string representations for these attribute types (e.g., telephoneNumber and rfc822Mailbox), and, in the interests of simplicity, LDAP prefers to use the string notation. Finally, attribute values, can, in theory, be arbitrarily complex binary structures in X.500. To make things tractable, LDAP uses equivalent string representations. Although one might argue that LDAP's use of strings is less efficient than a compact binary notation, implementation experience dictates otherwise. Specifically, strings are relatively easy to "get right" when coding a program, the same can't be said for a multitude of arbitrary binary structures.

Protocol Interactions

There are three parts to an LDAP session:

1. Bind to the server
2. Perform one or more directory operations
3. Unbind from the server

The client authenticates itself using the binding process. How it selects a particular server is outside of the LDAP specification. Authentication can occur by providing a plaintext password, or in more exotic environments by using Kerberos.

There are different kinds of directory operations available: searching and adding, deleting, or modifying. Of these, the search operation is particularly powerful.

The way search works is conceptually easy: You point the LDAP server at a particular node in the naming tree, you tell it how far down you want to search (either that one object, or just its immediate children or the entire subtree), and you provide a filter that is matched against every object being searched. Obviously, if you just want to read a particular object, the parameters to search are rather trivial. However, this needn't be the case. The filter specification allows you to test for the existence of attributes or particular attribute values, along with performing matches based on substrings, inequality and the like. Here's an example of what a filter might look like:

```
(& (sn=Strom) (cn=Dav*))
```

This says to look for objects with a surName of Strom and with a commonName starting with "Dav." One might also use

```
(cn=Dav*Strom)
```

which, depending on the implementation of the LDAP server, is probably slower. LDAP uses a binary representation for this filter, owing to historical reasons.

Finally, there are some other parameters that allow a limit to how much information the search can return or how long it can take to execute.

The other operations are less dazzling. Assuming the server authorizes your client, you can add, change or delete attribute values in existing objects; add new objects; or delete existing objects. The joy of LDAP is not that it provides a sophisticated mechanism for performing these operations, rather it merely provides a standardized means for conveying the semantics of these actions along with some conventions regarding how things are named.

Unbinding simply releases the underlying network connection between the client and server.

Lessons from LDAP

In many respects, LDAP is both a triumph and a failure for the Internet.

It is a triumph because it provides a basic mechanism for clients to look up information about people and other things, using servers that have been specifically configured for this purpose. This is quite an achievement and shouldn't be minimized. Before LDAP, only ad hoc, manual mechanisms existed for looking up information, such as mailbox addresses.

But, LDAP also represents a failure for the Internet community. Significant community resources were put into trying to provision an Internet-based directory service using X.500, but very little of X.500's promise was realized. Each LDAP server is really an island adrift in the Internet. There is no Internet-wide namespace, no mechanism for servers to communicate with each other, and so on. LDAP solves a local directory problem, not the global one.

SOLUTIONS

There is a rich series of products for solving some of the problems in sending enterprise messages. We look at various tips and hints on how to send email to unknown recipients, as well as how to use some of the LDAP-related tools. We also examine four categories of products that are useful in integrating enterprise email systems with other messaging services, including those that support fax, telephony and paging options.

Finding Someone's Address

We employ several strategies when trying to send email to our correspondents.

First, we look up the person in our own address book. If the person is there, we have a reasonable chance that his or her email address hasn't changed and that we have entered it correctly in our Rolodex. We also can sort and search our outgoing email folders and try to find the last time we corresponded, and use this address to begin.

If this is a new contact, we have to go looking for the address. We start with the Web page of the correspondent's company. If the company's name is the Example Corporation, then we try *www.example.com* and see if there is even a Web site. If that doesn't work, we go to one of the Internet search engines, such as Yahoo or Lycos, and try to track down the company. Once at the site, we surf around a few pages and see if there is a directory of names we can search or, better yet, a list of the corporate contacts reachable via email. If we can search a directory, all the better—that usually finds the right person. If there is just a listing, we look to see if there is any scheme to how the email addresses are listed. Is the pattern first initial, full last name? Or perhaps the first name, followed by a period, followed by the last name? Or is the company small enough or informal enough to have just the first name be the email address?

Sometimes we try CompuServe and AOL to see if we can track down our correspondents. As we have said earlier, we've had mixed results using these member search routines, but sometimes it can be worthwhile.

Next, we try sending mail to either the *webmaster@example.com* or *postmaster@example.com*. Both addresses are usually answered by a human being, and sometimes that person can be helpful.

Sometimes we use a colleague at the same company, or someone we know might know the whereabouts of the contact.

Searching Web LDAP Pages

These hints only go so far, so let's try to use some of the LDAP tools and see how useful they can be. There are two ways to get access to public LDAP directories of email users. You can use your browser (or if you are running Windows98, go to Start | Find | People) to search various public LDAP directories from their individual Web pages, using the search tools that are part of these directories. Or you can use your own email client to perform the lookups as you are composing your message.

And, there are several LDAP server products that we'll cover briefly.

The table below summarizes the various public LDAP directory providers available that come already installed with version 4 of Netscape Messenger, Outlook Express and Eudora software. Previous versions of these products had no LDAP lookup support, however, so if you want to make use of LDAP, you'll need to upgrade to these newer versions.

Public LDAP Directory Providers

Name, URL	Phone/Street Address? Email?	Partners
Bigfoot, *www.bigfoot.com*	P/S, E	
Four11, *www.four11.com*	P/S, E	Yahoo
Switchboard, *www.switchboard.com*	P/S, E	AltaVista
WhoWhere, *www.whowhere.com*	P/S, E	Excite
InfoSpace, *www.infospace.com*	P/S, E	

All of these providers have two different Web pages for your search—one for looking up email addresses, the other for looking up phone and postal addresses. Each vendor does this somewhat differently. Four11 asks you for city and other physical information, even when looking for an email address, while Bigfoot doesn't. InfoSpace has an interesting "reverse lookup" feature, whereby you type in an email address and it attempts to find the person behind the address. Some present results with just the email address and name, and you have to click on another screen to see the full street address and phone of that record. Others provide more information at once.

We had varying results with each system when we tried to search for ourselves in early January 1998. For example, Switchboard found six email addresses for David Strom, none of which was one of the author's. Bigfoot found 11 David Stroms, one of which was *the* David Strom. Four11 found 15 names, with David's displayed correctly. WhoWhere found 29 matches but only displayed the first 10 on the screen. If we wanted to see the additional listings, we had to perform the search from the WorldPages site (*www.worldpages.com*), which then brings up a screen where we can examine the other listings.

Some services listed exact matches for our name, while others provided names that were close matches or used "Dave" instead of "David" or just the initial D. With some listings, we could find out-of-date email addresses for ourselves. Some lists contained duplicates. All in all, it was not a very satisfying experience.

A group from Computer Center of Lower Saxony (Regionales Rechenzentrum für Niedersachsen, RRZN), University of Hannover, Germany, has put together a meta-search tool for these and some other LDAP directories called Meta Email Search Agent (MESA). If you go to *mesa.rrzn.uni-hannover.de* you can choose which of these directories you want to search and do a combined search. You must enter the surname, and the only other field is for a first name. There is no way to narrow the search by location, however. Still, this is a nice time-saver. You can compare results from the various public directory servers.

LDAP Searches Within Email Clients

But what about trying to access these servers from within your email clients? Outlook Express, Eudora and Messenger all come with the above five LDAP servers pre-configured. Of the three, Messenger is the most flexible in tailoring your searches, and it has a number of attractive features. First, you can decide on the appropriate order in which to search each of the LDAP directories, and also for your own private address book. In other words, if you find one directory more useful than others, you can move it up in your list. You change the order in Edit | Preferences | Mail&News | Directory. You can only search one directory at a time, however.

If you go into Edit | Search Addresses, you will see a dialogue box that asks you to search a particular LDAP server. It will go out and query the server in much the same fashion as we demonstrated with our Web browser. The difference here is that you can specify as many criteria or as few as you wish. For example, let's say I want to find all the David Stroms in New York. I could choose the Name field, choose "contains" and type in David Strom. Then I would click on the "more" button to add a field to the selection criteria. Finally, I would choose the city field, choose "contains" and type in New York.

It sounds more difficult than it really is, and Figure 6.1 shows how the dialogue box is configured. But neither Outlook Express or Eudora can match this flexibility if you want to narrow your searches. Messenger has seven different matching criteria. In addition to "contains," you can select "doesn't contain," "is," "isn't," "begins with," "ends with," or "sounds like" to try to match your name. In addition to name and city, you can also search for organization, email name, phone number and street. That is a lot of flexibility in matching, although you'll probably end up using one or two of these criteria and fields.

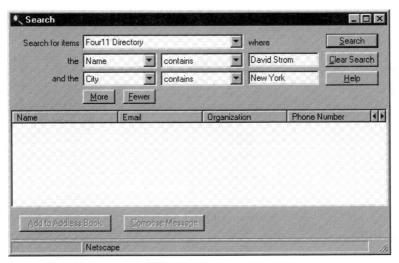

Figure 6.1   Messenger LDAP query

Outlook Express has a less functional search in Tools | Address Book | Find. You have exactly two fields to search, name and email address, and like Messenger you can only examine one LDAP directory at a time. You can't specify qualifying search criteria (like "sounds like") as you can in Messenger. And you can only search a name field, as shown in Figure 6.2.

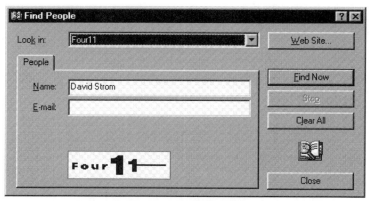

Figure 6.2   Outlook Express LDAP query

Eudora Pro lies somewhere between the two in its LDAP features. You can specify multiple LDAP servers to search automatically, and Eudora will go down the list and search them one after another. While the product comes with preconfigured servers as shown in Figure 6.3, you still have to manually check the box next to the server before you can perform any LDAP searches. Eudora only searches a single name field.

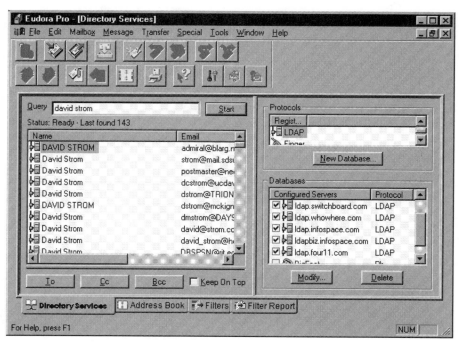

Figure 6.3   Eudora LDAP query

LDAP Servers

So far we have spoken only about the client side of LDAP. But there is the server side as well, and here we'll look at what Netscape is doing with its SuiteSpot server collection. The notion of an LDAP server is different from what we have been discussing. Instead of publishing or searching for public names and identities, we want to maintain our own directory of corporate resources that may not necessarily be visible from outside the firewall. Indeed, that is a big attraction of running one's own LDAP server.

When you first install any Netscape server, such as a Web server or an email server, the first question it asks is the location of your LDAP directory service. This should give you an idea of how important LDAP is to Netscape, and how key it is in its products. You can install and run Netscape servers without LDAP, of course, and make use of your own directories, but you have to enter them manually.

Another LDAP server is from Lotus. cc:Mail has an optional piece of software called the LDAP Connector, which allows LDAP clients the ability to search the cc:Mail address book and return the resulting Internet address. It runs as an NT service on the same machine as your cc:Mail router, which means it can automatically start up whenever you turn on your machine. You can set it up to allow anonymous access, or only those local cc:Mail users to search, along with a bunch of other parameters, such as the number of results to be returned from a search and the format in which they will be displayed.

Email Integration Products

Our other issue with sending enterprise email concerns integration of telephony services with the email systems to expand the range of recipients to those users of fax machines, telephones and pagers. These take the form of different kinds of products. First we'll look at what fax services are available to anyone with a 100% pure Internet email system, or the ability to access an Internet email address. These are good choices if you don't want to invest a great deal of money but want to obtain some of the functionality of integrating these services into your existing email systems.

Then we'll look at the various gateways and connections that email network vendors such as CompuServe and America Online offer as extensions to their basic email products and services.

Next we'll examine what the various paging network providers and third-party vendors are doing to integrate paging and email.

Finally, we'll review those gateways installed on your local mail server or other computers but run in-house and are maintained by the corporate IS staff. You'll need to consider the cost to maintain these gateways and also their limitations when it comes to supporting all of the features you require.

Internet-based Fax Services

Let's look at our first category of products, those that are third-party fax services that connect with standard Internet mail systems. There are many companies offering these options, and you can search Yahoo for "fax services" to find others. Let's cover a few examples.

One of the more notable companies in the fax arena is JFAX (*www.jfax.com*). Its offering is called JFAX Personal Telecom, which is a suite of products and services that integrates Internet email, telephony and faxing. The JFAX client is bundled with Eudora Pro version 4, or it can be downloaded from its Web site.

Here is how it works. JFAX has two different services: one for sending and one for receiving faxes. You set up an account with JFAX for an initial $15 fee. This entitles you to a local fax phone number in one of several dozen cities around the world. The phone number looks and feels like an ordinary fax machine. Anyone can send a fax to you by dialing this number. JFAX routes the fax to a specified email address tied to this phone number. The fax arrives as a TIFF file attached to an email message, which you can either view in your own viewer or with any graphics program. You are charged per fax received against your account, billed to your credit card. When your account balance falls below a specified level (e.g., $10), your credit card is billed to replenish the funds for more faxes.

Your same account is used for sending faxes as well. You put the fax number in the email To: field, appending @jfaxsend.com. For example, say you wish to send a fax to (212) 555-1212. You would use the following address in your email program: *12125551212@jfaxsend.com*. That's it. You'll receive a receipt indicating when the fax was sent and the amount charged to your account. Fees vary depending on the distance and country of the recipient, but are much less than direct international long distance calls. And you can send graphics in your documents as well as plain text messages.

JFAX has other services, including receiving voice messages on a personal 800 number. And the company has formed an alliance with CompuServe so that all CompuServe users can take advantage of these services as well.

Other vendors offer only the ability to send faxes. For example, faxSAV (*www.faxsav.com*) and Faxaway (*www.faxaway.com*) cover sending faxes from your Internet email client, using a syntax similar to JFAX by putting the phone number in the message header. And Interpage (*www.interpage.com*) has many offerings, including a service that will route received email to a specific fax machine or several fax machines.

Email Network Gateways

Let's look at what email network vendors are doing to enhance their systems, either by working with various Internet services or by connecting new services to their networks. These can get pricey, particularly as they charge by the message or on a monthly basis, but they can offer a great deal of functionality.

Two of the first email networks to provide a fax gateway were AT&T and MCIMail. They maintained a series of PCs with fax boards connected to their networks, wrote some custom software that would detect the fax number and convert the text of the message into a fax. Mail users on these systems would set up the fax address in the To: field of the message header, and it was relatively easy to use.

CompuServe offers a variety of programs for its users, including fax through the JFAX software. CompuServe also offers its own telephone-calling card. The card allows users to dial in remotely to receive voice mail, faxes and email. Messages are translated into speech for 25 cents a minute. AOL doesn't offer any telephony services for its users, other than what they can access via the Internet.

Paging Gateways

More people carry pagers than any other wireless device, and it is easy to see why. Pagers are small, they are easy to use, they provide instant connectivity (although just one-way) and you don't have to worry about running out of batteries every few hours. And to keep up with the popularity of pagers, many paging network providers have gotten the Internet religion in a big way.

Some of them, such as AirTouch Paging Northeast, have email addresses for all of their subscribers who carry alphanumeric pagers.

(Email to numeric pagers isn't very workable, as you might imagine.) To send a page to someone's system, you merely send email to *PIN@pager.mcb.com*, where PIN is the pager's ID number. PageNet offers a similar ability for its alphanumeric pager customers, but the syntax is somewhat more cumbersome. You need both a "terminal alpha modem number" along with the subscriber's PIN number.[11]

SkyTel has taken things a step further. On its web site (*www.skytel. com/Paging/*), you have a form that can be used to send a message to any of its alphanumeric subscribers. There are different forms for different types of pagers, which is initially confusing until you figure out which pager corresponds to which form. SkyTel also offers a series of Web forms to send custom responses to their two-way pagers.

With all of these services, there are limits to the size of the message, usually 80 to 250 characters. Email messages that get transmitted to your pager usually are billed as ordinary pages, with no extra monthly charges for the service.

The biggest advantage these network providers offer is that you as a customer don't have to do anything special. There is no software to install and no special procedures to follow. You get your pages in the same way as you always have, only now you get them directly from your correspondents' email programs. The only thing you need to know is the Internet email address of your pager.

However, this is also the biggest disadvantage. You are limited by the implementation of the provider's email gateway. If someone has done a poor job, you can't do much about it. For example, some systems may transmit the entire email header to your pager, rather than truncating extra-long headers and sending more of the message body. You can't change these implementations, unless the provider upgrades its gateway. And if your paging provider doesn't have a gateway, you are out of luck and you'll have to find someplace else that does.

There are many other companies that provide email-to-paging solutions that enhance the service offerings from the paging network providers. For example, PageMail (*www.airpost.com*) will sell you your own domain and address for your pager, or send messages simultaneously to pager, email and fax addresses. They also have a "follow-me" service that allows a paging user to specify which device can receive messages, so that a page will be sent to a fax machine, for example, if the user is out of range of the paging network.

InstantEmail (*www.instantemail.net*) offers a combination of email account, dialup access and pager, along with Web site hosting and other services.

In-house Email Enhancements

Another series of products involves those that work in-house to enhance your own email servers. These products include the ability to send and receive faxes, send alphanumeric pages and work in conjunction with Touch-Tone telephones to read and act upon your email. The difference here is that you purchase the product and run it yourself, rather than making use of a service provider or someone running a service via an Internet email gateway connection.

TenFour (*www.tenfour.com*) offers its TFS Gateway product that connects diverse email systems, including cc:Mail, Microsoft Exchange, Novell's GroupWise and others. TFS runs on either a Windows95 or Windows NT computer with LAN connections to the various email post offices. While you wouldn't buy TFS just for its paging access, if you have several in-house email systems and want a single paging gateway from all of them, this would be one of the better choices. Called the paging connection module, it supports up to 160-character messages and uses the National Dispatch Center in the U.S., among other paging networks in Europe. You connect a Hayes-compatible modem to the TFS Gateway computer and it then sends messages to the paging network.

Users of cc:Mail systems have many options when it comes to installing various gateways to fax and pagers, from both Lotus and third-party vendors. This is partly because cc:Mail has had a long history of encouraging third-party enhancements, and partly because there are so many users. For example, Lotus' cc:Mail Pager Gateway sells for $995 and runs on version 4 or 5 cc:Mail post offices. This could be an issue for users who have upgraded to later versions (currently, cc:Mail post offices are at version 8) and have to run multiple versions to offer this kind of connectivity.

The pager gateway (which, by the way, is still at version 1.0) runs on either DOS (yes, DOS!) or OS/2 machines. It can run on its own machine (which, given the resources needed to run a DOS machine, might be a good idea) or as another task on one of your existing cc:Mail post offices, provided that you are running the appropriate version of the post office and operating system.

It works by periodically checking the regular cc:Mail post office for any messages destined for pager users. When it finds one, it dials up the paging network provider with an ordinary modem attached to the gateway machine, sends the message and logs it to a file. Of course, the gateway can't confirm that the message was sent by the provider's network, nor can it track any other errors on the provider network.

The gateway is limited to a maximum of 200 recipients in a single message, and a maximum of 64 different paging providers. Attachments aren't transmitted to pagers, and only text items are delivered.

The cc:Mail administrator sets up the paging gateway and can create a series of aliases on your global address book, so you don't have to remember everyone's PIN number when you want to send a page. For example, your cc:Mail directory could list John's pager as one entry.

Lotus also sells a Fax Server product for $1,995 that connects to any version of cc:Mail server. It comes with a copy of the Notes (yes, Notes!) version 3.33 client, and it only runs on Windows 3.1 or NT. You'll need a second machine for the actual fax server, and, as you might suspect, it requires an attached fax modem. Does this sound cumbersome? You bet. This is one reason why this fax server product is still at version 1.1.

As with the paging gateway, your cc:Mail administrator makes entries in the global address book for the fax machines to which you wish to direct your email messages.

There are plenty of other cc:Mail enhancements and a variety of third-party vendors that offer gateways to other email systems. We'll discuss some of them in Chapter 7 concerning making cc:Mail Internet-ready.

Users of other LAN-based email systems such as GroupWise and Exchange have similar choices when it comes to adding fax and pager gateways to their mail systems. However, as with cc:Mail, these gateways don't always support all versions of the email server software and may have other restrictions. For example, GroupWise's fax and pager gateways only run on the NetWare servers and not on other platforms.

The fax gateways are mainly software products that work in conjunction with fax modems installed in the mail server. Another option is to purchase a special piece of hardware that can function as a fax server for your network. One of the longer-term players in this arena is Castelle (*www.castelle.com*). You buy a box with fax modems, network connections and software already installed. You tie it into your existing network and email system by configuring the software, and then the box will send faxes from any email or network user and receive faxes from the outside world. Having a separate box to do the faxing makes a great deal of sense, particularly if you are a cc:Mail administrator faced with the prospect of having to install Notes just to run your fax gateway.[12]

Besides these products, there is another group that works in conjunction with Touch-Tone telephones to read and act upon your email. GroupWise has such a product called PhoneAccess. You dial a special access number of your mail server. After entering your user name and password, you can hear the headings of your inbox read to you over the phone line, along with any meetings and other items that are part of the GroupWise system. You can delete messages you've read and also direct faxes to be forwarded to a nearby fax machine.

So far we have looked at products that work in conjunction with your mail servers. There are other products that can enhance the ability of your desktop to send pages and faxes. For example, Symantec's Win-Fax PRO can send faxes from many of the popular desktop applications over a desktop fax modem. It works in conjunction with your word processor or other office software and adds the ability to "print" to a remote fax machine. Some of the other fax gateways also use this metaphor and add printer drivers to your computer to send faxes.

However, the printer driver metaphor isn't very workable when it comes to receiving faxes. In this situation, you have to run the particular desktop fax software and view the faxes explicitly.

Microsoft includes a fax module as part of its Windows95 operating system. However, it isn't very useful, since it works inside its Windows Messaging software. We recommend you don't waste any time with this and get a copy of WinFax PRO or some other fax software client.

FUTURES

We are at a loss in making predictions for the future of sending mail in the enterprise. So many potential services rely on a ubiquitous directory service, and while LDAP provides robust access to a directory *server*, there is no Internet-wide directory *service*.

Although X.500 had numerous faults, one cannot help but wonder whether any directory service is doomed from the onset. Consider: For a directory service to be ubiquitous, there has to be strong agreement as to how objects are named, and how servers communicate, across enterprises.

It is unclear, however, if enterprises are willing to compromise on such weighty issues.

In December 1997, Internet standards were published for LDAP version 3, which included the notion of referrals to allow servers to indicate where a client should go looking for the data. Although the authors remain unconvinced as to the political reality of an Internet-wide directory service, this is a good technical underpinning. However, the naming issue remains unresolved, despite the fact that there are common-sense solutions to the problem. For example, Al Grimstad has suggested using mailbox addresses as the basis for distinguished names. For example, if you own the mailbox

    mrose@example.com

then you can also have an object in the directory named

    uid=mrose, dc=example, dc=com

This is a brilliant idea. We already know how to assign mailbox addresses, using a mix of local autonomy and coordinated registrations. So, the whole directory naming problem goes away, because we've already solved an earlier problem. Note that under such a scheme, you don't have to know someone's email address to find him or her (what would be the point?), rather you enter an LDAP search for something like:

    (sn=Rose)

and you'd get back one or more distinguished names, one of which would be

    uid=mrose, dc=example, dc=com

The magic of this approach is that we didn't have to argue with anyone regarding what the distinguished name should be—once you get a valid email address, you know what your distinguished name is for the directory. Alas, the standards process rarely appreciates either simplicity or elegance: This proposal was bound on the standards altar for a year before being withdrawn. Evidently, common sense is none too common.

This leads us to the following prediction. We will not see an Internet-wide directory service for a long, long time. At most like-minded communities may bind their servers together into a "community" service through the use of referrals and community naming agreements. However, we doubt that there will be global (or even national consensus) on naming schemes.

So, for now, expect a telephone call when we need to get your email address.

Endnotes

1. Thankfully, Internet email addresses are usually easy to input. Not all messaging technologies are so blessed. For example, during the OSI protocol wars, which raged at the beginning of the decade, the following observation was made. When two "Internet" people met at a conference, they could exchange business cards with their email addresses on them, and then either could send a message to the other; when an Internet person met an "OSI" person, the OSI person would have to start corresponding with the Internet person, because the OSI person's email address was incomprehensible; and, when two OSI people met, they would begin their correspondence by calling each other on the phone to figure out how to send email to each other. The moral of this parable is, hopefully, obvious.

2. To continue this analogy, one might view paging and facsimile as two species whose development took them down an evolutionary cul-de-sac. Clearly the notions of "two-way" paging, and (the ever-amusing) "file transfer via fax" are examples of solutions in search of problems.

3. Well, this is true for the most part. Look at the turmoil going on in North America over the past few years with splitting area codes in major cities. While this is nowhere near the level of change happening with email addresses, it is still difficult to keep track of new area codes, unless we make calls to those areas that have recently made the change.

4. This is a real problem for new America Online users, who often can't find a reasonable name that hasn't already been taken by one of its more than 11 million members. You often see addresses on AOL that are an odd assortment of numbers and letters. And there are cases of people deliberately using a mixture of letters, numbers and even nonprintable characters in their email addresses to foil search engines or spam harvesters. This of course makes them harder to remember or dictate to your correspondents, recalling the old Tom Lehrer routine of "Hen3ry" with the silent three.

5. Our friend Eric Hall would like to see LDAP become more pervasive, but he sees several obstacles. First, it needs to be a universal repository for any and all kinds of configuration information, from databases to Web pages. If it can be configured, these settings should be accessible via LDAP. Second, it needs a better syntax for retrieving information than the X.500 legacy structure that it inherited. LDAP needs better user interfaces for its queries and reporting results. Finally, it needs better management tools to manage multiple LDAP directories. You can read a full discussion of this on Eric Hall's Web site at *www.ehsco.com/opinion/ 19971227.html.*

6. Indeed, a celebrated case in the winter of 1998 demonstrated this situation all too well. A Defense Department lawyer had to make a special request (which unfortunately was granted) to track down the actual details of an AOL member who was also a member of the armed services. This information wasn't available on AOL's member directory.

7. When CompuServe first began, it gave out all addresses as two sets of numbers separated by commas, such as 77777,1234. Later on, it provided actual names for its users, but most of the CompuServe members still use the numbers.

8. The case of changing one's name is a particularly vexing problem for corporate email administrators. Do you change the email address to correspond to the new name, matching your corporate naming convention if you have one? Or do you keep an alias to the person's old name, so that email can continue to be delivered?

9. The case of changing one's name is a particularly vexing problem for corporate email administrators. Do you change the email address to correspond to the new name, matching your corporate naming convention if you have one? Or do you keep an alias to the person's old name, so that email can continue to be delivered?

10. Can you believe this stuff? Objects have distinguished names and contain attributes, while attributes are named with object identifiers. Sound circular? It isn't. Rather, it's just the deranged rambling of a standards committee.

11. These numbers are listed on PageNet's Web site at *www.pagenet.com/ sendpage/emailpage.htm*.

12. Of course, if Lotus has its way, you will probably be faced with having to install Notes for more than just the fax gateway. But that is the topic for some other forum. In any event, there are many choices for fax gateway products outside of those sold by Lotus.

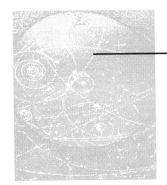

CHAPTER

7

Messaging in the Enterprise: 100% Pure Internet

In this chapter, we consider two central issues for enterprise email: how to determine the appropriate attachments for recipients and how to evaluate the Internet readiness of an enterprisewide messaging system. We also examine how to make the best use of groupware products, such as Lotus Notes and Microsoft Exchange, with Internet-based email.

These topics are a good place to end our discussion: As businesses rely more on messaging for extranet-style communications, being able to share information effectively is a key concern.

INTRODUCTION

To begin, let's ask ourselves about enabling information sharing between groups of users, whether those groups are workgroups or cooperating organizations.

As a first step, we have to agree on a common technology infrastructure—protocols and conventions. A workable infrastructure is one that allows for evolutionary change in a chaotic fashion. That is, while there may be a well-defined lowest common denominator—something that defines the "cost of entry" for using the infrastructure—there must also be a mechanism that allows for new technologies and approaches to be gradually introduced.

An easy example of such a workable infrastructure is the Internet and the Web. While much credit is due to the researchers who designed and the developers who implemented the Web protocols, even more credit is due the Internet architects for designing a networking infrastructure that is unaffected by new applications. This allowed the Web to grow organically. At first, only a small number of sites employed Web services. Over time, the technology achieved dominance within a powerful niche in the Internet. But, at no point did any Internet service provider (ISP) ever have to "turn a switch on" in order to allow Web-based traffic to flow in the Internet. Every site and computer made the choice, individually, one at a time.

However, this level of accommodation has a price: It allows two groups to make choices that conform to the infrastructure, but they are not compatible. Different groups often have different criteria and biases toward technological alternatives. An infrastructure that tries to choose winners, rather than letting user consensus drive toward resolution, often finds that it makes poor choices.[1]

Even so, the pain of having conforming but incompatible choices is considerable. Regrettably, while Internet messaging standards do a fine job of "strong typing" with respect to the attachments that are carried, there are few options available to determine the optimal, preferred or even readable format for the recipient.

This, however, raises an even more important issue: How can we be sure that we are building an enterprise infrastructure that supports Internet messaging to the fullest? How can we be sure that the products we select lead to cost-effective solutions that will work with the choices made by other enterprises?

These are thorny questions, and there are no easy answers. Having said that, we suggest a goal, which we term "100% pure Internet." As we mentioned in Chapter 1, this means you should select products that faithfully implement Internet standards as their native mode. If you can avoid using an application gateway, do so! If you can avoid converting between different messaging technologies, do so!

Naturally, many enterprises carry a significant legacy burden, and while it isn't realistic for many to adopt a 100% pure Internet strategy on day one, it is an appropriate goal.

So, let us now consider these issues in greater detail.

PROBLEMS

One of the first tasks attempted by email users beyond sending simple messages is exchanging attached files. Ranging from pictures to word processing documents to spreadsheets, it makes sense to use email in this fashion to deliver information. Indeed, this very book was created this way, with each of us emailing chapters back and forth to each other as attached Word documents.

The transfer of files is a very productive use of email. In the old days before universal Internet email connectivity was common (say, the late 1980s), you had to work a lot harder to transfer files. Usually, this involved modems to connect directly between two computers. This meant that you and your partner had to be ready to coordinate this operation. If you were separated by several time zones, someone was doing this either very late at night or early in the morning. And often the process took several phone calls to get everything working. We can remember giving up in frustration many times because we couldn't get our modems or software configured, or because the connection dropped in the middle of the transfer.

Sending files via email avoids synchronizing your movements. You create a new message, hit the attachment button or use the command to attach a file, find the file you desire and send the message. That's it. No muss, no fuss. No one has to know anything about parity bits and whether your modem is handshaking properly. You let the Internet handle getting the file from you to the recipient, and usually it does.

Well…yes and no. Sending attachments sounds easy in theory, but in practice it is a very difficult problem. It is made even more difficult because two people or enterprises may not be able to send and receive files to each other, even though they can exchange ordinary text messages. Compounding things further is the increased demands that email users have to exchange richer[2] email items, like those that include HTML pages or Java applets as part of the message. And the problem is made worse when you want to send multiple files in a single message, rather than attaching a single file per message.

Why Attachments Don't Attach

There isn't a single reason for this breakdown in communication, and often there is more than one possible cause for why attachments aren't delivered intact. If a corporation is running something less than a 100% pure Internet email system, there could be a failure in the gateway software from the corporate email network to the Internet. Or, the problem could be part of a design flaw in how the gateway translates the attachment from one system to another.

The attachment may not be delivered because of operator error. Your correspondent may not know what to do when receiving an attachment, and how to find it on his or her file system. Your correspondent may not have the appropriate application to open your file. Or your correspondent may have forgotten to attach a file to the message, and sent it on without noticing this omission.

Our problem could be, as Chapter 1 discusses, an issue of which particular application version is used to view the attachment. We often find correspondents sending us newer Word or PowerPoint files than we have running on our own machines.

And it could be that the email program isn't set up to view attachments properly, or can't handle them at all.

All of these problems demonstrate a very important point: You can't assume anything when you send someone a file. You can't assume that the recipient is running the same operating system version, let alone the right application software version, to open the file. You can't assume that the recipient will be able to receive anything bigger than a few kilobytes, and even if someone successfully received the data you can't assume that they know what to do with it and what applications to use to view the file. About the only thing you can assume is that some can receive your messages, although given the discussions in Chapter 2, we can't always assume that either.

With all of these problems, it is a wonder that attachments make it safely across the Internet at all!

Let's use a few examples to demonstrate these pitfalls.

We mentioned that sometimes your software doesn't handle attachments properly, but this situation was particularly vexing for us to solve.

We had two correspondents: one using Microsoft Network (MSN) and the other using a supposedly 100% pure Internet email product with a popular ISP. The person using the ISP sent a Word document as an attachment in his Eudora program to his MSN correspondent, who managed to save the file and open it in Word without any problems. Then the MSN person sent his changes back to our friend on Eudora. However, the attachment didn't attach and instead was encoded as part of his message. After much trial and error, we finally realized that our friend wasn't using the full Eudora software, but a version called Eudora Lite, which he had gotten from his ISP. Eudora Lite can't handle non-MIME attachment formats, which is what was supported by MSN.

One of the more popular uses of email is to exchange copies of Web pages. In the early days of the Web, you could just attach the page and let your correspondents fend for themselves. This was cumbersome, since it involved saving the file to disk, opening up your Web browser and finding the file to load it into the browser to view it. It took several steps and for some people it was too much effort. Many users of Web browsers had never used them to view pages on their own hard disks, and others couldn't find a file on their hard disks, despite all kinds of clues or hints.

Some email networks didn't work properly: If you use AOL's Macintosh software, for example, older versions would just throw away any attachments they received from Internet email correspondents. We often got messages from such users, asking us why we sent them a completely blank message. That was an indication that they were running Macs and using this particular AOL software. The later Mac versions and the AOL Windows programs worked fine.

As the Web became increasingly popular, more people started using HTML tags inside their own messages to highlight text, include URLs and do other things. Email vendors took note of this and began to incorporate various ways to interpret this special text. For example, version 3 of Eudora would underline the HTML tag and provide a means of automatically launching your preferred browser to view the link. It took some work to set this up, but once you did, you were literally a click away from viewing the page. You could just click on the highlighted text and the browser would come up, and load the link referenced in your email message. One-click viewing!

But just having a link isn't really very satisfying. Ideally, you'd like to see the actual page, in full color and with all the resulting graphics that the Web author intended. This is how the latest generation of products from Netscape, Microsoft and Qualcomm work. These products, as well as several others, can interpret HTML tags inside the message body and display the page properly, just as your browser would display the page. You don't have to load any browser software, and you don't even have to click on anything. It just appears as part of your message.

But not all products interpret all HTML tags as you might imagine. As new tags are invented, email vendors have to keep up and support them in their products in order to display properly. For example, Eudora 3 doesn't work with included HTML tables, but Messenger and Eudora version 4 do.[3] This is the same problem that the browser vendors have to deal with, since the HTML language continues to add new tags and support new features.

Sometimes the mail system can deal with attachments but not the people using them. Our favorite example is when a friend using AOL tried to view a photograph that was attached to the message. The photo was downloaded from AOL's computers to our friend's hard disk, and we could see the file sitting there innocently enough. However, the file arrived not as the JPEG format it began life as, but as a MIME-encoded message. For some reason, the AOL software didn't de-MIME it properly and convert it back into a JPEG photograph. Once we found WinZIP (a popular file compression utility), we were able to save the file as a JPEG image and view it without any problems.

But who is at fault here? The friend, who had never had any reason to do anything with MIME? Or AOL, which should have designed better software? Or the sender, who should have provided instructions on how to decode the MIME message? If we were going to pick a single party, we would suggest AOL. But it almost doesn't matter, really. You'd just like your attachments to arrive intact.[4]

There is a great deal of specific information—information that you may not be particularly inclined to divulge or necessarily know—in order to exchange attachments successfully. We'll have lots of tips and hints on how to do this later on in this chapter, but first we have some additional horror stories.

The Case of the Stuck Gateway

Attachment problems have a long legacy. One of the oldest email networks around is MCIMail. When it first was designed, attached files weren't even a consideration. The network was set up to send messages among users of character-mode terminals—and no one had files to attach, anyway. When PCs came along it made sense to extend the network to cover attachments, but this was done in a way to not pay any attention to Internet standards. MCI designed its own means of dealing with encoding and decoding attachments. When MCI established its Internet gateway, it left much of the implementation of attachments to various third-party vendors, who managed to muck things up royally.

In the early 1990s, we were avid users of MCIMail. It was the de facto means of communication among computer trade journalists, not to mention others in the high-tech industry. When we set up a new networking magazine, we made sure our email system (at the time, a precursor of Microsoft Exchange called Network Courier) would run an MCIMail gateway, so we could still communicate with the outside world.

This gateway was a problem child from day one. It ran on an ordinary DOS computer and had a network connection as well as an ordinary dialup modem (back then, we had 2,400-bits-per-second modems, if you really want to know). It would run a timer to do its tasks. Every 10 minutes, it would examine a particular set of directories on our network file server. When a message was stored as a file in the outgoing directory, the MCIMail gateway would dial the modem, connect to MCIMail's network, send its files and then receive anything waiting for our enterprise email system. It would then route these messages to the appropriate user.

This gateway was quirky and problematic. Sometimes the modem wouldn't connect to MCIMail's modems. Sometimes the machine would lose its network connection, or the machine would lose power and wouldn't boot to the right place. All of this had the same result: No mail would flow out to MCIMail, and no mail from MCIMail would come in. It got to the point where the first person into the office in the morning would check the gateway and make sure it was still living and breathing.

One day we got a call from one of our reporters, who had been trying to send us his story text via his MCIMail box. We hadn't yet received it, and we asked him to send it again.

It was an odd situation, because we were able to communicate *to* him. Our messages were being sent to MCIMail, but they were not being received. After much rebooting, sending some test messages out to ourselves and watching what the gateway was doing, we finally figured out the situation. We had a stuck gateway. Because the gateway first sent messages in its queue, these went out fine. But then it would try to download the inbound messages, and here we had a problem.

Someone had tried to send us a very large attachment. The way this particular gateway would work was that it would download the attachment into memory before saving it to disk. Since the attachment was larger than the puny 640 kilobytes that was in our DOS computer, it would never be downloaded. As a result, all the remaining inbound messages were stuck behind this one with the large attachment, and we couldn't get any of our MCIMail. Once we figured out this problem and deleted the offending message, our gateway system was back to normal and we could receive messages from the outside world as well as send them.

We weren't the only ones with this problem, and as we traveled around to other email administrators we found that they also kept a close watch over their gateway systems. Some even placed their gateway machines in their offices, where they could keep a very close eye on them and listen as they regularly dialed out for email. While it was nice to see so many people care about their communications, it did strike us as excessive that they had to live so close to their equipment.

The reason we recall this quaint piece of technology nearly a decade later is because many corporations still make use of this gateway, even with their so-called "advanced" Microsoft Exchange systems. The software that we used so long ago is still part and parcel to Exchange's MCI-Mail gateway. It casts a long shadow. And while the Internet gateways to Exchange are of more recent vintage, they are still prone to all sorts of problems, as we demonstrated in Chapter 2, where we presented different error reports from this gateway.

Microsoft isn't alone. Many vendors don't upgrade their gateways with the rest of their email network when they release new software. As we saw in Chapter 6, cc:Mail's gateways to fax and pagers run on older versions of their mail servers. If you want to make use of these gateways, you have to run both older and newer servers on your network—not a very satisfying experience. Novell's GroupWise has a similar problem.

The reason is relatively simple. Although a key piece of technology, the number of individual gateways that a Lotus, Novell or Microsoft can sell is fairly limited. While they might have millions of users of their software, they may only sell thousands or hundreds of copies of their particular gateways. There is very little incentive for these companies to improve and add features.

And, typically, a small outfit develops the gateway software—sometimes a single developer working as a contract programmer. There isn't any motivation for the developer to improve his or her software, mainly because the contract is up and he or she has moved on to other projects.

As the Internet has become popular, so have the gateways and connections to it from various email systems. That places an extra burden on the gateway to work reliably, as messages pass back and forth from the enterprise mail system to the Internet and back again.

This is no small matter. In some corporations, the Internet gateways have become so overloaded that if they go down for a few hours, the backlog of messages can take days to clear. This is even more of an issue for the email network providers. Witness the trials of Microsoft Network (MSN) and AOL: Often we've seen delays of days in getting messages to these users from the Internet.[5]

Almost every modern email system has a way to connect to the Internet and exchange email nowadays. That's great. But this universal connectivity has increased the possibility of problems when it comes to exchanging attachments.

And if more than one gateway is between you and your recipient, you could be in for some really interesting situations! For example, let's say that we have an MCIMail user sending a file to someone at AOL. But the sender addresses it to *joe@aol.com*, in the form of an Internet address. This message now goes from MCIMail, through its Internet gateway to the Internet, to the AOL Internet gateway and then on to the AOL user. That's a lot of postage and handling for a simple message, and chances are that some attachment will get mangled by one gateway post office or another, or will arrive in some format that the average AOL user wouldn't know what to do with it.

The trick for any email system, whether it is using 100% pure Internet standards or something less, is being able to recognize how attachments are encoded and then react properly when it comes time to decode the attached file. Chapter 3 discusses how messages are structured to contain attachments.

Mixing Macs and Windows

Another problem with sending attachments is trying to communicate between computers running different operating systems. Because email is so universally used these days, we tend to forget that not everyone will be using the particular version of operating system we use. Indeed, one of the nicer benefits of email is being able to send files that can be viewed or worked on from one computer to another, without regard for the operating system.

However, this cross-platform communication is difficult to do. Besides differences in how each email product encodes attachments, each operating system uses a different file format and character set. Something as simple as determining the end of a line of text could be just a carriage return, just a line feed or a combination of both characters, depending on whether you use Windows, Macintosh OS or UNIX, for example. And many Macs encode their attachments with something other than the MIME standard mentioned in Chapter 4.

If you have ever gotten a message that had strange characters at the beginning of a line or in place of where an apostrophe should be, then you know what we are talking about. While you can still read most of the message, it is annoying, and this could ruin an entire day for some people (or at least it seems to do so, based on the flames they send). We'll cover how these character sets are implemented in our next section on standards.

This means trouble when a Mac user sends a file to a Windows user, or vice-versa. It may mean it's time to upgrade an older version of your email software, because many of these products didn't implement the MIME standards properly and won't be able to decode your attachments.

Compounding this problem is that each operating system has its favorite way of compressing files—a common practice for correspondents who want to save bandwidth and time in moving data around the Internet. For example, Macintosh users like StuffIt, Windows users are fans of WinZIP, and UNIX has its compressor gzip. If you have all of these utilities and know how to use them, count yourself lucky. Some of the newer versions of these utilities can interpret compressed files in the other formats and uncompress them properly, but many of the older versions can't. We'll talk about how to make use of compression utilities later on in this chapter.

We experienced an odd situation as we were writing this chapter. One of us was working on a PowerPoint presentation with a correspondent using the Mac version. We were able to exchange an initial file without any problems, but when we tried a second (and much larger) file, the Windows version of PowerPoint couldn't read the attachment. It turns out this is a bug in PowerPoint, and not related to email! Our correspondent had to first divide her file into pieces, and then reassemble them on a Windows machine!

Fear of Infection

One of the biggest problems with attachments, once you actually can receive them and read them, is catching a virus from the attached file. Since the file arrives intact (hopefully), there is a chance that it could be an executable program. And if your luck has run out, these executable programs could contain a virus that could make your computing life miserable.

Viruses have lots of ways of operating. Some just have to be saved to your hard disk before they go about their dirty business. Some have to be explicitly opened by you or your application before they start doing whatever their inventor programmed. Some attack specific parts of your hard disk, such as the system files or the boot records, which can make your disk inoperable at worst or very unstable at best. It is really difficult to generalize, but there is one sure bet: You want to keep your machine as virus-free as possible, and that means practicing safe computing.

It is almost like the strictures for safe sex. You don't exchange files freely, whether they are on a floppy disk or email attachments. You don't let others make use of your machine or install software on it without understanding what they are doing. You run special protection software on your machine as a matter of course, no matter how safe you think you are.

Executable files can take many forms, and two of the more insidious are thanks to Microsoft.[6] Both Word macros and Active X applications are really nothing more than programs. Both can be found in many places, and Word has now become the standard for exchanging text files. This means you are in a more vulnerable situation when it comes to catching a virus, because you may not realize that your document or Web page contains a program that can erase files from your disk until it is too late and the damage is done.[7]

Word macros are programs, just like anything else. Indeed, part of the Word software itself makes use of macros. They are written in a version of BASIC programming language—a language that has been around since the early 1960s—almost ancient history in Internet time. And if you are running a version of Word later than version 2, you have the ability to become infected from a malicious or poorly written macro virus.[8]

This doesn't happen that often, but when it does you certainly remember it. We've seen this a number of times, including a friend's badly infected Macintosh. We managed to track down its infection to an email attachment that was a Word document sent to our friend. It turns out this Word document was infected with a virus, not a very nasty one but an annoying one nonetheless. Unbeknownst to our friend, every Word file that he had created or opened since viewing this file had been infected. This was no small matter: The infection occurred nine months prior to our examination and had touched several hundred files. It took the better part of the day to clear up this contagion and protect his machine against future infections.

So, how do you know ahead of time whether or not a file contains a virus? You don't; there aren't any symptoms or obvious signs. And sometimes even the most respectable of correspondents can turn out to infect you with a virus. We have seen email from Microsoft employees that contain infected attachments. Again, you may be lucky. These viruses may not do much more than announce their presence. Or you may not be as lucky. They could trash your entire hard disk without warning. Do you really want to take that chance?

In our section on solutions, we'll go into details about how you should take extra precautions against the kinds of attachments you receive and how you should operate on a day-to-day basis to stay protected.

Securing Your Messages

The issue of viruses brings up an important point: how to send something to your correspondent securely, without you both having to worry that someone has tampered or viewed the message in transit. While this has the air of cloak-and-dagger mystery to it, or illegality, as we said in Chapter 4, lots of people use encryption technologies to keep their messages away from the eyes of the world.

A relatively easy task would be for someone to try to guess your password, and attempt to log in to your email account and collect your mail. If your password is just a few characters long, or if it is a common word, there are computer programs that can try to figure this out. This is why all network administrators suggest using a combination of numbers and letters instead of choosing things like your birthday, street address or your spouse's name as your password.

In any event, there are many ways to secure your messages. You can encrypt the entire message with a set of keys, so that only someone who has the right key can decrypt and read it. You can sign your message with a special digital signature, so that your recipients can be sure that they actually got the message from you and not some impostor. You can secure your own network from the public Internet, so that all messages never leave your own wires and modems. These issues are discussed in Chapter 4.

Internet Readiness

Before we get to standards, there is one final issue to explore for general enterprise email users. How Internet-ready is your email network? In our case, running Network Courier with a bad MCIMail gateway, the answer was "not very Internet-ready." We had a second gateway on that email system that connected to the Internet, and that would work somewhat better. But still, we had our share of mangled attachments.

In our ideal world, every email system would support 100% of the various Internet standards and protocols and work predictably. By this we mean that every email user runs software that makes use of TCP/IP protocols and SMTP mail servers. We think this is an ideal world because it allows for freedom of choice of desktop software: Being 100% Internet means never having to stay locked into a particular piece of software if something better comes along.

Certainly, proprietary email systems such as Notes, Exchange and cc:Mail have more features and functions than most Internet email programs. They work with their own database of users and are tightly coupled to their own software for forms, routing of messages, and so forth. Products such as GroupWise and PROFS have long had the ability to recall a sent message before it could be read by anyone, what one IS manager calls the "save your skin" feature.

Another GroupWise feature is integrated calendars and schedules with its email functions, making it easier to reserve conference rooms and keep track of your workgroup. These and other features are not currently found in 100% pure Internet products. This could be an important justification of why you should choose these products over more Internet-ready ones, but there is a downside to this choice: relying on the Internet gateway for your correspondence outside the corporation.

The problem is how to connect such a proprietary system to the rest of the world. If all of your customers are running cc:Mail servers, that's great. You can then connect your servers to their servers via an ordinary phone line and never have to worry about passing messages through the public Internet. But that is more fantasy than reality.[9]

There isn't a single email system that everyone is using, even everyone within the strict confines of a single corporation. And the moment you mix and match email systems, you are stuck with implementing gateways and using the Internet as a common carrier to connect them.

Our ideal world is still very much a goal. While there are email products that are very Internet-savvy, protocols are implemented differently by different programs. Standards are subject to interpretation or, worse, ignored. And older email systems, as we have seen, have little or no motivation to change or to increase their Internet readiness.

Often, as we have seen in our examples, you can't determine your email system's level of Internet-readiness until you attempt a particular task that bangs up against some wall. Or you aren't running TCP/IP throughout your enterprise network, so you have to rely on some other protocol to move your message from your desktop to your email server, and perhaps on some gateway to move it out to the Internet.

And, as we have already discussed, relying on an Internet gateway can be a single choke point for your enterprise messaging traffic. If your gateway gets stuck or becomes temperamental, then your messaging traffic slows or stops to the outside world. As corporations become more reliant on communicating across the Internet, this can be an issue for those enterprises using less than 100% pure Internet products.

STANDARDS

In a broad sense, Chapters 2 through 6 have described the Internet standards that pertain to messaging. So, what can be said about standardizing Internet-readiness? For our purposes, there are three topics we can expand on: Internet architecture, which describes how things fit together; extensibility of content types and character sets, which describes how you can send new kinds of attachments; and the multipart/related content type, which allows you to send groups of attachments together.

The Internet Architecture

To begin, while there is an Internet "architecture," it does not exist in a formal sense. Technological change is continuous, and seemingly ever increasing. In such an environment, it would be folly to attempt to codify a static set of principles. Rather, there are more rules than axioms, more guidelines than rules, and they are all subject to change. This doesn't suggest a happy future for the corporate professional trying to plan and anticipate technology changes. Fortunately, there are two very basic axioms that have withstood the test of Internet time.

First, functionality should always be placed as close to the user as possible. The corollary is that the messaging infrastructure should be as simple as possible.

For example, consider the task of securing email from unauthorized disclosure in transit. One approach is to ensure a secure channel between each message relay in the infrastructure and make no requirements on the sender or recipient. The alternative approach is for the sender to encrypt the message and make no requirements on the messaging infrastructure. Which approach will actually work in practice? Quick, no peeking ahead to the next sentence! The answer is to carefully avoid putting security features into the message infrastructure. Add them to software under the user's control instead.

The reason is simple. You're never going to get all the stakeholders in the infrastructure to agree on key management issues, or even basic cryptographic algorithms. Are these stakeholders nefarious? No, of course not. They are simply numerous entities playing different roles without any centralized authority. Some are service providers, some are corporations, some are public institutions and some are running a business out of their garage. They all "own" their own little slice of the Internet. They are never going to agree on a single standard to be provisioned. If multiple standards are offered, then they'll tend to make incompatible choices. By putting security features in the desktop software, the sender and receiver will implement the appropriate level of security. Different communications will have different requirements, and one size simply doesn't fit all. Provide the user with a variety of options, if need be, and let them choose.

Second, don't "standardize" on anything until it's running on platforms shipped by two different vendors.

The simple fact of the matter is that even the simplest protocols and services are complex. Until two independent groups implement a standard into a product, and until they interoperate in your environment, any talk of a "solution" is entirely speculative. It is worth noting that in "Internet speak," one of the requirements for something to be called a "standard" is that it has multiple, interoperable implementations.

Content Types and Character Sets

The lesson from the two preceding axioms is that extensibility in the messaging infrastructure will largely occur in the introduction of new content types and character sets. Chapter 3 discusses content types in depth. A content type is a designation used to mark an attachment within a message. With that designation, you know what kind of application to use to process them. Chapter 3 discusses character sets briefly. We will flesh out that description here.

Content Types

A key concept with respect to content types is that they are user definable. Anyone can define a content type and then register it with the Internet Assigned Numbers Authority (IANA).

Registration is meant to achieve one very important goal: If someone encounters your content type in a message, he or she can go to a repository to find out more about it. In general, this won't be a user but a vendor programmer or systems administrator. Typically, whoever "owns" the data definition of the file being marked with a content type does the registration. However, this isn't a requirement. So, before defining your own content type, you should visit the IANA's Web site[10] to see if it's already registered. There's just one note: The IANA uses the term "media type" instead of content type. Content type is the term introduced originally by MIME; as the MIME standard was updated, the term media type was introduced. However, since the header remains Content-Type:, we continue to use that term.

Character Sets

A character set is simply a convention for identifying the glyphs associated with digitally rendered text. In other words, if you've got a file containing text, you need to know how to interpret each character in the file. For example, perhaps it takes more than one octet to represent a character. The definition of a character set says how to interpret the stream of octets that make up the text and how to render them for reading by a human.

The Internet had a very gentle introduction to character sets. In the beginning, it only used one of them! The choice was the "US ASCII" set. Each character is represented in a single octet, and high-order bit of each octet is zero-valued. Over time, of course, other character sets had to be supported.

Today's solution is rather direct:

1. The US ASCII set continues to be used for protocol syntax. After all, programs, not people, interpret these.

2. The US ASCII set is the default character set used in message headers. Those parts of message headers that are meaningful by people can be encoded using different character sets. For example, the value associated with the Subject: header can be encoded using an arbitrary character set. However, the keyword of this header ("Subject") is always in ASCII. Again, the reason is that programs, not people, interpret the "Subject:," while people interpret the value that follows. A subtler example deals with email addresses. For example, looking at

Marshall Rose <mrose@example.com>

it is clear that the mailbox (everything between the angle-brackets) must be machine-readable; in contrast, the textual phrase (everything else) is meaningful only to humans.

3. Textual body parts (e.g., text/plain) are explicitly tagged with a character set. This may very well be "us-ascii," but the tagging is necessary nonetheless.

As Chapter 3 notes, product support for character sets, particularly character set support in headers, is spotty. However, the situation continues to improve over time.

Once again, the IANA maintains a registry of character sets. Check out the IANA's Web site[11] to see what's registered.

Grouping Attachments

Chapter 3 introduces the concept of structured message bodies. Key among these is the multipart content that is used to group body parts. For example, a multipart/mixed content contains several seemingly unrelated subordinate body parts. Now, we introduce the final content type, multipart/related, which is used to group several body parts together that comprise a unitary set of data.

For example, if you wanted to send an HTML page to someone, there may be various images contained within the page. Although you could send just the one HTML file in a message (as a text/html content), the recipient needs network connectivity in order to view the images. The alternative is to send the images (as image/gif or image/jpeg contents) with the HTML file. All of these body parts are sent inside a multipart/related content.

There are only two tricks to understanding how multipart/related works: First, it defines a base type that is used to direct processing of the parts; and, second, there is a mechanism for referencing different body parts within a message.[12]

The multipart/related content type has two mandatory parameters. One defines the base type of the related objects and the other points to the "root" object. So, in the case of our "sending a Web page" example, the type parameter would indicate text/html. The key thing to appreciate here is that the type parameter is telling the recipient's software that the entire multipart/related structure should be handed off to the recipient's HTML software for rendering. This differs from the way a multipart/mixed content would be handled. In that scenario, the HTML software would get invoked on just the text/html body part, and then the recipient's image display software would get invoked for each image/gif and image/jpeg body part.

The second trick deals with how the recipient's HTML software can resolve links from the HTML file to the various images. The answer is astonishingly easy: Each body part containing an image has a Content-ID: header, and the HTML file uses a cid: URL in order to reference the image contained in that body part.

Let's look at a brief example. Suppose you had an HTML file that contained a fragment like this:

```
<img src="logo.gif">
```

When you sent that HTML file to someone, your software constructs a multipart/related content containing two subordinate body parts. The first is a text/html, the second is an image/gif. The type parameter of the multipart/related is text/html and the base parameter points to the text/html body part. The headers of the image/gif body part might look like this:

```
Content-Type: image/gif
Content-Transfer-Encoding: base64
Content-ID: <008001bd2915$7b710b60$13c743cf@example.com>
```

Chapter 3 discusses all of these headers, and there is nothing particularly out of the ordinary about them. What is special is how your software will modify

```
<img src="logo.gif">
```

when it builds the text/html body part:

```
<img src="cid:008001bd2915$7b710b60$13c743cf@example.com">
```

The magic, of course, is that the recipient's HTML software will see the cid: URL and know to look around for a body part having the same value for its Content-ID:. For completeness, we note that there is also a mid: URL, used for referencing a message having a certain value as its Message-ID:.

Essentially, that's it! This is a very straightforward way of relating the objects that you send in a very transparent way. Of course, your software might allow options as to whether images should be included in the messages you send. On the plus side, the recipient doesn't need network connectivity to view the whole page. But, on the minus side, your messages are going to be considerably larger.

Attachment File Formats

As much as we'd like every email program to use MIME for attachments, some older and/or clueless software does not. Some support other formats in addition to MIME.

There are five basic attachment formats: MIME, which we have already discussed in Chapter 3, is one of the five. The others?

> [The] four options for encoding attachments [are]: BinHex, Uuencode, AppleSingle and AppleDouble. The two Apple options are methods of sending a Macintosh file, with its two forks, as a binary attachment. If I send a file encoded with AppleSingle to a Netscape Messenger user, they're stymied. Netscape Messenger doesn't understand how to reassemble a MIME attachment that identifies itself as AppleSingle. Likewise, if I send a uuencoded file, the recipient is still stymied. Even more irritating is that uuencode is fairly universally supported-- but it's not an option in the freeware Eudora Light on the Mac, though Eudora Light under Windows does support it.[13]

We recommend that you use MIME method whenever possible, unless you are communicating with users running older Macintosh or UNIX mail programs. In that case, you'd choose BinHex (for the Mac users) or uuencode (for the UNIX users).

BinHex[14] is a special form of encoding made popular on Macs and has since spread to other operating systems. Like uuencoding, it takes an 8-bit file and turns it into 7-bit formats so that the file can be transferred by programs that were designed to deal with ordinary text. Uuencoding was popular in those early days before MIME became a standard, and is still used by many partly functional Internet gateways.

SOLUTIONS

We offer several strategies, tips and tools in this section to help solve some of the problems mentioned earlier. First, we'll look at how to send attachments and the various methods used by each of our featured software products. We'll then take this information and show you how to successfully receive and decode your own attachments. Next, we'll look at the range of virus scanning software available to protect your enterprise and your own desktop from infection. We'll also look at strategies for selecting and managing the appropriate email server technologies, whether they be 100% pure Internet or something less standard.

How to Send Attachments

Let's look at how you actually can send a file using one of the featured software programs. With WinCIM, there are two ways to send files. Mail | Create New Mail | Attach File will bring up a window where you can browse your hard disk file system and find the file you desire. Or, you can do Mail | Send File and get to the window, shown in Figure 7.1, directly. You can choose one of your files and add it to your message. If you want to attach more than one file, you click on the Add to list button and select another file. You may want to adjust the file type once you have chosen your files, and here you have four choices: text, JPEG and GIF for image files in these formats, and binary (for everything else). These choices for the file types aren't really that important, as WinCIM will still send them the same way.

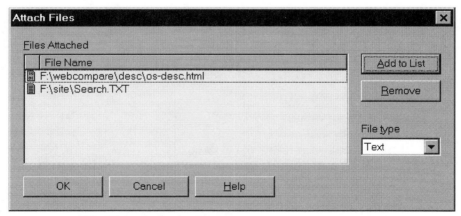

Figure 7.1   WinCIM attachment options

With America Online, you go to Mail | Compose Mail | Attach and you'll see a window on your file system. We would recommend that you select a single file to attach to a message, so if you want to send more than one you'll have to send multiple messages. The same is true when it comes time to send any AOL recipients any files: It's best to send a single file at a time, because sending multiple files can cause problems with earlier AOL software.

If you are using WinCIM or AOL, you don't have any choice in how your attachment gets sent. Anything that you attach to your message has the format specified by what these network operators are using to move things around. And the particular version of software you are using could change what attachment method you use. We recommend that if you are having trouble sending or receiving attachments you make sure to upgrade to the most recent version of WinCIM and AOL software.

In cc:Mail, you have several ways to attach a file. The easiest is to click on the paper clip icon at the top of the toolbar. You can also go to the File | Attach menu. Or if you are inside the lower window pane of the message body, right-click your mouse and choose the Attach option. All of these have the same result: You'll get the window to browse your file system and select the file. Once you do, it is placed inside the message body with an icon as shown in Figure 7.2. If you want to select more than one file, hold down the Shift key while you choose the first and last files and every file in between them on your directory list with your mouse, and you'll see their names and icons added to your message. If you want to choose files that aren't in a particular sequence, hold down the Control key and then click on them with your mouse.

Baward.gif   amazon.html   IMC.bmp

Figure 7.2   cc:Mail attachments shown as icons inside your message

The issue with using cc:Mail is that you have to trust whatever gateway you are using for your corporate cc:Mail network to get the attachment to your destination. If your correspondent is on the same cc:Mail system as you, chances are he or she will be able to read the attachment without a problem. The trouble comes when the correspondent is running on something else, or when there is more than one gateway between you two. More on Internet gateways later.

Let's look at our Internet-based products and the choices of attachment formats. First is Eudora. Go to Tools | Options | Attachments, and you'll see three different formats: MIME, BinHex and uuencode. See Figure 7.3. (Other versions of Eudora, including the Eudora Lite freeware program, only support MIME and BinHex.)

There are other options on this screen, including where you want your received attachments to land on your hard disk and whether you want attached text files to appear in the message body or not. We recommend that you don't change this option unless your correspondents are having problems receiving your files. Also, if you do change the directory location, all of your stored messages will no longer have the correct information about where they stored their past attachments. These pointers aren't updated when you change the directory, so choose it wisely and try not to change it.

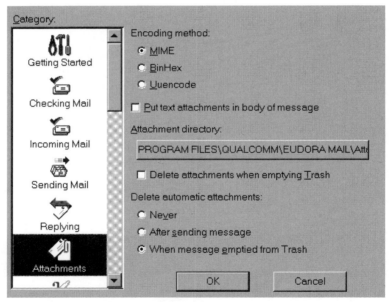

Figure 7.3   Eudora attachment options

Once you select your options on this screen, it is time to now send a file. As with cc:Mail, you can choose the menus (Message | Attach File), click on the paper clip icon on the toolbar, or use the keystroke shortcut of Control-H to bring up the window to select your file. And you can select more than one file by holding down the Shift or Control keys while you click your mouse on the files you want to send. You'll see their names added to your message header under the Attached: line.

What about Outlook Express? To set up your sending options, go to Tools | Options | Send window. There you'll see a choice of one of two boxes, HTML or Text. Each has a further Settings window with other options, as shown in Figure 7.4.

We recommend you use HTML, but regardless of whether you prefer HTML or Text, please set the encoding to "none," so that running older programs can read just the plain text without any encoding hassles!

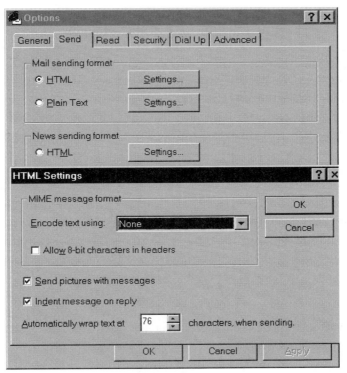

Figure 7.4   Outlook Express attachment options

Finally, Netscape Messenger sets up its attachment options in two places. First is the choice at Edit | Preferences | Mail | Messages | More Options. You have a simple choice here: either send messages "as is" or use the quoted printable characters. We recommend you use the first choice. Again, the reason is that if you correspond with people using old, pre-MIME software, they will see the plain text portion of the message without any encodings.

Second is the choice you have during message composition. Go to View | Options or click on the bottom of the three tabs in the header window, and you'll see a check box to choose Uuencode instead of MIME to send attachments. We recommend you leave this box unchecked and use MIME, unless your correspondents are having trouble receiving your files.

Where Are Those Attachments Kept, Anyway?

Now that you know how to send a file, let's talk about how you find the files that are sent to you. Each program stores its attachments in a different place, naturally. With Eudora, attachments are stored separately from the message that carries them to you. This is handy for checking viruses, but it can be difficult to manage if the original message is deleted and the attachment remains behind.

This directory is set up in Tools | Options | Attachments | Attachment Directory. If you haven't specified anything here, you're attachments are probably in c:\Program Files\Qualcomm\Eudora mail\attach. (Note the embedded spaces in that path name!) In Outlook Express, attachments are stored as part of the message. If you want to save them to another location on your hard disk, you need to view the message, right-click on the attachment icon and specify where you wish to save it.

In Messenger, attachments are also stored as part of the message when you initially receive them. You can set up where you want all your messages stored in Edit | Preferences | Mail | Mail Server | More Options. You typically place this folder in C:\Program Files\Netscape\Users\default\mail. With Messenger, you can detach the attachment and save it to any location on your hard disk when you are viewing the file, again by right-clicking on the icon.

AOL, WinCIM and cc:Mail don't treat attachments any differently than regular messages. See our descriptions in Chapter 2 on how they store their messages.

Setting Up Your Attachment Strategy[15]

Now that you know the basics, it is time to talk about formulating a strategy for successfully exchanging attachments. Before you do anything, send email to your potential correspondents and find out the following things. First, what email software and version number are they using? What is the version of their operating system platform? What kinds of files are you likely to exchange—word processing documents, spread-sheets, images or presentations? Do you both have the right kind of soft-ware to view the files you wish to exchange? Are you going to make use of any file compression software to save the time it takes to move the file across the Internet?

Now this seems like a great deal of work, and hardly anyone does this before sending a file. Typically, we go our merry way, attaching the file and hoping for the best—leaving the recipient up to his or her own devices to deal with what pops out on the other end. So, let's say you ask your questions and get back a thoughtful and truthful response. Now what?

1. Pick your common file format. In the ideal world, you and your correspondents would have the same version of applications software to make this exchanging easier. But we know this isn't the case. As an example, one person is working on Word 97 on Windows95, another on Word 6 for the Macintosh and the third is using Word 95 on Windows NT. Is there any way these three people can exchange documents? Yes.

It turns out that the common format among all three is Word 6, or you can use the Rich Text Format (RTF). Both versions of Word on Windows can read and write to these formats, although you have to remember to use the Save As command and scroll down a long list of file formats until you find either of them. So, before you start working on some common document, you can agree to use Word 6 (or RTF) as your file format. You can imagine the same sort of negotiation happening for sending image files. One popular choice is the Windows Bitmap format, which is supported by a number of applications.

This sounds more complicated than it is, and often the best strategy is to exchange a small test file to prove that it will be sent and received without any problems. Make sure each person can modify and send their changes back and forth before you get any further.

2. Pick your encoding method. If you are using different email products and you can configure your software to send and receive MIME attachments, by all means use this as your starting point. If MIME doesn't work, then try uuencoding. If neither works, then you'll probably have no choice but to forget about email and use the file transfer protocol (ftp) to send your files. More on that option later.

You may need to upgrade your email software to work properly. This is particularly true when it comes to using older versions of Netscape email products. We had attachment problems with version 3 that were solved when we received the same files using version 4. And, if you are running the free Eudora Lite software, we strongly recommend you spend a few dollars and obtain Eudora Pro. The Lite version doesn't handle attachments very well.

3. Pick your file viewing tools. Once you have established a common file format, you need to get your tools in order. If you don't have the right software to view your correspondents' files, look at what tools are available already on your machine. If you are running Windows95, there are already some applications that come with the computer that can help. The two we'll mention here are WordPad and Imaging. They are both very useful applications and come free as part of the Windows95 and Windows NT operating systems.

WordPad is great for viewing Word 6 files you receive via attachments, mainly because you can't get infected from any potential Word macro viruses (WordPad doesn't run any macros at all). It is found under Start | Programs | Accessories | Wordpad.

Most Windows machines have an image viewer, under Start | Programs | Accessories | Imaging. It can view and print a few different image file formats, including TIF, Windows Bitmaps (.BMPs) and JPEG. If your file is damaged, it doesn't always work, but we have found it a very reliable way to view images.

There are several products on the market that claim to be able to view almost anything in almost any version. We have tried many of these products and haven't found anything that really works without a great deal of fuss and bother. With one product, for example, you need to cut and paste the data from the file into the Windows clipboard, and then use the product to interpret the information. Your best strategy is to find something that will work for a particular file format. If you really must try something, the Eudora Pro version 4 package includes Verity's Key-View Pro file viewers.

4. Send a single file per message if you can. Many email programs don't deal well with sending more than a single attached file. You can send multiple messages, each with a single file attached, but that gets tedious quickly. A better way is to make use of a file compression program, and collect all the files you wish to exchange into what is called an archive. This also has the advantage of saving space and transmission time when you are sending the file. See our tips on compression utilities section for more details.

5. Keep the file names short. Remember those early DOS-based 8.3 character file names? Well, you might want to keep your own file names within those limits, because some of your correspondents may still be running DOS or 16-bit Windows. Sure, most modern operating systems can deal with longer file names, but why take the chance on something so simple? You also might wish to name the file with the appropriate extension, since some software programs can't recognize all extensions easily.

For example, use file.doc for word processing documents, file.ppt for PowerPoint presentations, file.tif for TIFF files, and so forth. An alternative suggestion is to rename the file when you receive it to one of these extensions based on what you believe the file to be. We have received PowerPoint presentations, for example, that wouldn't open up inside PowerPoint until they were renamed .PPT files.

6. Keep the files short. Many email systems place limits (as we saw in our earlier example of the stuck gateway) on file sizes. Anything more than 1 megabyte will cause you trouble on these systems, and you are better off using file transfer software to move the file. If you can't compress the file, or if the file is just too big, you'll find you should do a file transfer anyway.

7. Try several encoding formats when all else fails. You may need to encode or decode the file because of MIME/uuencode issues, as we mentioned earlier. You might try to send several test files, each one encoded in a different format, and see which one makes it intact at the other end. (It is a good idea to label each file with the encoding format, so you will be able to interpret your results.) We'll get into more details on this later.

Tips on Sending and Receiving Attachments

You should have a good idea of what to keep in mind when using one of the featured email programs to send an attachment. But that isn't the end of the story, of course. Sometimes, despite our best efforts, attachments won't go through. We have put together a chart showing you the chances of success when sending and receiving attachments using the products we mention. We cover cc:Mail in a separate section below, since the success or failure of any of its attachments is largely due to the particular Internet gateway employed by the enterprise.

You'll notice in our table that you might need to first encode the file before you send it, or decode the file after you receive it. We cover utilities that you can use for these tasks in a later section.

Can You Get There from Here?

Receiver	Sender				
	AOL	WinCIM	Eudora v4	Messenger v4	Outlook Express
AOL	Always*	Encoder***	MIME****	Always	Always
WinCIM	Decoder**	Always	MIME, Decoder	MIME, Decoder	MIME, Decoder
Eudora v4	Always	Encoder, Decoder	Always	Always	Always
Messenger v4	Always	Encoder, Decoder	MIME	Always	Always
Outlook Express	Always	Encoder, Decoder	MIME	Always	Always

NOTES: This table is based on the article "File Attachments Made Easy," which appeared in *MacUser* magazine, February 1997. This article contains additional Macintosh, UNIX and Windows email products and can be found at *www.zdnet.com/ macuser/mu_0297/handson/table.html.*

* *Always*: Sender/receiver pair should always transmit attachments correctly. Earlier versions of this software may not work, however.

** *Decoder*: Recipient will first need to save a copy of the message as a text file, then make use of one of the decoder programs such as XferPro.

*** *Encoder*: Sender will first need to encode the file with one of the utilities such as XferPro before attaching it to a message.

**** *MIME*: Sender should follow our instructions to make sure to set attachment type to MIME before attaching the file.

File Compression and Decoding Utilities

Earlier in this chapter we mentioned two kinds of products you might want to have to help you through the attachment maze. The first is file compression software. If you have more than two files you wish to send, or if you are concerned at all about the amount of time it takes to transfer your files and the size of your Internet pipe to send them, you should consider this software. There are several shareware or freely available products, all of which can be downloaded from many sites around the Internet.[16]

These utilities operate very simply. They make a copy of a file you select, squeezing the nonessential space and redundant data out of the file. In the case of some graphics files, this space can be significant— we've seen files reduced to a tenth or less of their original size. You select which files you want squeezed, and they are collected in what is called an archive. You then save this archive file to someplace on your hard disk. This is the file you send to your correspondents. Of course, if you choose to compress your files, your correspondents need to have a copy of the same software, or some equivalent, to go through the process to uncompress the files back to their original usable state before they can work on them.

Let's look at one of the most popular Windows products, WinZIP, as an example of how to prepare your files for sending.

We assume you can find a copy of this software, download it and install it on your machine. You are asked whether to start WinZIP with a wizard or in the classic interface. Choose classic, and you'll see a screen with an empty window. Click on the New button to create a new archive, and type the name and location where you'll remember it. Now you'll see a screen that is browsing your local hard disk. Choose the file or files you want to compress and include in that archive. You can use the Shift and Control keys to specify more than one file. If you return back to the control window, you can use the Add button to place additional files into the archive. When you are finished, choose the File | Close Archive command. Now go to your email program and attach this file, which should have a .ZIP extension, to your email message.

When your recipients receive this message, he or she needs to save the attached .ZIP file someplace on the local hard disk, and then run Win-ZIP and open this archive. The recipient will need to extract the files before using them.

If you or your correspondents are using Macintoshes, they should obtain a copy of StuffIt Deluxe. This software can uncompress ZIP files that you receive, but it can't create them. For this task, you'll need another utility such as ZipIt.[17]

So much for compression software. There is a second kind of utility that is useful for decoding files. If you are using an older email program, or if your file has gotten mangled through a gateway, you might want to investigate using one of these products to try to reassemble your data.

Nothing can ruin your email day more than receiving an unreadable attachment. We've spent more time than we care to admit decoding, resending and trying all sorts of tools on the files we get from others, with a mixture of success and failure.

Let's look at an example message fragment below:

```
--------------40D012293FF4Content-Type: image/tiff;
name="2.tif"Content-Transfer-Encoding:
base64Content-Disposition: inline; filename="2.tif"
```

```
SUkqAJDkBgAAAACAAAAAgAAAAIAAAADAAMAApgAEAAgADAAARABY
AHAAiACkAVQBNAEIAOQD/AP8A1gDMAO8A5wCtADMAZgCZAMwAAA
AzAGYAmQDMAP8AAAAzAGYAmQDMAP8AAAAzAGYAmQDMAP8AAAAzA
GYAmQDMAP8AZgCZAMwAAAAzAGYAmQDMAP8AAAAzAGYAmQDMAP8A
AAAzAGYAmQDMAP8AAAAzAGYAmQDMAP8AAAAzAGYAmQDMAP8AMwB
mAJkAzAD/AAAAMwBmAJkAzAD/AAAAMwBmAJkAzAD/AAAAMwBmAJ
kAzAAAADMAZgCZAMwA/wAAADMAmQDMAP8AAAAzAJkAzAD/AMwAA
ACZAJkAzAAAADMAZgDMAP8AAAAzAGYAmQDMAP8AMwBmAJkAzAD/
AAAAMwBmAJkAzAD/AAAAMwBmm...
```

What is odd about this message, apart from the fact that it isn't readable, is that each line is exactly the same length. This is your first clue that your attachment didn't come through properly. You also can see that the file name of this attachment is "2.tif," which could indicate an image file. Our diagnosis here is an email program that couldn't interpret the MIME-encoded message, which is what the line containing "base 64" is referring to. What to do?

You could first try to save this message as a separate text file.

Next, remembering where you saved the file, you can bring up your decoder program and see if it can recognize the file coding scheme and try to decode it. Sometimes you need to save the file with an extension of .UU, and sometimes any extension will work. Sometimes you need to bring up your word processor and delete all of the message header information from the file before you can process it with the decoder program. (Eudora offers you the option of saving your file without any of the email headers when you go to save your message.)

Both WinZIP and StuffIt Deluxe can decode files—some of the time. But if these two programs don't work, or if you need something to first encode the file before you send it, you might try one of the following:

- XferPro (Windows) www.sabasoft.com/info/xferpro.htm
- UULite (Mac) www.peanutsw.com
- PMPrep (OS/2) users.informatik.fh-hamburg.de/~radlof_k/ PMPrepEnglish

The Trouble with Gateways

We've already described several times in this book the trouble of using Internet email gateways. Nevertheless, if you are using email within a large corporation, chances are there is some division, subsidiary or far-off company that will be using a less than 100% pure Internet email system, and you'll want to send messages to that group.

Here is a note we received from one of our correspondents, whose company switched from a 100% pure Internet email to Lotus Notes. Sometimes, it is the little things that you miss:

```
Notes doesn't mark the previous message which you
reply to with ">" symbols, for example, something
that I really miss. It also does not have signature
files, and it tries to stick graphics into the
message body. Finally, I can't sort the message
display by subject.
```

If you are using Notes, cc:Mail, Exchange or some other non-100% pure product, chances are your attachment problems are caused by your gateway software. You might want to investigate if there are alternative products that can do a better job with handling the gateways.

You have two basic choices in how you install your email gateway. If you want complete control over both the local mail system and the Internet mail, you'll need to install an SMTP mail server at your corporation and connect it to the gateway server via your local area network. With this situation, you can use the gateway software from your email vendor (Lotus, Microsoft or Novell), or you can purchase a third-party product that will work with multiple email products.

Why would you want to buy a gateway when it comes free with the email package? A few reasons: performance, features and reliability. Some of the gateways don't scale well as the number of messages passing to and from the Internet increases, as you know it will over time. Some gateways aren't very reliable and need some serious babysitting to keep running, which is one of the reasons why we've seen them located in the email manager's office. And some don't have as many features as the third-party products do.

As an example, Novell's own STMP gateway for GroupWise requires two pieces of software: one that gets installed on the GroupWise post office (either running NetWare or OS/2), and one that gets installed and replaces the sendmail program running on a UNIX computer that handles the Internet mail service. These two machines must be connected on the same local area network, which means that you must be able to have a continuous Internet connection to make use of Novell's gateway. Other gateways, including the ones from Lotus and Microsoft, do not have this requirement.[18]

All four of the free gateways have a feature that you should know: being set up to send either MIME or uuencoded attachments. This is a global setting for all of your enterprise email users running messages across this gateway—meaning, if you change this parameter, you change it for all of your email users communicating to the Internet. As you have seen earlier in this chapter, we recommend using the MIME setting whenever possible.

Here are some products to consider. Many of them have versions that are freely downloaded from their Web sites and usable for a limited time, usually 30 days.

Internet Email Gateway Products

Company/URL	Product Name, Price	Platform OS [email system] supported
Gateways included in enterprise email systems		
Lotus cc:Mail www.ccmail.com/overview/ r8smtpdata.htm	cc:Mail Link to SMTP	NT
Novell GroupWise www.novell.com/	GroupWise/html/ smtp.html GroupWise SMTP/MIME Gateway	NetWare NLM,* OS/2*
Lotus Notes www.lotus.com	Notes SMTP MTA	NT
Microsoft Exchange www.microsoft.com/exchange	Internet Mail Service	NT

Internet Email Gateway Products (Continued)

Company/URL	Product Name, Price	Platform OS [email system] supported
Third-party gateways		
TenFour *www.tenfour.com/tfs*	TFS Gateway, $400	NT, 95 [1, 2, 3, 4, MS Mail]
International Messaging Associates *www.ima.com*	Internet Exchange, $1,495 (100 users)	NT, 95 [1, 3] (separate products for cc:Mail and Notes)
Computer Mail Services *www.cmsconnect.com/sbridge/sbv3.htm*	S-Bridge, $495 (15 users) and up	NT, 95 [1, MS Mail]
Wingra *www.wingra.com/Products/facts/summary2.html*	Missive, pricing varies	UNIX [1, 2, 3, 4, many others]
Worldtalk *www.worldtalk.com/html/nettalk/ntlknfo.htm*	NetTalk, pricing varies	NT [1, 2, 3, 4, MS Mail]
U.S. Computer *www.usc.com/products.htm*	Internet Mail Center, $750	NT [1, 3]

NOTES: Numbers in brackets in last column refer to the message system supported by the third-party gateway vendor (i.e., 1 refers to cc:Mail, 2 to GroupWise, etc.)

* GroupWise SMTP/MIME Gateway requires a constant Internet connection and has a separate component that runs on a UNIX server to communicate with the gateway.

If you don't want to configure and install a gateway, a second choice is to make use of one of the outsourcing vendors. This entails using a native post office-to-post office connection between your local email system and the vendor's network. In this situation, messages are taken from you and are sent to an outsourcing vendor's own SMTP mail server, then out onto the Internet. Using an outsourcing vendor means you don't have to own your own Internet connection and maintain your own Internet servers, but you do have to pay a per-message fee and other fees to the outsourcing vendor.

Three examples of these outsourcing vendors for cc:Mail users are Lansoft Jazz (*www.lansoft.com*), Fabrik Connect (*www.fabrik.com*) and

ESPMail (*www.espmail.com*). Fabrik charges $150 per cc:Mail post office per month, along with fees starting at 20 cents per message sent. ESPMail charges $3 per user per month. Lansoft charges a $50 registration fee, along with $28 per month for two post offices and 5 megabytes of messages transferred per month. Beyond that limit are additional fees. Lansoft has support for Exchange, GroupWise and Notes. All services receive messages for free, and they set up a trial account for the first 30 days.

MCI recently started its own outsourcing service called Connect. It handles a variety of LAN-based email systems, including cc:Mail, Notes, GroupWise, Exchange, MS Mail and even MHS. The pricing details are complex, and corporations must pay an initial fee of $500 plus usage charges. While we couldn't find a Web site with the details, you can get more information by sending email to *connect.sales@mcimail.com*.

Non-Internet Addressing

One issue using gateways is dealing with how they transform addresses when they deliver the messages. You might wonder if it is too much to ask to leave Internet addresses in the style local@domain. Many times gateways end up mangling addresses, making it almost impossible for you to figure out the original address to reply. This is one of the reasons we warned you in Chapter 2 to pay attention when replying to messages that come from systems running gateways or less than 100% pure Internet email. And it is worth repeating here: Look at your message header before you hit the send key. You might save yourself some time and aggravation trying to interpret some error report a few hours or days later.

Why is this the case? The answer lies in how the gateway maps the email address of its native users and how that relates to the domain-style addresses of the Internet.

If you are new to sending email outside of your corporation, here are a few pointers. First, users on email networks such as America Online, CompuServe and others have a basically standardized Internet domain style for addressing messages. Let's take the example of a user named Rose on each system. To reach Rose on AOL, you would address email to rose@aol.com. To reach him on CompuServe, you would address email to rose@compuserve.com (or more likely, some series of numbers).[19] To reach Rose on MCIMail, you would use rose@mcimail.com. On AT&T Mail, he would be rose@attmail.com.

What you are doing by assembling these addresses is using the Internet gateway to these proprietary email networks. You might first want to check with your corporate email administrator and find out if your company maintains a separate gateway directly to these systems. Some enterprises prefer these gateways, assuming that because they don't make use of the Internet they are more secure or more easy to use (both assumptions aren't necessarily true).

What about going the other way, say from AOL or CompuServe to Internet users? With AOL, this is a trivial task. You type in the address, say rose@example.com, in the TO: field of the message box. With CompuServe, as we have shown in Chapter 3, you can assemble the right syntax of the message inside WinCIM, by first choosing the destination email network.[20]

Sending HTML-enabled Messages

As the Web has become more popular, more people and products are making use of the hypertext markup language (HTML) to format messages. Depending on the email software you and your messaging partners use, you may be able to send a URL referencing a Web page and have the page appear on your recipient's computer somehow. Let's talk about how to accomplish this.

First, we should mention that sending HTML messages is different from viewing your email from inside a browser, making use of the various services mentioned in Chapter 5 to read your mail when you are on the road. We are talking about composing formatted messages, complete with pictures, Java applets and other nontextual elements. You might want to do this for emphasis, to preserve the original look of a particular document, or because you are excited about the Web and want to use it whenever you can.

HTML messages have some other problems. Your embedded links may not work unless you are connected to the Internet at the time you view your message, or they may generate more network traffic than you intend. And some people could use the HTML links to embed a unique URL or applet. This link could track who receives and opens messages, which could impact your own privacy.

Before you start sending HTML messages, first find out what software your correspondents are using. This is one of those situations where you really need to upgrade to the latest version of your email software. Earlier versions didn't do HTML very well or at all, and there is no sense in using these older products if you intend to make extensive use of this feature. This also means that your correspondents who want to view HTML pages also need to upgrade this software.

If you don't want to upgrade your email software, then we recommend against using HTML-enabled email. Best to stick with just plain text, otherwise you'll draw the ire of your correspondents who can't view your messages.

There are several ways you can make use of HTML email. If you are trying to draw attention to a particular page out on the Web, you can place a link with a URL of this page inside the body of the message, or place the actual page inside your message if you are using Messenger.

If you want to format your message with boldface, multiple links and type fonts, each of the three products (Eudora, Messenger and Outlook Express) has a miniature HTML editor as part of its respective message composition screens. The toolbar is directly over the message screen, and looks like a toolbar from a word processor: You can use boldface, italics, underscores, different colors and text sizes. If you can't remember what the small icons on the toolbar do, hold your mouse over them until the help message pops up at the bottom of the window. The toolbars look like the following (Figure 7.5 for Outlook Express, Figure 7.6 for Messenger, and Figure 7.7 for Eudora):

Figure 7.5   Outlook Express message composition toolbar

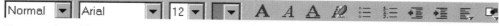

Figure 7.6   Messenger message composition toolbar

Figure 7.7   Eudora message composition toolbar

Most of these buttons are familiar to users of modern word processors. You don't have to know anything about HTML tags, but use the toolbar buttons and menu choices to boldface and change font styles. You also could compose a message in an HTML editor and cut and paste the resulting tags and markup into the body of your message.

Each product operates with HTML mail somewhat differently, of course. Outlook Express takes backgrounds and pictures and converts them to HTML markup tags, along with your text formatting tags. It also has stationary that you can use to create your own customized documents with backgrounds and type faces; these choices can be sent as HTML to non-Outlook users who will then be able to view the graphics more or less according to your original design.

Outlook Express needs to know who is going to be getting which type of message, and generally you need to set this up in the address book and the configuration options first before composing your messages.

In Outlook Express, at the bottom of each address book entry is an option to Send email using plain text only. This means that the default behavior for each recipient is what you have specified in the Tools | Options | Send window, unless this box is checked for each of your correspondents who may be using older email programs. In the options window, as we have mentioned earlier in this section, you can choose to send messages in either HTML or plain text, and pick the various encoding options for either.

Netscape Messenger can import an actual page from any URL you specify, and if you type in a URL as an attachment, it will include the page at the bottom of your email message, along with all the graphics and links on that page. This is somewhat handy, particularly if you are exchanging Web pages with someone and want to do more than just send them the link.

After you are finished composing your message, with all the tags and formats and fonts you desire, Messenger brings up a dialogue box asking you what you'd like to do, as shown in Figure 7.8. You have three choices: You can send your message in both plain text and HTML, send plain text only, or send HTML only. Choose one of the options and the message will be queued.

Messenger also has a place in its address book where you can specify whether you wish a particular recipient to receive HTML email. If you have checked this box, then the dialogue box does not appear and the mail is sent with the HTML tags intact.

Figure 7.8   Messenger HTML mail choices

In Eudora, you need to make sure two options are turned off. Under Tools | Options | Miscellaneous Options, Discard styles before sending messages should be unchecked, otherwise you won't be able to send anything other than plain text in your messages. And under Tools | Options | Extra Warnings, also make sure to uncheck Warn me when I queue a message with styled text. Eudora doesn't have any option to specify how a particular recipient is to receive mail, and indeed the default is to send mail with HTML formatting. There may be a way to turn this off in future versions of Eudora, but in our version we would have to do this for each message.

How about adding links and images to your messages? There are two ways to do this. The first instance is when you need to send email to users running older versions of products that don't necessarily make use of HTML email. In Eudora, you place your URLs inside angle brackets as part of the message text, such as

There is an interesting site to visit at <http://www.example.com>.

Notice that you don't completely follow HTML markup rules here. You just need the angle brackets surrounding your URL. For images, go to Edit | Insert | Picture and you'll see a window browsing your hard disk for the particular picture you wish to send. If you are sending this to Eudora version 3, it will recognize this as a link and open it in your default browser.

For correspondents who can make use of HTML-enabled email, there is another way to enrich your messages. In Eudora, you can create hyperlinks as part of your message by highlighting the text and going to

Edit | Text | Make Hyperlink. You'll see a small window with the http:// reference, and you can type in the URL there. When you are finished, your text is now underlined and the link is part of the message.

In Outlook Express, there are two ways to add links. First, highlight a portion of text you wish to serve as the basis for the link. Then choose Insert | Hyperlink from the menus, or press the chain link icon at the right end of the composition toolbar above the message body. You'll see something like Figure 7.9, and then scroll down to enter the right protocol and URL for the link.

Figure 7.9   Outlook Express HTML mail options

In Messenger, there are two ways to add links. Insert | HTML Tag from the menus will bring up a screen where you can type the actual HTML tag and link. Of course, you have to know the correct syntax here. Or you can right-click in the message body and choose the Insert New Link option, and fill out the window with the appropriate link syntax. Both are very cumbersome, however.

Using the Internet File Transfer Protocol

If you absolutely have to send a file across the Internet, sometimes email isn't the best solution. This is especially true if you have to send many smaller files and don't have the time to fool around with a file compression utility, or have to send many large files to several people. This is where the file transfer protocol (ftp) comes in handy. While this is a book about email, you may not be aware of how to use ftp. It could be a big time-saver, particularly if you have tried to send files as attachments but something isn't working out. Here is an example:

```
A couple of years ago, I was regularly sending
Microsoft Word files to my editor at Adobe
Magazine, part of Adobe Systems. At that time,
Adobe used cc:Mail with a gateway server that
handled Internet mail and interacted with the
```

```
proprietary cc:Mail servers. No matter what
combination of encoding formats I tried and no
matter what my recipient did, the files rarely came
through intact.21
```

There was a time when ftp servers used to be more popular than the Web, if you can remember back to the time when the Web was nothing more than a research project. They are fast, they are simple to use and the software comes built into Windows95 and Windows NT.

Many Web servers are also ftp servers, including ones from Netscape, Microsoft and Apache. This means that you can set them up for what is called anonymous transfers, or where no user authentication is needed to copy the file from the server to your local hard disk. (You still need appropriate rights to post the files to the ftp server.)

If you think that ftp is still exotic, consider that every AOL member has two megabytes of ftp storage space per screen name as part of his or her membership. Anyone who needs to send you a file can upload them to your AOL ftp site. (The reverse isn't true: Only AOL members can download files from this site.)

Say your AOL screen name is example. You tell all your correspondents that if they want to send you some file, they need to go to

    ftp://members.aol.com/example/incoming/

If one of your friends is running Windows95, make a copy of the following instructions. First, your friend needs to bring up an MS DOS prompt window and type the following commands. Change directories and go to the place where your file is located by using the cd\ "directory" name command. (If your directory name has spaces embedded in it, you'll need the quotation marks.) Then type:

    ftp members.aol.com

Your friend will be asked to type in a user name. Type anonymous. Then a password. Type the email address, such as test@example.com. Then type the following commands:

```
cd \example\incoming
binary
put test.doc
```

Your friend will see a short message indicating that the file has been sent to your ftp server. Keep in mind that the file names are case sensitive: We recommend you use all lowercase letters in naming the files.

Now, how do you retrieve this file? Start up your AOL software, log in and go to the keyword MYPLACE. This will take you to a series of screens introducing you to both the Web and ftp server space that you are entitled to as an AOL member. Go to the subdirectory incoming. Press the button to download files to your hard disk.

Our AOL example is just a small introduction to ftp.[22] Another way to use protocol is to store files on your Web server in a directory that isn't referenced on any of your Web pages. You will need to set up your ftp server security so that your friends can gain access to this particular directory. You can tell your friends the URL of this directory, and they can bring it up in their Web browsers. Remember to start the URL with ftp://, as in:

```
ftp://www.mywebserver.com/directory
```

If you don't want to make use of ftp to deliver your files, there is another solution that involves a proprietary product called DropChute+ from Hilgraeve (*www.hilgraeve.com*). It only runs on Windows NT and Windows95, so that may be a limitation. But if users on both ends have the product, they can exchange files with a minimum of fuss and bother. If you find yourself doing lots of file transfers with a small number of people, this may be an answer.

If all this seems too much for you, we have one further recommendation: There is always overnight package delivery! Of course, this presents other technical challenges, such as how to fit large files on a single disk, and whether your recipient has the same kind of disk format as you. We'll leave that for now and move on.

Exchange, Notes or GroupWise: Which One for You?[23]

We have taken the position in our discussions in this book that 100% pure Internet email is desirable and a worthy goal. Nevertheless, there are times when you might want to consider other alternatives, and the three groupware products (Microsoft Exchange, Lotus Notes and Novell's GroupWise) are the most likely suspects. Which one should you choose?

We have several recommendations, based on our own use of the products over their lifetimes. First, some perspective. Notes came about as the first product with the label groupware, and, while the current version is showing its age, its strength lies in being a collaborative applications delivery tool. Notes is still the best product of the three for developing custom applications, such as tracking client correspondence or automating particular business processes. It has the widest array of scripting tools and the oldest and deepest third-party development community. Its user interface, however, leaves a lot to be desired and can still confuse new users.

Exchange began its life as a DOS-based email product, and has done the most work in integrating Internet standards and combining scheduling with messaging. Microsoft continues to work on the server scripting tools that come with the product, although we think its biggest attraction is the user interface innovations brought about in its Outlook desktop software. Outlook continues to be an attraction, although the latest 98 version seems to be fat and bloated with features. (Outlook Express, which is Microsoft's attempt at a 100% pure Internet email product, has features that weren't found in earlier Outlook software but have been added to the Outlook 98 version.)

And GroupWise, which has always had an integrated scheduling feature, has continued to add to its roots in document management. You can easily publish documents to the Web with an add-on module. Long ago, GroupWise pioneered the message recall feature and the ability to easily turn an email message into a task or scheduled item—things that only recently have been added to products by the other two vendors. Unfortunately, it continues to be closely tied to NetWare's Directory Services, which is required to run the product.

As we said earlier, each of the products now comes with its own SMTP gateway. Moreover, each product can make use of standard POP and IMAP email programs such as Eudora and Messenger to read and respond to email created by the native desktop software. This is a nice touch, although we aren't sure that anyone would implement one of these products strictly for supporting POP email users. Of course, POP and IMAP users don't have access to the nonmessaging functions, such as adding schedule items and reviewing discussions, but it is nice to know that the three vendors are concerned about the Internet.

Each of the products also comes with a module that allows ordinary Web browsers access to many, but not all, of the features found with the native desktop software. Of the three products, GroupWise's Web access has the closest look and feel to its own desktop software; Notes' Web access is the least similar.

Speaking of the Web, don't look for innovations in HTML-enabled email with these products. GroupWise lacks the ability to view this kind of formatting entirely, and Notes and Exchange lag behind the features discussed earlier in this chapter for Outlook Express and Messenger.

Lotus has done the most work in the Web remake of Notes, and indeed the product now goes under the Domino rubric to try to differentiate it from its humbler, non-Internet upbringing. But some of the Web features are worth noting. For example, Notes servers can be administered with a Web browser, and the browser-based administration tool includes features that are lacking in the native Notes administration software, such as the ability to display disk space usage statistics.

Both Notes and Exchange have also opened up their products when it comes to viewing public discussion folders with Network News transport software, such as Netscape's Communicator news reader. GroupWise lacks this feature.

Finally, if you decide to make use of any of these products, you'll find out that support for remote users leaves something to be desired. Each of the products requires a roaming user to carry his or her laptop with them to truly be productive. None of the products works well with storing user profiles and messages on the server.

Anti-Virus Software and Strategies

We recommend that everyone install some kind of virus protection software for email systems. As email usage continues to climb, the chances and cost of infection will increase. Certainly email attachments can contain viruses. We've seen it many times on our own computers and on friends' computers. Adding the correct level of protection to your email servers and desktops is tricky, depending on what you want to protect, what kind of email systems you are running and what kinds of protection features are available in any particular virus scanning software.

The best course of action is to protect all of your desktops within your enterprise and then move on to protect standard SMTP mail servers. A nice touch is the McAfee desktop scanning software included with Eudora version 4.

The three biggest vendors are Symantec, Network Associates and Trend Micro. They offer a wide line of virus protection products, including desktop protection (which we recommend buying from the same vendor whenever possible) and others.

Each vendor's SMTP protection software runs on Windows NT, and Trend also offers UNIX-based products. Each product scans incoming email traffic from your SMTP server, including attachments and compressed files. Unlike desktop virus protection software, these SMTP products don't necessarily have to reside on your actual SMTP server, but can run on another machine if you so desire (or if you are running an SMTP mail server on some other platform).

The software warns you of potential problems when it matches a virus signature with one in its database, and can automatically clean the infected file, place it under quarantine until a network administrator can examine it, or delete it.

Trend's product comes with scanning routines for Web and ftp servers; Network Associates offer similar protection in its WebShield LX product.

These products aren't perfect. For example, in tests of Exchange scanning software at *PC Week*,

```
If an email recipient happens to be working in his
or her mail client and opens an incoming message
immediately upon its arrival, the recipient can
infect the PC by running an infected attachment….
Products scan mail after it is delivered to the
user's mailbox.24
```

Features to examine in evaluating these products include enterprise administration, the mechanics of upgrades and overall price.

Each product has various strengths in centralized and remote administration. Since Norton's product is administered from a browser, it is relatively easy to set up across your enterprise. The others require NT machines to run them. Some products require you to visit each mail server in your enterprise, which could be cumbersome.

Of course, you would want to keep up-to-date with the latest signatures and upgrades to these products. But before you purchase a virus scanning product, find out how these updates are administered. For some products, such as Dr. Solomon's Anti-Virus for Microsoft Exchange, the updates arrive on floppies, and you must walk around and install the update on each Exchange server in your enterprise. That gets old fast, and you might be tempted to skip an update.

And when it comes to price, it will be difficult to pin down the exact figure unless you call the vendor. Consider that each of the three vendors also offers other virus-scanning products for Notes (Symantec, Network Associates), Exchange (Network Associates), and desktop and server products. If you are planning on protecting your entire enterprise, you might be better off trying to contact a sales representative at one of these vendors and cutting a deal for equipping all of your desktops at once.

If you need one of the Exchange or Notes scanning products, it could get pricey: to protect a typical 500-user configuration could easily wind up costing $6,000. The SMTP products are a bit less expensive, but still end up costing several thousand dollars for a medium-sized installation.

You can get more information and download trial versions of these and other products from the Web locations listed below in the table.[25]

SMTP Server Anti-Virus Software

Vendor, URL	Product Name	Platforms
Symantec/Norton *www.symantec.com/nav/fs_navieg.html*	Norton AntiVirus for Internet Email Gateway	NT
Network Associates/McAfee *www.nai.com/products/antivirus/* *webshield_smtp*	WebShield SMTP	NT
Trend Micro *www.antivirus.com/products/isvw*	InterScan VirusWall	NT (Intel, Alpha), UNIX
eSafe Technologies *www.eliashim.com*	ViruSafe	NT
Data Fellows *www.datafellows.com*	F-Secure Anti-Virus Mail Gateway	NT, UNIX
Integralis *www.mimesweeper.com*	MIMEsweeper	NT

Installing anti-virus software is just one piece of the protection puzzle. Ideally, you want to adopt a few other good working habits in your day-to-day email life. For example, even though we make use of various protective software, we still tend to open any received Word files with the built-in WordPad in Windows95. It can read most Word 6-formatted documents without any problems, and because it doesn't have the ability to run macros, it is just another layer of safety if any attachments come with a macro virus.

We also tend to not run any attached executables that we receive via email, unless we have requested a particular file and know the person who is sending it to us. Finally, we avoid running other's floppies on our computers whenever possible, again to minimize the chance of infection.

FUTURES

The key lesson of this chapter demonstrates the richness of Internet email and its ability to carry text, Web objects, arbitrary files and the like. There is a commensurate amount of responsibility that goes with this freedom.

Our first prediction deals with the use of gateways. In brief, their usage will decline in favor of 100% pure Internet systems. There are two reasons for this. First, many gateways exist as legacy deployments; and, second, in view of the increasing capabilities of systems built using Internet technology from the ground up, all gateways exist as future legacy systems.

Of course, there remain valid reasons for gateways—a gateway is something you deploy when you're locked into a vendor-specific architecture or implementation. Examples include Microsoft Exchange and Outlook 98, although "modern" products, they are hardly 100% Internet. In their defense, they do have a lot of good value-added features. As a consequence, deployment of these products yields a short-term productivity gain but a long-term headache as the "cows come home to roost."

Our second prediction deals with the use of attachments. In brief, they will remain a problem, but the nature of the problem will change. We think that soon virtually all email software will be able to use MIME for transporting attachments and the interoperability problems we've discussed will disappear. However, we also think that additional security issues will be raised. For starters, some data files have the potential to be quite harmful. In general, the problem exists whenever you receive files for a program whose data language allows for extensibility and access to platform services. Popularized examples include things like Microsoft Word, which has a macro facility that meets these requirements.

While we might be careful when exchanging files of this sort, we are extremely concerned about the increasing tendency of vendors to write programs that mail executable (.exe) files about. For example, one vendor of a video email product offers this option: If you're not sure if your recipient has the vendor's video player, rather than just sending the video file, you can send a .exe file that contains the player and the video. One of our colleagues sent us such a file—we returned it unopened on general principle.

Endnotes

1. Consider, for example, the ill-fated attempt of several western governments to pick technology winners through the procurement process.

2. Microsoft calls this "rich messaging." We are not sure if the term refers to the fact that Microsoft will be rich by the time the rest of its competitors figure this out, or because there are other data types besides plain text included in the message.

3. The frustrating part is that Eudora 3 interprets the tables anyway, formatting them rather poorly. Web designers who have built pages with tables and then mailed those pages to someone running Eudora 3 have actually burst into tears because Eudora's rendering was so bad.

4. Rose finds it easy to assign blame with AOL. If you're going to run with the big dogs (play in the Internet space), then try to get it right, okay?

5. Here again, MCIMail raises its ugly head. To this day, MCIMail's connection to the Internet remains under-provisioned and functionally stunted. One of the authors has an automated tool to measure email delay times.

6. In fairness, the leading desktop operating system and word processing software comes from Microsoft, so their mistakes are usually highly visible.

7. One enterprising programmer, Fred McLain, demonstrated how you could browse a Web page with a rogue Active X program that when run would reboot your Windows95 desktop. You can check it out at *www.halcyon.com/mclain/ActiveX*. Microsoft has tried to counter this by setting up a complex series of security zones inside Internet Explorer. However, the fact remains that Active X applications are programs, and still could do unexpected damage.

8. Word version 2 did not have this ability to run macros. One way of being absolutely safe when exchanging documents is to just run Word version 2. The problem here is that this version doesn't contain many of the features found in more recent versions, and some recent versions can't save Word version 2-formatted files, making it difficult to exchange documents with someone who is only running this version. An alternative, which we sometimes use, is to open all of your emailed Word files in WordPad. (Go to Programs | Accessories | WordPad.) This is included on all Windows95 and Windows NT machines, and cannot run macros. However, it cannot read Word 97 formatted files, just Word 6.0.

9. And some email or network administrators may object to connecting your mail systems in this fashion, since your enterprise directory is now available to your customers. At one corporation where we worked, we had a particularly paranoid email administrator who refused to allow such connections.

10. *www.isi.edu/in-notes/iana/assignments/media-types/*

11. *www.isi.edu/in-notes/iana/assignments/character-sets*

12. Actually, there's a third trick. The committee, which defined the documents that describe multipart/related, provided for two mechanisms for links between body parts. We describe the simplest of the alternatives. The more complex alternative, which adds two new headers, Content-Base: and Content-Location:, is best left unsaid. We note in passing that providing two mechanisms to do essentially the same thing is a violation of Internet architectural principles. Better to have one way of doing something, and best if it's a simple way.

13. This is taken from the NetBITS online newsletter (*www.netbits.net/nb-issues/Net-BITS-016.html*).

14. If you ever receive a BinHex file and you can't decode it, go to this site: *www.natural-innovations/com/boo/binhex.html* and check out one of the various utilities mentioned there.

15. More details about these strategies can be found in the *MacUser* article "Foolproof File Enclosures," February 1997, *www.zdnet.com/macuser/mu_0297/handson/hotech.html*.

16. Try *www.shareware.com* as a starting point in locating any of the software mentioned in this section. WinZIP can also be found at *www.winzip.com* and StuffIt Deluxe can be found at *www.aladdinsys.com/deluxe*.

17. Other Macintosh compression software can be found at *wwwhost.ots.utexas.edu/mac/pub-mac-compression.html*. ZipIt can be found at *www.awa.com/softlock/zipit/zipit.html*.

18. Lest you think we are singling out Novell here, we should point out a 13-page document on Microsoft's Web site. The paper, with a 15-step installation procedure along with other details about how to install the Internet Mail Service SMTP gateway for Exchange, begins: "Connecting Exchange to the Internet is a very quick and simple process." A good explanation of how to set up Exchange's Internet services can be found in *"Mastering Microsoft Exchange Server,"* by Barry Gerber, Sybex, 1996.

19. CompuServe assigns two numbers to most of its users, although more recently you can make use of more sensible names. But the two numbers are usually displayed separated by a comma, such as 77777,1234. This would translate to an Internet address of *77777.1234@compuserve.com*. In other words, replace the comma with a period and append the @compuserve.com to the end.

20. More details on constructing these non-Internet addresses can be found in the book *!%@::, A Directory of Electronic Mail*, by Donnalyn Frey and Rick Adams, O'Reilly and Associates, 1994.

21. From NetBITS online newsletter (*www.netbits.net/nb-issues/NetBITS-016.html*).

22. If you want more details about using this protocol and how to use the various command options, we recommend *The Internet Guide for New Users*, Daniel P. Dern, McGraw Hill, 1994.

23. While there have been many articles written on this topic, one of the best analyses we've read is by *PC Week*'s Matt Kramer: "Groupware Systems Are Growing Up," published November 17, 1997. The article can be found at *www.zdnet.com/pcweek/reviews/1117/17group.html*.

24. "GroupShield 3.2.1 Routs Rivals," by Ken Phillips, *PC Week*, January 26, 1998.

25. And for more complete information along with a good page of anti-virus links, see Eutron's site at *www.eutron.it/link/html/7.htm*.

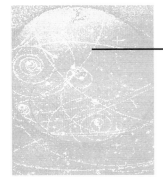

8

Closing

In this chapter, we reflect on the state of Internet messaging and consider some areas in which the infrastructure will evolve.

EMAIL TECHNOLOGY TODAY

If we would have to pick a year as the birth of Internet email, we would pick 1982. That's the year the document describing headers for messaging was written. Given the scope of applications we've discussed in the previous six chapters, it is clear that the Internet messaging infrastructure has evolved considerably over the past 15 years.

Perhaps the most significant advance is that practically anything you can do on the Web today can be done in email. Since you can send messages that are HTML formatted, all of the Web's presentation qualities are now available in email. Just as you can have beautifully designed Web pages, you can also have beautifully designed messages. To the extent that you can present concepts and information in a friendly and intuitive fashion on the Web, you can also do so in email. Of course, nothing prevents you from having poorly designed Web pages, or poorly designed messages. You can put a pig in a suit, but it still acts every bit the pig.

To appreciate the power of this marriage, you need only consider that messages can carry images and applets. Signature blocks are *de rigeur* in messages. We think of them as textual entities containing contact information at the bottom of a message. Of course, they could just as easily be little self-contained programs. Figure 8.1 has an example of a VirtualSIG, used by Marshall Rose:

Figure 8.1   VirtualSIG, initial view

If you click on one of the tabs next to the photo, the corresponding information animates onto the screen, as shown in Figure 8.2.

Figure 8.2   VirtualSIG, another view

There are a lot of cool things you can do with technologies like this, and they work as well on the Web as they do in email.

Of course, this brave new world is not without intrigue. For example, let's say someone sends you a message that references an image residing on a Web server (rather than embedding the image using the technique described in Chapter 7), and you are connected when you read that message. The image automatically will be downloaded by your mail reader and displayed. That's great, but the URL pointing to the image could be "unique" in that it was generated specifically for use by your message. When your mail reader downloads the image, the Web server now knows that you opened the message. You may not want people to know when you read mail from them. Let the reader beware!

EVOLVING EMAIL STANDARDS

Advances in email didn't happen all at once—they were part of a continuing evolution of the technology. This evolution continues. Many times throughout this book we've discussed desirable features in proprietary systems that are lacking in the standards-based infrastructure. Slowly, this is changing.

For example, at the beginning of 1998, standardization work was underway for:

- Remote configuration of applications (so you can keep preferences for your email software on a server, which you can then access regardless of what system you happen to be using to read email)

- Scheduling of appointments and meetings through Internet messaging

- Using Internet messaging to transfer electronic documents

- Supporting facsimile with Internet messaging (so your mailbox becomes your fax machine)

- Adding "return receipt" facilities to Internet messaging

- Remote management of Internet messaging services

The challenge, of course, is to balance engineering requirements and commercial interests. The Internet's standards process has had mixed results in the past. Perhaps it will do better in the next few years. However, some standards pundits are rather pessimistic. The argument goes like this: There are more people than ever working on messaging standardization and the quality of the resulting standards are demonstrably lower than in the past. Perhaps quality of help is more important than the quantity.

THE ROLE OF EMAIL ON THE DESKTOP

The role of email has increased as a desktop application. Not too long ago, email was considered something extra and above the standard desktop configuration. Now you can't buy a new computer without several email products preinstalled on its hard disk. And most corporations include email as a matter of course in their supported desktop applications.

We've seen how email can become the nexus for all sorts of communications—for faxing, paging and sending documents to colleagues and coworkers. Email integration with other desktop applications is still far from perfect, and with luck will see more improvement in the years to come.

What remains unclear is whether functionality will increase for desktop software, or whether server-based solutions will dominate. For example, one solution to the attachment problem discussed in Chapter 7 is to have a universal standard for revisable documents. Although end users in different constituencies may not agree on the same standard, server-based solutions can simply pick one format (e.g., Adobe's Acrobat) and then map all attachments to that one format. Such an approach requires that all communication between users go through the server, which does the conversion. It also requires that all end users be able to render that one format. Clearly, it is preferable to avoid a server-based solution, since it introduces a whole new set of issues (scalability, security, usability, ad nauseam). However, unless the folks doing desktop software get their act together (and we're not referring to the folks doing email software), server-based solutions may become more attractive.

THE ROLE OF EMAIL IN THE ENTERPRISE

Email has become the lifeblood of many corporations. It connects far-flung offices and provides the role once reserved for printed communications. It creates and sustains a corporate culture, provides motivation to workers to share more than just their work product. As we have said earlier, email has arrived.

There are three true challenges to email in the enterprise. First is manageability. We suspect that outsourcing may become key. The resource investment required to run a world-class enterprise email system isn't modest. Quite the contrary! As a consequence, we imagine that just as telecommunications infrastructure is often outsourced, so too will the corporate email infrastructure. What remains unclear, at least as of this writing, is what kind of organization is capable of undertaking such a task. There is still a lot of "work in progress" with respect to the nature of hardened email.

Second is unification and interoperability. Almost no corporation has the luxury of administering a system using software from a single email vendor. Whether by design, by accident, by acquisition or by some belligerent end-user department, running multiple email systems is a necessary fact of life for most corporate IS managers. The trick is making them communicate among each other with a minimum of fuss and bother, and running as few different systems as possible. Several email administators told us how hard they worked to reduce the number of disparate systems and products.

Finally, there is our favorite subject: 100% pure Internet email. This actually is both a challenge and an opportunity for corporate email administrators. It is a challenge because these administrators (and end users too) need more functionality than is currently available from the pure Internet systems. Having an integrated calendar to schedule meetings, or an integrated discussion group that shares the same directory as your email system is something that isn't yet part and parcel to the 100% pure Internet product space. This is a good reason why Lotus Notes, Microsoft Exchange and Novell GroupWise are so popular, and will continue to be popular. All three products continue to grow in number and we don't think this growth will change anytime soon.

But obtaining 100% purity is also an opportunity, since Internet-based products will continue to gain functions to compete. It is also an opportunity for the "impure" products to take on these Internet protocols and embrace them as their own. Witness how you can now run IMAP, POP, LDAP and other Internet protocols as part of a standard Notes, Exchange and GroupWise server. This certainly wasn't the case prior to 1996. While we will certainly hear of corporations that will replace their proprietary email servers with Internet ones (as our friends at Netscape will continue to remind us), we think a more likely situation would be the continued operation of both Internet and proprietary products for a long time to come. The challenge will be to make them work together.

Index